Introduction to Islamic Banking and Finance
An Economic Analysis

INTRODUCTION TO ISLAMIC BANKING AND FINANCE
An Economic Analysis

M Kabir Hassan
University of New Orleans, USA

Salman Ahmed Shaikh
SZABIST University, Pakistan

Selim Kayhan
Necemettin Erbakan University, Turkey

World Scientific

NEW JERSEY · LONDON · SINGAPORE · BEIJING · SHANGHAI · HONG KONG · TAIPEI · CHENNAI · TOKYO

Published by

World Scientific Publishing Co. Pte. Ltd.
5 Toh Tuck Link, Singapore 596224
USA office: 27 Warren Street, Suite 401-402, Hackensack, NJ 07601
UK office: 57 Shelton Street, Covent Garden, London WC2H 9HE

Library of Congress Cataloging-in-Publication Data
Names: Hassan, Kabir, author. | Shaikh, Salman Ahmed, author. | Kayhan, Selim, author.
Title: Introduction to Islamic banking and finance : an economic analysis /
    M. Kabir Hassan, University of New Orleans, USA, Salman Ahmed Shaikh,
    SZABIST University, Pakistan, Selim Kayhan, Necemettin Erbakan University, Turkey.
Description: New Jersey : World Scientific, [2020] | Includes bibliographical references and index.
Identifiers: LCCN 2020028767 | ISBN 9789811222689 (hardcover) |
    ISBN 9789811224218 (paperback) | ISBN 9789811222696 (ebook) |
    ISBN 9789811222702 (ebook other)
Subjects: LCSH: Finance--Islamic countries. | Finance--Religious aspects--Islam. |
    Banks and banking--Islamic countries. | Banks and banking--Religious aspects--Islam. |
    Economics--Religious aspects--Islam.
Classification: LCC HG187.4 .H396 2020 | DDC 332.0917/67--dc23
LC record available at https://lccn.loc.gov/2020028767

British Library Cataloguing-in-Publication Data
A catalogue record for this book is available from the British Library.

For any available supplementary material, please visit
https://www.worldscientific.com/worldscibooks/10.1142/11895#t=suppl

Desk Editors: Balamurugan Rajendran/Karimah Samsudin

Typeset by Stallion Press
Email: enquiries@stallionpress.com

Printed in Singapore

Foreword

Islamic banking and finance is an estimated $2.6 trillion dollar industry as of the end of 2018 with major footsteps in the Middle East, South Asia, East Asia, Far East, North Africa, and Europe. After the global financial crisis of 2007–2009, this nascent field has exhibited resilience, stability, and strong growth. The economic and sound commercial competitiveness alone has generated interest in the use of Islamic finance instruments as alternate finance. The principles of risk-sharing, financial transparency, and responsible use of funds for identified asset acquisition have increased its appeal as a form of ethical and socially responsible finance.

This book covers the basic principles of Islamic economics and finance. It discusses both the theory of Islamic economics and finance as well as the applications in the design of instruments of finance as well as Islamic financial institutions. It enables the readers to gain an understanding of the structures and operations of Islamic banking, Islamic capital market investments, and risk management for Islamic banking contracts.

The book sets forth the following objectives:

- To get an overview of the principles of Islamic economics and understand their contrast with mainstream economics.
- To get an overview of the basic rules of commercial law in Islamic jurisprudence.
- To get an overview of basic principles, structures, and operations of Islamic banking both in the liability-side and asset-side operations.

- To gain an understanding of Islamic capital market instruments and investment management including some unique activities peculiar to Islamic investments, such as stock screening and income purification.

This book features chapters covering Islamic finance products and their applications. The book highlights how the distinguishing features in Islamic finance do not hamper the economic purpose in most product structures, thus, it makes a strong case for using it to enable access to finance in developing countries, foster financial inclusion of voluntarily excluded faith-conscious people, and to bring competitiveness in the financial industry.

The book is focused on the theoretical and academic treatment of Islamic finance theory and practice. It does not get into jurisprudential debates within Islamic banking product developers and regulators. Rather, it presents the mainstream consensus in theory and practice with well-supported mainstream literature and the latest statistics.

The text avoids the normative discussions and evaluation of arguments in issues which are less well settled and agreed upon in the research literature. It focuses on the mainstream theory and practice and elaborates it for the audience who is interested to know about Islamic banking and finance the way it is being practiced. The book provides a global perspective on Islamic finance instruments, especially those that are applied in the financial industry currently.

The book is beneficial to academicians, researchers, practitioners, and legal experts who wish to get a global perspective on Islamic banking and finance products and their contemporary applications. The updated content makes the information useful for pedagogical purposes in training and academic programmes. The book is beneficial to be used in Islamic banking and finance courses in academia and executive learning programmes that cover Islamic banking and finance practice.

Among the individual readers, the book will be useful to practitioners, academicians, legal experts, and university students, especially those majoring in finance, accountancy, and law. This book can also be used as a reference text in these courses, such as:

- Fundamentals of Islamic Banking and Finance
- Applied Islamic Banking and Finance

- Risk Management in Islamic Banking
- Islamic Capital Markets and Investments.

The book attempts to provide an exposition to the research and practice in the area of Islamic banking and finance. The chapters and the contents are organized and adequately elaborated for a variety of technical and non-technical audiences in academia and industry.

Lastly, we would like to acknowledge the patronage and assistance provided by World Scientific Group Company to publish this book. We thank the entire team that worked on this book project, especially Balamurugan Rajendran and Karimah Samsudin for their assistance in various stages of the editing and printing process.

About the Authors

 **M. Kabir Hassan** is a Professor of Finance in the Department of Economics and Finance in the University of New Orleans. He currently holds three endowed positions of Chairs-Hibernia Professor of Economics and Finance, Hancock Whitney Chair Professor in Business, and Bank One Professor in Business in the University of New Orleans. Professor Hassan is the winner of the 2016 Islamic Development Bank (IDB) Prize in Islamic Banking and Finance. Professor Hassan has done consulting work for the World Bank, International Monetary Fund, African Development Bank, Transparency International-Bangladesh (TIB), Islamic Development Bank, United Nations Development Program (UNDP), Government of Turkey and many private organizations. Professor Hassan has over 350 papers published as book chapters and in refereed academic journals. For his outstanding research and scholarly work, Dr. Hassan has been recognized with Lifetime Achievement Award by UNO Research Council in 2019.

 **Salman Ahmed Shaikh** holds a PhD in Economics from the National University of Malaysia. He has published research papers on Islamic Economics in top international journals; presented research papers in conferences held in Malaysia, Turkey, Brunei, Indonesia, and Pakistan; and has also contributed several book chapters in books published by Routledge, Springer, Palgrave, Edward Elgar, and Gower Publishing. He is also on the Editorial Advisory Board of several research journals. He also worked as Editor for the 2019 Global Islamic Finance Report for the Cambridge Islamic Institute of Islamic Finance. Furthermore, Emerald editorial team selected two of his papers for two separate journals as Highly Commended Paper in the 2018 Emerald Literati Awards. He also won paper prize in the World Islamic Finance Forum in 2018.

 **Selim Kayhan** is a Professor of Economics at Necmettin Erbakan University, Turkey. He earned his PhD in Economics from Erciyes University, Turkey. He spent 2 years as Visiting Professor at Michigan State University and University of New Orleans. He specializes in monetary macroeconomics and has published a good number of articles in highly reputed journals. He has also worked as a consultant to the Turkish Government and presented papers in international conferences.

Contents

List of Figures

List of Tables

List of Abbreviations

AAOIFI	Accounting and Auditing Organization for Islamic Financial Institutions
ADB	Asian Development Bank
AT1	Additional Tier 1 Capital
ATMs	Automated Teller Machines
AUM	Assets under Management
BCBS	Basel Committee on Banking Supervision
CAGR	Compound Annual Growth Rate
CAPM	Capital Asset Pricing Model
CAR	Capital Adequacy Ratio
CDS	Credit Default Swaps
CET1	Common Equity Tier 1 Capital
DJIM	Dow Jones Islamic Market Index
DPO	Dividend Payout Ratio
FSP	Financial Service Providers
FTSE	Financial Times Stock Exchange
FX	Foreign Exchange
GCC	Gulf Cooperation Council
GDP	Gross Domestic Product
GST	Goods and Services Tax
IAS	International Accounting Standards
IDB	Islamic Development Bank
IFIs	Islamic Financial Institutions
IMF	International Monetary Fund
IMFIs	Islamic Microfinance Institutions

LC	Letter of Credit
LCR	Liquidity Coverage Ratio
LIBOR	London Interbank Offered Rate
LR	Leverage Ratio
MDGs	Millennium Development Goals
MFIs	Microfinance Institutions
MPC	Marginal Propensity to Consume
MUIS	Majlis Ugama Islam Singapura
NPLs	Non-Performing Loans
NSFR	Net Stable Funding Ratio
OECD	Organization of Economic Cooperation and Development
OIC	Organisation of Islamic Cooperation
OTP	One-Time Passwords
PLS	Profit and Loss Sharing
PPP	Purchasing Power Parity
PSIA	Profit-Sharing Investment Account
PSR	Profit-Sharing Ratio
ROA	Return on Assets
ROE	Return on Equity
RPGT	Real Property Gains Tax
RWA	Risk-Weighted Assets
SC	Securities Commission
SDGs	Sustainable Development Goals
SDLT	Stamp Duty Land Tax
SDU	Saving Deficient Units
SOP	Standard Operating Procedures
SP500	Standard & Poor's 500 Index
SPV	Special Purpose Vehicle
SRB	*Shari'ah* Review Bureau
SSU	Saving Surplus Units
T2	Tier 2 Capital
VAT	Value Added Tax
WB	World Bank
ZSR	*Zakat* Savings Rate

PART I

Foundations of Islamic Finance

Chapter 1

Introduction to Islamic Finance

1.1 Normative Foundations of Productive Enterprise in Islam

1.1.1 *Emphasis on economic pursuits*

We start with a discussion on how Islamic teachings guide in the quest to earn a livelihood. Islamic principles inspire individuals to make an effort for *Halal* means of earning as long as they refrain from the prohibited means and ways of earning, such as *Riba* (interest),[1] bribery,[2] fraud,[3] *Maysir* (gambling),[4] theft,[5] the trade of intoxicants,[6] and prostitution.[7] In general, excluding the above and similar modes of earning incomes, the *Qur'an* permits mutually beneficial and voluntary exchange.[8] As per Islamic principles, endowments granted by Allah are to be used for personal use as well as for societal causes to earn *Falah* (welfare in this world and hereafter). Prophet Muhammad (pbuh) said, *The truthful and*

---

[1] *Al-Qur'an*, Al-Baqarah: 276.
[2] *Al-Qur'an*, Al-Baqarah: 188.
[3] *Al-Qur'an*, Al-Mutaffifeen: 1–4.
[4] *Al-Qur'an*, Al-Maida: 90.
[5] *Al-Qur'an*, Al-Maida: 38.
[6] *Al-Qur'an*, Al-Maida: 90.
[7] *Al-Qur'an*, Al-Nur: 19.
[8] *Al-Qur'an*, Al-Nisa: 29.

trustworthy businessman will be in the company of Prophets, saints and martyrs on the Day of Judgment.[9]

Islamic teachings compel one to avoid idleness and dependence on others without becoming part of the labour force or engaging in entrepreneurship. Prophet Muhammad (pbuh) said, *For one of you to go out early to gather firewood and carry it on his back so that he can give charity from it and be free of need from the people, is better for him than to ask a man who may give that to him or refuse. Indeed, the upper hand (giving) is more virtuous than the lower hand (receiving), and begin with (those who are) your dependents.*[10] In yet another *Hadith*, Prophet Muhammad (pbuh) explained, *The upper hand is better than the lower hand, and the upper hand is the one that spends, and the lower hand is the one that asks.*[11] Prophet Muhammad (pbuh) said that begging is not allowed for the physically fit and rich persons except for those who are facing extreme poverty or indebtedness.[12]

1.1.2 *Filter of Halal (permissible) and Haram (impermissible) in productive enterprise*

This section discusses the Islamic guidelines for the consumption behaviour of individuals. These teachings are also relevant for firms to ensure that their product offerings, marketing strategies and sales promotions are consistent with Islamic teachings. Islamic teachings make a distinction between allowable (*Halal*) and non-allowable (*Haram*) goods and services. The *Qur'an* says . . . *Eat of that which is lawful and good on the earth* . . .[13] Therefore, the consumer would only make a choice among *Halal* consumption goods and *Halal* investment products. For instance, Islam forbids intoxicants like alcohol or drugs.[14] In financial services, Islam forbids *Riba* (interest)[15] and *Maysir* (gambling),[16] for instance.

---

[9] *Jami-al-Tirmizi*, Vol. 3, Chapter on Business, Hadith Number 1209.

[10] *Jami-at-Tirmidhi*, Vol. 2, Chapters on *Zakat*, Hadith Number 680.

[11] *Sunan Abu Daud*, Vol. 2, Book of *Zakat*, Hadith Number 1648.

[12] *Jami-at-Tirmidhi*, Vol. 2, Chapters on *Zakat*, Hadith Number 653.

[13] *Al-Qur'an*, Al-Baqarah: 168.

[14] *Al-Qur'an*, Al-Baqarah: 219.

[15] *Al-Qur'an*, Al-Baqarah: 276.

[16] *Al-Qur'an*, Al-Maida: 90.

Islamic juristic experts have classified needs in a hierarchical structure. Al-Raysuni states that Imam Al-Shatibi has classified needs into three categories, i.e. (i) Necessities (*Dharuriyah*), (ii) Conveniences (*Hajiyah*), and (iii) Refinements (*Tahsiniyah*).[17] In the hierarchical structure of needs espoused by Imam Al-Shatibi, necessities include such things and activities that are vital to safeguard (i) Faith (*Iman*), (ii) Life (*Nafs*), (iii) Wealth (*Mal*), (iv) Intellect (*Aqal*), and (v) Progeny (*Nasl*).[18]

1.1.3 *Islamic teachings governing conduct of producer*

In the Islamic social framework, wealth inequality does not imply that one segment of the population has any superiority over the other segment of the population. Wealth inequality is only meant to test gratitude, forbearance and fairness in socio-economic relations and exchanges. The *Qur'an* says: *Is it they who would portion out the Mercy of your Lord? It is We Who portion out between them their livelihood in this world, and We raised some of them above others in ranks, so that some may employ others in their work. But the Mercy (Paradise) of your Lord (O Muhammad — PBUH) is better than the (wealth of this world) which they amass.*[19]

Islam permits trade, but warns people to refrain from exploitation, unfairness and deceit. The *Qur'an* says: *Do not devour one another's property wrongfully, nor throw it before the judges in order to devour a portion of other's property sinfully and knowingly.*[20] In another verse, the *Qur'an* says: *Do not devour another's property wrongfully — unless it is by trade based on mutual consent.*[21]

Islamic teachings on commercial trade strongly prescribe observing fairness in economic exchange. The *Qur'an* says: *And measure full when you measure. And weigh with an even balance. This is better and its end*

---

[17] Al-Raysuni, A. (2005). *Imam Al-Shatibi's. Theory of the Higher Objectives and Intents of Islamic Law*. Malaysia: The International Institute of Islamic Thought (IIIT).

[18] Quoquab, F., Abdullah, N. L. *et al.* (2015). "Epicureanism & Global Consumerism in Shaping Muslim Buyers' Consumption Pattern: An Islamic Perspective", *International Journal of Innovation & Business Strategy, 3,* 1–12.

[19] *Al-Qur'an*, Al Zukhruf: 32.

[20] *Al-Qur'an*, Al-Baqarah: 188.

[21] *Al-Qur'an*, Al-Nisa: 29.

is good.[22] In another verse, the *Qur'an* says: *Woe to those that deal in fraud, those who, when they have to receive by measure from men, exact full measure, but, when they have to give by measure or weight to men, give less than due. Do they not think that they will be called to account?*[23] Moreover, Islam stresses on completing terms of the contracts in letter and spirit in commercial contracts. The *Qur'an* says: *O you who believe! Fulfil [your] obligations.*[24]

Islam permits the motive to earn profit and using the earned profits for consumption and investment. Nonetheless, Islamic teachings discourage wealth accumulation. The *Qur'an* says: *They who hoard up gold and silver and spend it not in the way of Allah, unto them give tidings (O Muhammad) of a painful doom.*[25]

Islamic teachings on commercial trade condemn taking false oaths in order to deceive people. The *Qur'an* says: *You resort to oaths as instruments of mutual deceit, so that a person might take greater advantage than another; although, Allah puts you to the test through this. Surely, on the Day of Resurrection, He will make clear the truth concerning the matters over which you differed.*[26]

In intertemporal trade and commerce, Islam encourages recording the terms of the contract in order to diminish the risk of ambiguity, conflicts and misunderstandings. The *Qur'an* says: *O Believers! Whenever you lend money for a particular period, write and someone among you must write it justly. And the one who can write must not refuse.*[27]

Islamic principles of commercial trade permit transactions on credit, but denounce reneging on debt obligations. Prophet Muhammad (pbuh) said: *Any, who takes out a loan, having resolved not to pay it back, will meet Allah as a thief.*[28]

Islamic principles of trade allow competitive bidding and bargaining, but suggest softness and gentleness in executing trade deals in order to avoid exploitation and undue advantage or disadvantage to others. Prophet Muhammad (pbuh) said: *May Allah's mercy be on him who is*

---

[22] *Al-Qur'an*, Al-Bani-Israel: 35.
[23] *Al-Qur'an*, Al-Mutaffifin: 1–4.
[24] *Al-Qur'an*, Al-Maida: 1.
[25] *Al-Qur'an*, Al-Tauba: 34.
[26] *Al-Qur'an*, Al-Nahl: 92.
[27] *Al-Qur'an*, Al-Baqarah: 282.
[28] *Sunan Ibn-e-Maja*, Vol. 3, Chapters on Charity, Hadith Number 2410.

lenient in his buying, selling, and in demanding back his money [or debts].[29]

While selling goods, Islam highly recommends that deceit be avoided. Islamic moral teachings compel the seller to reduce information asymmetry for the buyer in order to allow him a fair chance to evaluate his/her course of action transparently. Prophet Muhammad (pbuh) said: *It is not permissible for a Muslim to sell his brother goods in which there is a defect without pointing that out to him.*[30]

On another occasion, Prophet Muhammad (pbuh) stated: *The seller and the buyer have the right to keep or return the goods as long as they have not parted or till they part; and if both the parties spoke the truth and described the defects and qualities [of the goods], then they would be blessed in their transaction, and if they told lies or hid something, then the blessings of their transaction would be lost.*[31]

Islamic teachings also discourage getting an unfair advantage over the counterparty. Prophet Muhammad (pbuh) said: *Whoever takes a false oath to deprive somebody of his property will meet Allah while He will be angry with him.*[32]

Islamic teachings allow the price mechanism and determination of prices to be driven by market forces without any influences, hindrances, and frictions. To make sure that market price is determined competitively without asymmetric information between the counterparties, Prophet Muhammad (pbuh) forbade a town resident to sell on behalf of a nomad and to manipulate prices upwards.[33] Prophet Muhammad (pbuh) disallowed intercepting unsophisticated growers and sellers until these sellers reached the markets with their supply of goods.[34] Moreover, in making bids for the acquisition of assets or businesses, it is disallowed to engage in overbidding without having any earnest intention to purchase (*Al-Najash*).

It is well known that excessive speculation in markets can artificially raise prices and cause the formation of price bubbles. In financial and asset markets, when these bubbles burst, the markets suffer crises. To promote

---

[29] *Sahih Bukhari*, Vol. 3, Book of Sales, Hadith Number 2076.

[30] *Sunan Ibn-e-Maja*, Vol. 3, Chapter on Business Transactions, Hadith Number 2246.

[31] *Sahih Bukhari*, Vol. 3, Book of Sales, Hadith Number 2079.

[32] *Sahih Bukhari*, Vol. 3, Book of Watering, Hadith Number 2356.

[33] *Sahih Muslim*, Vol. 4, Book of Marriage, Hadith Number 3459.

[34] *Sahih Muslim*, Vol. 4, Book of Financial Transactions, Hadith Number 3821.

authenticity of trades and weaken the motive of speculation, Prophet Muhammad (pbuh) said: *He who buys food grain should not sell it until he has taken possession of it.*[35]

In modern day businesses, often, there is a need to employ labour to produce goods by working over some capital goods like machinery. In labour-management and relations, Islam, gives significant protection and rights to labour. In order to educate people on the significance of fair treatment of labour, Prophet Muhammad (pbuh) said: *I will be a foe to three persons on the Last Day: one of them being the one who, when he employs a person that has accomplished his duty, does not give him his due.*[36] Prophet Muhammad (pbuh) emphasized timely compensation to the labourer for his/her services: *Give the labour his wage before his sweat dries.*[37]

In another *narration*, Prophet Muhammad (pbuh) stated, *Those are your brothers [workers under you] who are around you; Allah has placed them under you. So, if any one of you has someone under him, he should feed him out of what he himself eats, clothe him like what he himself puts on, and let him not put so much burden on him that he is not able to bear, [and if that be the case], then lend your help to him.*[38]

1.1.4 *Building blocks of Islamic finance*

One of the most distinctive elements of Islamic finance is the non-existence of *Riba* (interest) in financial transactions. Islamic law forbids *Riba* (interest) just like all monotheistic faiths, including Christianity and Judaism. This view on interest is taken up by all Abrahamic faiths and other distinguished scholars in history.

Aristotle commented on interest as follows: *Of all modes of getting wealth, this is the most unnatural.* Moreover, Thomas Aquinas said: *To take usury for money lent is unjust in itself, because this is **to sell what does not exist** and this evidently leads to inequality which is contrary to justice.*

In mainstream economics literature, we also find criticism of interest. John Maynard Keynes in his seminal book *General Theory of Income, Employment, Interest and Money* commented as follows:

---

[35] *Sahih Muslim*, Vol. 4, Book of Financial Transactions, Hadith Number 3836.

[36] *Sahih Bukhari*, Vol. 3, Book of Hiring, Hadith Number 2270.

[37] *Sunan Ibn-e-Maja*, Vol. 3, Book of Pawning, Hadith Number 2443.

[38] *Sahih Bukhari*, Vol. 3, Book of Manumission, Hadith Number 2545.

> *Interest to-day rewards no genuine sacrifice, any more than does the rent of land. The owner of capital can obtain interest because capital is scarce, just as the owner of land can obtain rent because land is scarce. But whilst there may be intrinsic reasons for the scarcity of land, there are no intrinsic reasons for the scarcity of capital.*[39]

The term *Riba* in Islamic finance refers to any stipulated increase over the principal amount of loan. Thus, the term *Riba* incorporates usurious loans as well as modern-day interest in banking, debt markets, and contracts.

Islamic law does not guard capitalists with a fixed return on money capital to accumulate more wealth without bearing any potential loss in the commercial undertaking for which the loan was provided. Instead, Islamic law makes it necessary for money-capital owners to bear the risk of the productive enterprise to earn any legitimate growth in money capital. Islamic law permits profit on the trade of assets including consumer goods and capital goods if the seller has the ownership and risk of the goods prior to bringing them for selling to others. In Islamic law, *Bai* means a sale transaction between buyer and seller in consideration for a price. After executing *Bai*, the ownership and risk transfer from the seller to the buyer. Islam permits *Bai;* however, Islamic law does not permit earning money from lending money without undertaking risk in a productive enterprise.

Further, Islam emphasizes transparency in relations and economic exchanges. Thus, it prohibits *Gharar* (uncertainty) in a transaction that can potentially lead to significant losses down the road due to misinformation.

Gharar implies significant uncertainty in any contract regarding the details of the contract, such as specification, quantity, and quality of the subject matter. *Gharar* is also there when there is ambiguity about price, mode of delivery, and payment terms.

Islam also forbids *Maysir* (gambling) due to its negative effects on distributive justice as well as on the moral standards of earning a livelihood. Since Islam forbids *Maysir*, it implies that most contemporary financial derivatives, convertible securities and the contemporary system of insurance also stand prohibited if they involve an element of *Maysir*. In contrast, Islam encourages striving to earn a livelihood through labour,

---

[39] Keynes, J. M. (1936). *Theory of Income, Employment, Interest & Money*. New York: Polygraphic Company of America.

and if there is surplus wealth, Islam encourages that it is invested in real productive enterprise and the payoffs shared from the productive enterprise equitably. This ensures distributive justice, employment of idle resources and circulation of wealth through growing real sector economic activities.

In the financial contracts, Islam emphasizes transparency, full disclosures, rule abidance, justice, truthfulness, and excellence in conduct, both in letter and spirit as elaborated in the previous section.

Islamic financial institutions comply with Islamic rules to offer financial services in the areas of (i) financing real assets through sale, lease and equity-based modes of financing, (ii) investments in real assets and enterprise, and (iii) risk management through mutual risk sharing.

Finally, Islamic social finance comprises institutions which aim to perform the redistributive function by wealth and asset reallocation from the rich to the poor, from the haves to the have-nots, and from the wealthy to the deserving people through institutions, such as *Zakat* (a wealth tax on people owning wealth above a threshold amount known as *Nisab*) and *Waqf* (Islamic endowments). Property-based *Waqf* can earn income through the rents on properties. In turn, these proceeds can be used to finance the needs for social development. Cash *Waqf* can provide *Qard Hassan* (interest-free loans) to the needy in sectors like education, health, and agriculture.

Thus, we see that the Islamic finance ecosystem has sufficient variety of institutions as rules and product structures to meet the contemporary financial needs responsibly and ethically in line with Islamic principles. Figure 1.1 shows the major institutions in Islamic finance architecture. Islamic finance can be divided into commercial and social finance, which together cater to the needs of all the broad sections of the society.

1.1.5 *Economic value proposition of Islamic finance*

Financial institutions provide facilitation in intertemporal exchange of funds between saving-surplus and saving-deficient units by providing delegated monitoring and investment management services efficiently.[40] In the direct potential exchange between saving-surplus and saving-deficient

---

[40]Diamond, D. W. (1984). "Financial Intermediation as Delegated Monitoring: A Simple Example", *Review of Economic Studies*, *51*(3), 393–414.

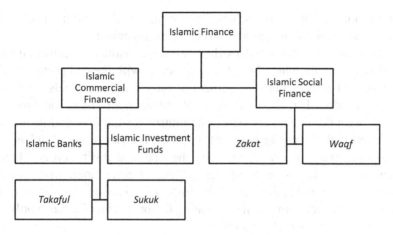

Figure 1.1.   Islamic finance architecture.

units, there is a double coincidence problem in terms of (i) matching cash flow needs and availability and (ii) the preference for maturity in investment and financing. Unlike in spot exchange, information asymmetry between the counterparties in an intertemporal exchange of funds requires diligent monitoring and enforcement of contract terms. Financial institutions provide intermediation services to reduce these transaction costs for both counterparties.

From the Islamic viewpoint, the critical element is that the intertemporal exchange of funds shall not include any increase over the principal amount of the loan. There are two alternatives to meet this restriction. One alternative is that if a money loan is provided, then no increase over the principal amount is charged. The second option is to provide financing for the acquisition of an asset by either selling it or providing it on lease. In both cases, the financial institution has to own, possess, and bear the risk of an asset in possession before selling it or providing it on lease. In such a way of financing, the Islamic financial institution can earn a profit on credit sale or rents on providing the usufruct of an asset in its ownership to the client.

To enable households and firms to meet various financial goals in conformity with *Shari'ah* principles, Islamic finance was theorized and then practically implemented as an alternative financial system in the twentieth century. The first modern Islamic commercial bank, Dubai Islamic Bank, was established in 1975. Since the year 1975, several

Islamic financial institutions have been established in different financial sectors like banking, insurance, and asset management.

According to some scholars, there are some distinctive features inbuilt in Islamic banking which link it automatically with the real sectors of the economy. The necessary requirement of only providing funds for assets that are produced in the real sector of the economy links the financial payoffs with the real assets. Since the returns for the financial institution are linked with the performance of the asset, it ensures more prudence in monitoring and risk management by the financial institution and hence safeguards the investments of depositors.[41] Furthermore, asset-backed financing ensures that the size of the financial sector does not exceed the real size of the economy by necessitating the provision of finance only for the genuine purchase of assets.[42]

1.1.6 *Islamic banking: Growth and profitability*

At the global level, Islamic banking started as social finance in the middle of the twentieth century. In Egypt, Mit Ghamr Islamic Savings Bank was established in 1963 by El-Naggar. Almost at the same time, Tabung Haji or Pilgrims Fund Corporation started operations in 1963 in Malaysia to help Muslims save to meet expenses of the Hajj journey.[43]

Then, the Islamic Development Bank (IDB) was established in 1974 to provide financial support to member countries for economic and community development. After that, commercial banking started in 1970s with the establishment of the Dubai Islamic Bank. Ever since then, the Islamic financial institutions penetrated different parts of the world including the Middle East, East Asia, South Asia, Northern Africa, and Europe.

Thomson Reuters reports that there were as many as 1,389 Islamic financial institutions operating globally by the end of 2017 and at least 45 countries have regulations supporting Islamic finance operations.[44]

---

[41]Ahmed, A. (2010). "Global Financial Crisis: An Islamic Finance Perspective", *International Journal of Islamic and Middle Eastern Finance and Management, 3*(4), 306–320.

[42]Chapra, M. U. (2007). "The Case against Interest: Is it Compelling?" *Thunderbird International Business Review, 49*(2), 161–186.

[43]Chachi, A. (2005). "Origin and Development of Commercial and Islamic Banking Operations", *Journal of King Abdul Aziz University: Islamic Economics, 18*(2), 3–25.

[44]Thomson Reuters (2018). *Islamic Finance Development Report*. Salaam Gateway.

Table 1.1. Growth in Islamic banking and finance (2012–2017).

Year	Islamic Banking Assets ($ Billion)	Islamic Finance Assets ($ Billion)
2012	1,305	1,746
2013	1,565	2,050
2014	1,445	1,965
2015	1,604	2,190
2016	1,675	2,290
2017	1,721	2,438
2023	2,441 (Projected)	3,809 (Projected)

Source: Thomson Reuters Global Islamic Finance Report 2018.

According to the Global Islamic Finance Report 2019, global Islamic finance assets reached $2.6 trillion in 2018.[45] Table 1.1 gives a snapshot of growth in Islamic banking and Islamic finance since 2012.

As much as 71% of the global Islamic financial assets are held by Islamic banking institutions including full-fledged Islamic banks and Islamic banking windows of conventional banks. The total number of Islamic banks and Islamic windows operating globally has reached 505 in 2017.

Among individual countries, the market share of Islamic banking in national banking in Saudi Arabia, Kuwait, Bahrain, Qatar, United Arab Emirates, Malaysia, Pakistan, and Indonesia remains at 52%, 46%, 30%, 26%, 22%, 26%, 15%, and 6%, respectively. Table 1.2 gives the share of different countries in the global Islamic banking assets.

In more recent years, Islamic finance industry assets grew by a Compound Annual Growth Rate (CAGR) of 6% to $2.6 trillion in 2018 as compared to 2012. Quarterly panel data from 2013 to 2018Q1 in Table 1.3 reveal that profitability in Islamic banks has generally been impressive. Furthermore, in Brunei, Egypt, Kuwait, Malaysia, Sudan, and Turkey, the cost to income ratio is below 50%. Except in Bahrain, the gross non-performing finance ratio is lower than 10% in all countries. It shows high asset quality in Islamic banking with low infection ratios. Finally, the capital adequacy ratio on average is greater than 13% in all countries.

---

[45]Global Islamic Finance Report (2019). *Global Islamic Finance Report*. London: Edbiz Consulting Group.

Table 1.2.   Share of countries in global Islamic banking assets.

Country	Share in Global Islamic Banking Assets (%)
Iran	34.40
Saudi Arabia	20.40
UAE	9.30
Malaysia	9.10
Qatar	6.00
Kuwait	6.00
Turkey	2.60
Bangladesh	1.90
Indonesia	1.80
Bahrain	1.70
Sudan	1.60
Pakistan	1.20
Egypt	0.80
Jordan	0.70
Oman	0.60
Brunei	0.50
Others	1.40

Source: Islamic Financial Services Industry Stability Report 2018.

This shows that Islamic banks are solvent and have the ability to withstand financial shocks.

There is a significant potential for further growth in enabling financial inclusion in Muslim majority developing countries. A survey of 65,000 people from 64 countries highlights that Muslims are comparatively less likely than non-Muslims to have a formal account or save at a formal financial institution.[46] In countries like Afghanistan, Morocco, Iraq, Niger, and Djibouti, the percentage of the adult population with no bank

---

[46]Demirgüç-Kunt, A., Klapper, L. *et al.* (2013). *Islamic Finance and Financial Inclusion: Measuring Use of and Demand for Formal Financial Services among Muslim Adults.* Policy Research Working Chapter No. 6642.

Table 1.3.   Islamic banking indicators globally.

Country/ Indicators	Capital Adequacy Ratio (%)	Gross Non-Performing Financing (%)	Return on Assets (%)	Return on Equity (%)	Net Profit Margin (%)	Cost to Income (%)	Liquid Assets to Total Assets (%)
Bahrain	19.0	12.1	1.3	9.8	26.5	82.3	17.6
Brunei	21.2	5.7	1.7	12.3	52.4	40.5	49.9
Egypt	13.5	7.6	2.7	47.9	59.2	31.5	68.4
Indonesia	15.7	4.7	0.9	9.4	9.0	91.1	12.9
Jordan	22.3	3.0	1.7	17.9	48.3	51.7	36.7
Kuwait	18.0	3.0	1.2	10.3	21.4	36.7	32.0
Malaysia	15.7	1.3	1.1	15.2	39.4	41.6	11.2
Nigeria	38.3	1.7	0.1	0.7	4.9	89.9	21.1
Oman	40.7	0.1	−2.0	−3.4	−71.0	158.2	20.4
Pakistan	14.1	6.0	1.0	15.9	24.6	74.8	30.7
KSA	20.3	1.2	2.1	14.4	47.7	52.0	26.3
Sudan	18.7	6.0	2.6	25.7	52.9	43.8	37.1
Turkey	15.5	4.3	1.1	12.4	18.7	49.3	48.7
UAE	16.5	7.9	1.5	12.6	33.9	66.2	15.0

Source: Authors' calculations from IFSB Data.

accounts for religious reasons stands at 33.6%, 26.8%, 25.6%, 23.6%, and 22.8%, respectively.[47]

Furthermore, Sub-Saharan Africa accounts for less than 2% of the Islamic finance assets globally even though the continent's Muslim population is 250 million, and according to the World Bank, as many as 350 million Africans do not have a bank account.[48]

In June 2014, Britain became the first non-Muslim country to issue *Sukuk*, which is an Islamic substitute for the bond. Besides that, Singapore and Hong Kong are other non-Muslim-majority countries that have also issued *Sukuk* in the past. Among the major companies, Goldman Sachs and General Electric's GE Capital have also sold Islamic bonds in the past few years. The Economist reports that some non-Muslims may be drawn to pious banks for ethical reasons since Islamic law forbids investments in stocks of companies which deal in arms, alcoholic drinks, and tobacco.[49]

1.1.7 *Islamic investments*

In *Shari'ah*-compliant asset management, there are more than 1,410 *Shari'ah*-compliant mutual funds operating globally. By the end of 2017, the total global Islamic assets under management (AUM) stood at $110 billion as shown in Table 1.4.

In Islamic capital markets, *Sukuk* is an instrument representing ownership in the underlying asset to the proportion of investment in that underlying asset. The underlying physical asset can be financed using Islamic trade- and lease-based modes of financing. The funding for the asset comes from issuing participation certificates (i.e. *Sukuk*) to the investors. The returns on these assets come in the form of profit on sale or rentals on the use of the assets, which are paid by the issuer of *Sukuk*. *Sukuk* is one of the significant contributors to the total assets of the Islamic finance industry with a total outstanding value of $426 billion in 2017. Overall, 19 countries observed *Sukuk* issuances, amounting to $85 billion in 2017. Among these, agency *Sukuk* constituted a 6% share,

---

[47]Naceur, S. B., Barajas, A. *et al.* (2015). *Can Islamic Banking Increase Financial Inclusion?* IMF Working Chapter, WP/15/31.

[48]*The Economist* (2017). *Africa is Islamic Banking's New Frontier*. Print Edition, July 13, 2017.

[49]*The Economist* (2018). *Why Non-Muslims Are Converting to Sharia Finance*. Print Edition, October 20, 2018.

Table 1.4.   Growth in Islamic fund assets.

Year	Islamic Funds ($ Billion)	*Sukuk* ($ Billion)
2012	46	260
2013	54	284
2014	59	299
2015	66	342
2016	91	345
2017	110	426
2023	325	783

Source: Thomson Reuters Global Islamic Finance Report 2018.

whereas sovereign issuances and corporate issuances constituted 31% and 63% shares, respectively.

In Islamic investments, to determine the eligibility of a company with regard to *Shari'ah* compliance, two sets of criteria are employed. The first step is the qualitative screening. In this process, the companies are screened on the basis of whether their core business is in conformity with Islamic principles or not. Companies dealing in prohibited goods and services are considered non-eligible for selection in the Islamic index or portfolios. For instance, if a company sells goods and services such as alcoholic drinks, arms, pork, intoxicants, pornography, or betting, the company is considered *Shari'ah* non-compliant. If a company engages in interest and gambling-based financial products, such as conventional banking, leasing, and insurance, the company is rendered non-eligible for selection in the Islamic index or portfolios.

After eliminating firms with *Shari'ah*-non-compliant business operations, the remaining firms are evaluated on quantitative indicators. These quantitative indicators are related to *Shari'ah*-non-compliant leverage, *Shari'ah*-non-compliant investments and *Shari'ah*-non-compliant income. Finally, the dividend income obtained on *Halal* stocks is purified to exclude the *Shari'ah*-non-compliant portion of the income from dividends.

Figure 1.2 plots the daily closing index values of the Dow Jones Islamic Market World Index from May 2009 to May 2019. The holding period return for the overall period was 135% during the 10-year period. The average annual return during the period is clocked at 10% per annum, whereas the CAGR has remained at 9% per annum.

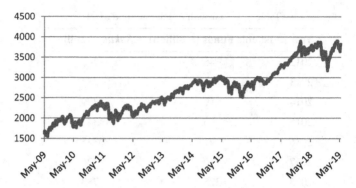

Figure 1.2.   Dow Jones Islamic Market Index closing values (May 2009–2019).

Source: S&P Dow Jones Indices.

1.1.8 *Islamic insurance*

Takaful is an Islamic substitute for conventional insurance. The conventional insurance includes the element of interest-based investments as well as resemblance to gambling since the payoffs are contingent on some future probabilistic events. *Takaful* avoids the element of interest by only resorting to investments that are permissible in Islamic law and which avoid *Riba* (interest), *Maysir* (gambling), and *Gharar* (uncertainty). Rather than paying premiums to a company, the clients contribute voluntary donations (*Tabarru*) in a pool of funds in *Takaful*. This pool of funds is managed by a *Takaful* operator or managing firm. In practice, if the *Takaful* operator only works as an investment agent and to process claims on behalf of all clients, then the agency (*Wakalah*) model is used to organize and structure the *Takaful*. On the contrary, if the *Takaful* operator not only works as an investment agent and to process claims on behalf of all clients as an agent but also as a partner, then the *Mudarabah* model is used to organize and structure the *Takaful*. In the *Mudarabah* model, the compensation to the *Takaful* operator is primarily based on the performance of investments. On the contrary, in the *Wakalah* model, the compensation to the *Takaful* operator is fee based.

In global Islamic finance assets, the share of *Takaful* is 2%. With a CAGR of 6%, *Takaful* assets have grown from $31 billion to $46 billion in 2017 as compared to 2012. Globally, there are 322 *Takaful* operators working in 47 countries.

Table 1.5. The distinction of *Waqf* from other social finance institutions.

Zakat	*Waqf*	Ordinary *Sadaqah*
Obligatory.	Not obligatory.	Not obligatory.
The heads in which *Zakat* funds are to be allocated are clearly specified in *Qur'an*.	Any person can benefit from the *Waqf* assets depending on the purpose for which *Waqf* was established.	Any person can benefit from *Sadaqah*.
Recipients of *Zakat* do not have a consistent and regular source of disbursement to them.	The benefits flow from *Waqf* assets on a regular basis.	Benefits only flow when *Sadaqah* is paid, which maybe regular or irregular.
Zakat collected for a period is usually disbursed in the same period.	It is open to institutionalization due to the non-consumable nature of the *Waqf* assets and their permanent dedication.	The irregular nature of *Sadaqah* renders it less suitable to institutionalization unless the flow of *Sadaqah* is on a regular basis.

1.1.9 *Islamic Awqaf*

Waqf is one of the important institutions in Islamic social finance. In *Waqf*, the owner of some asset or property permanently dedicates an asset along with its usufruct and benefits to a particular social cause voluntarily. This enables the society at large to benefit from *Waqf* assets. In modern practice, *Waqf* can be established through movable as well as immovable assets. Using liquid assets like cash, *Waqf* can be used to mobilize funds for establishing institutions like schools and hospitals. It can also enable the divisibility of the social investments in *Waqf* and enable people at large to contribute to *Waqf* even if they do not wholly own a valuable tangible fixed asset or property. Table 1.5 gives the distinctive features of *Waqf* in comparison to *Zakat* and *Sadaqah*.

1.2 Conclusion

This chapter has introduced the basic foundational principles and economic value proposition of Islamic finance. It has provided a brief look at the variety of Islamic finance institutions that are operating globally. The recent statistics on the Islamic finance industry exhibit exemplary growth and penetration in the Muslim as well as non-Muslim customer base in banking, investments, and insurance. In later chapters, the product structures on which these institutions operate will be explained in more detail.

Self-Assessment Quiz

1. *Riba* encompasses usury as well as:
   (a) Any stipulated amount charged over the principal amount in a loan contract
   (b) Any profit or mark-up in the credit sale of commodities
   (c) Any amount of profit in a commercial contract
   (d) All of the above

2. The economic rationale of prohibiting *Gharar* is to avoid:
   (a) Uncertainty in the contract
   (b) Adverse selection
   (c) Any party gaining some additional return
   (d) Both (a) and (b)

3. Prohibition of *Maysir* implies that:
   (a) Gambling and lottery are disallowed
   (b) All credit sales are disallowed
   (c) All types of speculative trades on forecasts are disallowed
   (d) All of the above

4. In a direct potential exchange between saving-surplus and saving-deficient units, there is a problem of
   (a) Double coincidence of wants in terms of matching cash flow needs
   (b) Matching preference for maturity in investment and financing
   (c) Both (a) and (b)
   (d) None of the above

5. *Takaful* is an Islamic alternative of insurance which avoids
   (a) *Riba*
   (b) *Maysir*
   (c) Both (a) and (b)
   (d) None of the above

Self-Assessment Questions

1. List any two examples of goods and services that are not *Halal* in terms of (i) consumption and (ii) investment.
2. List any five means of earning income that are not permissible in Islamic economics.
3. List the five important elements in the hierarchy of needs in Islamic jurisprudence.
4. Define the term *Riba*. How does bank interest constitute *Riba*?
5. Illustrate the Islamic finance ecosystem by identifying institutions in Islamic commercial finance and Islamic social finance.
6. What is the size of assets in (i) Islamic banking, (ii) Islamic asset management, and (iii) *Takaful* globally.
7. Differentiate between *Zakat*, *Waqf*, and *Sadaqah*.
8. How is *Takaful* different from conventional insurance?
9. Identify social welfare projects which can be funded by mobilizing funds through Cash *Waqf*.
10. Briefly explain the economic demerits of *Gharar* and *Maysir* in economic activities.

Chapter 2

Islamic View on Capital Allocation

2.1 Islamic View on Interest as Price of Capital

In modern mainstream economics, the definition of physical capital stock implies that it includes "produced means of production". Some examples of physical capital stock in contemporary businesses include equipment, tools, machinery, buildings, furniture, infrastructures, installations, and production plants.

As per the definition of physical capital stock, it does not include money capital. However, since there is interest-based banking operating everywhere, the opportunity cost of buying physical capital stock with money capital is considered to be the market interest rate forgone on an alternate interest-based investment of money capital.

The cost of using physical capital stock in the production process is the real interest rate plus the depreciation rate. The real interest rate is the opportunity cost of using money capital in buying the physical capital good. If the interest rate on money capital investments is 10%, then it is considered that the physical capital investment should yield at least 10% for it to be a comparatively better investment decision. Else, if physical capital investment yields a lower return than the return expected on money capital investment, then a rational investor taking into account only the self-interest shall choose money capital investment over physical capital investment in the production process. The argument goes as follows. If an entrepreneur has an option to invest $1,000 with a bank and earn 10% rate of interest on it, then the $1,000 invested in buying equipment for the production process should generate a minimum of 10% return for the justification of efficient allocation of resources.

Apart from the real interest rate, the other component in the user cost of capital is the depreciation rate. It is the rate per period at which there is wear and tear in the physical capital good when it is used in the production process for a period.

The user cost of capital per period as explained by Hall and Jorgenson[1] can be expressed as follows:

$$UC = P_k\,(r + d) \tag{2.1}$$

where UC represents user cost of capital, P_k represents the price of physical capital stock, r represents the real rate of interest, and d represents the rate of depreciation.

Even from the perspective of economics, there are several issues in interest-based financial intermediation. It creates distributive inequity, concentration of wealth, limiting potential investments and as a result it may give rise to unemployment, financial exclusion, rising income inequalities and even ecological imbalances when producers strive hard to pay off debts without considering the external social costs of their operations on the environment.

Since collateral based lending in interest-based financial intermediation mostly entertains large scale businesses, they are able to gain scale advantage and beat the competition from the smaller entrepreneurs. With a greater degree of pricing power in imperfect markets, the producers pass on the cost of capital to the consumers by raising the prices. This fuels inflation in the economy which is not driven by real variables or supply shocks. Rather, it is the result of providing risk free return to the money capital in the economy. Thus, the cost of interest is also by and large paid by the consumers.

Table 2.1 gives an illustration of how interest cost adds in the price and adds to increase in the prices of goods and services. Panel A lists the assumed values for the numerical example. Product's ex-factory cost per unit is the sum of direct material cost per unit, direct labour cost per unit and factory overhead cost per unit. The market price is the cost plus profit markup in the case when no leverage is used and no interest cost is paid. In the case of leverage, the interest expense is calculated as follows:

---

[1]Hall, R. E. and Jorgenson, D. W. (1967). "Tax Policy and Investment Behavior", *American Economic Review*, 57(3), 391–414.

Table 2.1.   Increase in price due to interest cost.

Panel A: Assumptions	
Interest rate	10%
Debt to asset ratio	0.5
Number of units produced	1,000
Direct material cost per unit	$40
Direct labour cost per unit	$20
Factory overhead cost per unit	$20
Desired profit markup	25%
Total assets	$100,000
Panel B: Market Price with No Leverage	
Ex-factory cost per unit	$80
Profit margin per unit	$20
Initial market price	$100
Panel C: Working of Interest per Unit	
Sales revenue	$100,000
Total debt	$50,000
Interest expense	$5,000
Interest per unit	$5
Panel D: Market Price with Leverage	
Ex-factory cost per unit	$80
Interest per unit	$5
Total cost per unit	$85
Profit margin per unit	$21.3
Initial market price	$106.25

$$\text{Interest expense per unit} = \frac{\text{Interest rate} \times \text{Total debt}}{\text{Total units produced}} \qquad (2.2)$$

Interest expense per unit increases with leverage, interest rate and decreases with the number of units of goods produced. Panel C computes the interest expense incurred per unit. Thus, financial institutions also prefer to serve big corporates that are able to absorb the cost of capital over a larger output. Finally, Panel D shows how the additional interest expense per unit raises the cost price as well as market price. It shows how the interest expense incurred by profitable and larger firms is eventually recouped from the pockets of consumers when they purchase the goods and services from the goods market. Furthermore, profitable and larger firms have preferable asymmetric access to credit services in comparison to small firms and micro-entrepreneurs.

On the other hand, in the interest-based financial intermediation, the market interest rate becomes a benchmark return or hurdle rate of return. Social and environment friendly investment projects yielding a lower rate of return than the market rate of return remain unfunded as a result.

In addition to that, firms having an obligation to service debts with fixed payments regardless of their profitability are compelled to push growth in revenues. Often, this results in aggressive advertising and promoting consumerism to meet the cost of interest on borrowed funds. If the demand remains sluggish, then the surplus output remains unsold and causes a recession in the economy leading to unemployment.

Furthermore, since interest is an additional cost in the production process, there is lesser chunk of cost budget available to invest in environmental friendly technologies. Thus, firms squeeze budget by paying less to unskilled labour and overuse other resources which may cause environmental problems. Rather than internalizing the cost of damaging ecological imbalance, firms free ride on whatever leeway they obtain to use and overuse public goods and common property resources.

Finally, since the loans are usually provided to richer segments of the population who can furnish collateral and already have sufficient incomes to service the cost of debts, the gap in incomes between those who are able to access credit services and those who are not able to access credit services rises overtime.

2.2 Critical Analysis of Arguments in Favour of Interest

Sometimes, arguments are made in favour of the justification of interest. These arguments are not potent from the perspective of economics. This section looks at some of these arguments and shows how they do not justify the institution of interest from even the economics standpoint.

2.2.1 *Interest is the price of risk*

Lending money for stipulated interest does not involve risk. The lender gets interest in any situation, no matter whether the borrower earns profit or loss. Even when the borrower takes a loan for meeting health expense or buys essential food intake from the borrowed money, the borrower is required to pay interest. Even when the loans are provided to commercial businesses, the returns from enterprise in the real economy are uncertain. After taking the risk, businesses either earn profit or incur loss.

2.2.2 *Share in the profit of the borrower*

Interest cannot be regarded as the profit share in the business of the borrower. Not all borrowing is for commercial purposes. Even when borrowing is sought for commercial undertakings, the lender does not agree on sharing profits. Rather, the lender stipulates a pre-determined rate of increase demanded over the principal amount of loan. For sharing in the profit and loss of the business, the appropriate way of engagement is to provide investment funds on equity financing basis. In genuine equity financing, profit-sharing ratio is agreed at the beginning. If the profit is earned, it is shared on the basis of profit-sharing ratio. If there is a loss, it is shared on the basis of investment share.

2.2.3 *Interest is a rent on money*

It must be noted that the assets on which rent is charged are used and given back in the same existing condition after the use, such as homes or cars. On the other hand, money and other consumption goods are consumed. When we borrow money, we consume it and then regenerate it to repay our liabilities. In a loan transaction, when the money is used by the borrower, it is consumed. The borrower has to regenerate it and the lender without taking any risk is entitled to receive the consumed money with interest. An example here would illustrate the difference between rentable and non-rentable goods. Can we borrow apples or mangoes on rent? The answer is "no" since these are consumption goods. Thus, we can borrow a hammer, but not the nails based on the above classification between rentable and non-rentable goods.

2.3   Flow of Funds in the Islamic Capital Market

On the choice of financial architecture, we have two major systems: bank based and market based. Market-based systems are characterized by large and active capital markets where firms are able to raise external funds by issuing debt and equity securities. On the contrary, bank-based systems are characterized by financial systems where a major source of external finance is banks.

Several researchers deliberated on the relative merits of both systems, but the consensus view of recent research is that classifying countries as bank based or market based is not important. Bank-based view holds that bank-based systems — particularly at early stages of economic development and in weak institutional settings — do a better job than market-based financial systems at mobilizing savings, allocating capital and exerting corporate control. In contrast, the market-based view emphasizes that markets provide key financial services that stimulate innovation and long-run growth. This section discusses the flow and allocation of investible funds in the Islamic capital market.

The Islamic capital market avoids the elements of interest and instead allocates capital investments based on the profit-sharing ratio. In any typical economy, there are some consumers who have income which is more than their consumption for the period. Such individuals are known as saving surplus units where the savings in a period are the portion of income that is not consumed in the same period. These consumers are required to pay *Zakat* on their surplus wealth endowment in every period if their wealth is above the value of *Nisab*. In contrast to the interest-based asset market, there is no fixed return that they can earn at the prevailing rate of interest by simply lending their surplus savings to a financial institution or debt issuer in the interest-based capital markets. Thus, in order to avoid a reduction in wealth and to earn any legitimate return on their surplus savings, these saving surplus units have to undertake investment in the real economy.

In making investments, these consumers forgo present consumption for possibly higher future consumption. In the light of economic theory and empirical evidence in both mainstream and behavioural finance literature, the amount of investments they make would depend on their (i) marginal rate of substitution between current and future consumption, (ii) reward to variability ratio of the investment undertaking, and (iii) the degree of loss aversion in their preferences. They will reveal their preferences by responding in terms of making different levels of capital investments at different levels of profit-sharing ratio. Steep indifferences curves, i.e. higher marginal rate of substitution for intertemporal consumption and loss aversion, would make them demand a higher profit-sharing ratio for themselves. On the other hand, a higher Sharpe ratio (i.e. higher reward to variability ratio) of a potential investment undertaking would enable them to reap the target level of return even with a lower profit-sharing ratio. Sharpe ratio is the excess return on investment divided by the standard deviation of the return.

In addition to that, in an economy, there will be individuals or groups of individuals who would be looking to pursue productive investments, but remain short of funds. Such individuals would require capital investments. In return, they would offer profit sharing in the investment undertaking. As is the practice, the *ex-ante* profit-sharing ratio is offered by saving deficient units looking to source finance. The factors that determine this offered profit-sharing ratio include the (i) amount of capital needed, (ii) duration of investment, and (iii) reward to variability ratio of the investment undertaking. The greater the capital requirement and the duration of investment undertaking, the higher will be the offered profit-sharing ratio. However, the higher the reward to variability ratio, the lower will be the offered profit-sharing ratio.

Unlike the debt based financing where the savers and investors have the opposite reaction to the rate of return since the return for savers is the cost to the investors, the interest-free equity financing based capital markets do not have an inherent tension between savings and investments. Both react uniformly to the internal strength of the investment undertaking, i.e. reward to variability ratio.

Since there is no fixed return to money capital alone in the loanable funds market, all savings must necessarily be invested in the real economy to earn any return. If no return is required, then surplus savings can be either paid to the charity or given as interest-free loan. However, any return on investments will have to be earned in the real economy. The equilibrium is shown in Figure 2.1 where the horizontal line represents the saving deficient units demand for capital investments whereas the upward sloping line illustrates the saving surplus units supply of investable funds at the different levels of profit-sharing ratios. Equilibrium occurs where at the equilibrium profit-sharing ratio the amount of capital invested by the investors equals the capital investment required by the firms.

The higher capital requirement, longer duration of investment and lower Sharpe ratio will compel the firms to offer a higher profit-sharing

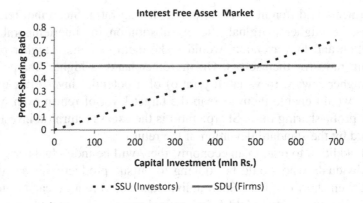

Figure 2.1.   Equilibrium in the interest-free asset market.

Figure 2.2.   Downward shift in SDU curve.

ratio and vice versa. Figures 2.2 and 2.3 show both the downward and upward shift in SDU investment demand curves.

An increase in the Sharpe ratio of an investment indicating greater strength of the project will shift the SDU curve down as well as shift the SSU curve to the right. Thus, firms sourcing funds can source the required

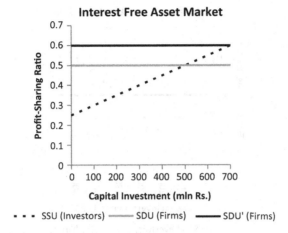

Figure 2.3. Upward shift in SDU curve.

funds at a lower profit-sharing ratio as the SSU curve becomes flatter and shifts to right following an increase in Sharpe ratio.

On the other hand, greater impatience in the consumers would make their indifference curves steeper and hence shift the SSU curve to the left. Furthermore, higher loss aversion would also result in the SSU curve becoming steeper. As a result, firms will have to respond by increasing the profit-sharing ratio for inducing patient and loss averse consumers to engage in capital investments. Figures 2.4 and 2.5 show both the rightward and leftward shift in SSU investment supply curves.

Thus, the preceding analysis shows that movement in the profit-sharing ratio can perform the asset allocation function in the interest-free capital market. Furthermore, investment acceleration can be achieved through institutionalizing *Zakat* which levies a charge on idle wealth. In an economy where there is a prohibition of interest, the surplus and idle wealth would accelerate the conversion of saving into investment. Thus, it can enhance the scale of decent employment opportunities and contribute to economic growth. Even those savers who would not like to directly invest in stocks of new start-ups or small companies, they will invest through financial intermediaries like banks and mutual funds to minimize their risk by diversification and effective asset reallocation by skilful fund managers who could monitor the performance more effectively and efficiently on investors' behalf.

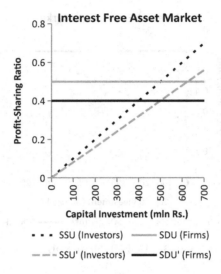

Figure 2.4.   Rightward shift in SSU curve.

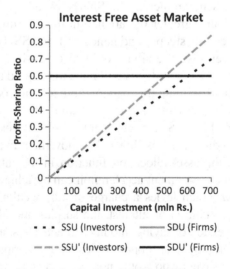

Figure 2.5.   Leftward shift in SSU curve.

In addition to that, since there is no return on money balances and direct participation possibilities in the investment projects through asset markets, there will be a lower risk for the economy to fall in a liquidity trap. The liquidity trap is a situation in economy when people tend to hold onto their cash balances rather than investing them in return-generating investments when the return on such investments is very low. The Haque and Mirakhor show that due to no compulsion of paying interest as a cost, the rate of return to both saving surplus units and saving deficient units from the productive enterprise will increase and will cause the aggregate savings to increase.[2] Due to the prohibition of interest, these savings will be converted into investments and will contribute to employment generation rather than sitting idle and earning stipulated increase at the rate of interest without any regard to the real economic activities.

The effects of Islamic capital market operations on the macro economy are also positive. There is less pressure on the current account balance if there is no or limited gap between savings and investments. In an open market economy, the gap between savings and investments is filled by the current account balance. Thus, a stable current account can have a stabilizing effect on the exchange rate and on domestic currency as a store of value in the interest-free economy. In an empirical study of 15 Muslim majority countries, it has been found that interest-free money is more stable than interest-bearing money.[3]

2.4 Islamic Banking for Short-Term Financing and Investments

Academic literature that discusses the philosophy and rationale of banking as an institution explains the rationale for having banks as institutions that bring efficiency in intertemporal trade, distribute risk, deal effectively with asymmetric information and provide an effective means of monitoring.

Islamic banking enables short-term intertemporal finance between risk averse investors and individual and corporate clients who require short-term finance. Risk averse investors want to minimize risk and delegate the responsibility of credit portfolio monitoring to the Islamic banks.

---

[2] Haque, N. and Mirakhor, A. (1986). *Saving Behaviour in an Economy without Fixed Interest*. Discussion Paper, Development and Research Department, Economics and Research Staff, Report No. DRD184.
[3] Hassan, M. K. and Aldayel, A. Q. (1998). "Stability of Money Demand Under Interest-Free Versus Interest-Based Banking System", *Humanomics*, *14*(4), 166–185.

There are certain short-term finance needs that might be difficult to finance through long-term equity finance or which can be more efficiently funded through employing trade and lease based modes of financing. Interest-free Islamic banking primarily caters to short-term finance needs involving an asset and the investor client base of Islamic banks are investors who want to smooth the path of consumption through regular incomes with limited chances of risk. Thus, Islamic banking investments are suitable for impatient, risk averse and loss averse investors who invest in a limited way by sharing in the financing of real assets where the returns are linked to the asset's sale or use rather than their long-term productivity.

At the outset, it is important to know that Islamic banking is a set of principles, rules and product structures that are compliant with Islamic laws and principles. Islamic law or *Shari'ah* is embodied in the *Qur'an* and the *Sunnah* (teachings) of Prophet Muhammad (pbuh). Since the contemporary financial and banking system did not exist 1,400 years ago, the foundational principles in Islamic *Shari'ah* are used to prescribe the true Islamic viewpoint with regard to contemporary products and practices by the *Shari'ah* advisors. The term *Shari'ah* compliant in Islamic finance refers to an instrument, transaction or contract which is compliant with the principles of *Shari'ah*.

The basic structure of Islamic banking looks like this. First, an Islamic bank establishes an asset pool. In that asset pool, the investment comes in the form of the bank's equity and deposits. The deposits in Islamic banks have two further categories, i.e. return-generating deposits and non-return-generating deposits. Investors expect to gain profits on return-generating deposit accounts, such as savings deposits and fixed/time deposit accounts. On the other hand, investors expect to gain no profit on non-return-generating deposit accounts, such as the current account. Such accounts are used for safekeeping of deposits as well as facilitating payments and remittances.

Return-generating deposits are mobilized by using *Mudarabah* structure. It is a form of partnership in which one party *Mudarib* provides management expertise and the other party *Rabb-ul-Maal* provides the investment capital for the partnership. Profits are shared between the two partners on the basis of a pre-agreed profit-sharing ratio. In case, there is a loss in partnership, it is exclusively borne by the investing partner, i.e. *Rabb-ul-Maal*.

In deposit mobilization operations of Islamic banking, bank's shareholders act as *Mudarib*, i.e. working partner and depositors act as

Rabb-ul-Maal, i.e. investing partner to form the partnership. Profit-sharing ratio is agreed at the start of this partnership. Non-return-generating deposits are mobilized by using *Qard* (interest-free loan) or *Wadiah* (safe-keeping deposits).

The pool of assets established for the investment purpose is then used to provide asset backed financing to the individual and corporate clients. In accounting terminology, the asset pool is the liability side of the Islamic bank's balance sheet; whereas, the asset backed financing assets and receivables comprise the asset side of the Islamic bank's balance sheet. Asset backed financing comprises various financing assets based on different underlying lease and trade based modes of financing.

Islamic banks generate income through rents and profit on credit sale. The distribution of income takes place first between the shareholders of the bank and the depositors as one category. Then, the income is distributed among the different category of deposits based on a weightage mechanism. Among the depositors, the horizontal distribution of profits makes the use of a weighting mechanism to provide an opportunity to earn higher profits on larger and long-term deposits. Weights are pre-assigned to different types of depositors depending on the magnitude and maturity profile of the deposit category. The detailed illustration of profit distribution will be discussed in Chapter 3.

2.5 Islamic Banks in the Islamic Economic Framework

Islamic economic principles are very much open and favourable towards a market-based economy. By enabling the market economy to run competitively, an Islamic economy provides market-based solutions for employment creation and improvement in living standards through effective and efficient utilization of resources. The market competitiveness is achieved by removing from the economy those factors which lead to concentration of wealth and underutilization of given labour and non-labour resources in the economy. In an Islamic economic framework, private investment is incentivized by the institution of *Zakat* which favours private investment/spending rather than hoarding wealth.

In a market following Islamic norms and values, the market forces will determine which *Halal* goods and services should be produced and offered at what price. Firms produce goods with resources provided by the household sector. Households are paid a return on their labour. If households provide investment capital, then they are provided a share in profits. Firms produce and sell goods in the goods market which are purchased by the households. These households obtain purchasing power by providing rentable factors of production like labour services (*Ijarat-ul-Ashkhas*) or usufruct of a naturally existing or produced real asset (*Ijarat-ul-A'yan*) in the production process and earn compensation in terms of wage and rent, respectively. As per Islamic rules of trade, the subject matter should be *Halal* and the price once determined cannot be changed in a credit sale after the sale is executed.

Since contemporary businesses require expensive and long duration capital goods for achieving efficiency and economies of scale, sourcing capital from individual households having surplus investible capital might be cumbersome. Islamic banks exist to reduce transaction cost, mitigate moral hazard and provide asset backed financing. Islamic banks monitor the investments made by households and share the profits on investments with them.

Since there is no provision of earning money by simply loaning fiat money, all the financing provided is backed by real assets in the Islamic economic framework. This mitigates the moral hazard problem and the misuse of funds. It also ensures that the real assets are traded or leased when a financing contract is executed. Thus, it strengthens the link with the real economy and links the payoffs with the outcome of real economic transactions rather than fixing profit for one party in investments.

As per Islamic principles, for earning money on monetary investments, the money capital has to be invested in a productive enterprise to earn a share in actual profit/loss out of the productive enterprise in which it is used. Rather than concentrating risk with only the borrower, the risk is widely shared in Islamic banking instruments and contracts.

By ensuring that financial intermediaries cannot simply earn interest on money capital alone, they necessarily have to ensure that they provide asset backed financing and these assets are purchased from the resource markets (such as raw materials, equipment, and machinery) or goods market (such as cars and consumer appliances).

Finally, the institution of *Zakat* ensures that the poor and hungry people who earn below subsistence level incomes are provided with income support so that they can fulfil their basic needs. Producers and rich households who are required to pay *Zakat*, *Ushr* (10% levy on the value of produce requiring either labour or capital for production), *Khamsa* (5% levy or half

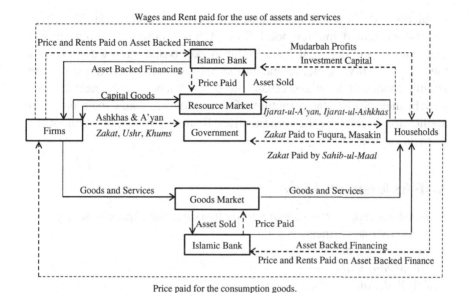

Figure 2.6. Islamic economics framework.

Ushr on value of produce requiring both labour and capital for production), and *Khums* (20% levy on value of produce requiring neither labour nor capital for production) share their incomes with the poor households.

Thus, the Islamic economic framework ensures that the investible capital is invested in the real economy and through which, a greater magnitude of employment opportunities are created against an interest-based financial system in which the funds can be invested in financial derivatives and money market to earn a risk-free return. Finally, those households which remain unable to earn sufficient incomes to meet their needs are supported through the second phase of circulation of endowments which is not based on the profit motive, but which is driven by pure altruism. Figure 2.6 shows the Islamic economic framework in which the dashed lines represent monetary flows and the solid lines represent the commodity flows.

2.6 Conclusion

This chapter discussed the Islamic viewpoint on interest and its economic rationale. It also introduced how the institution of interest causes problems in the allocation of resources and income distribution. The chapter also presented intertemporal flow of funds between saving surplus units and saving deficient units in the market-based intermediation with the use of equity financing and in the bank-based intermediation using Islamic modes of lease and credit sale based financing. The next chapter will further discuss the structure of these contracts and their practical application in meeting the contemporary financing needs, but without the element of interest.

Self-Assessment Quiz

1. In which type of the investment partnership, the capital is solely provided by one partner:
   (a) *Musharakah*
   (b) *Mudarabah*
   (c) *Wakalah*
   (d) All of the above

2. In the conventional capitalist system, the user cost of capital assigns real rate of interest as compensation of:
   (a) Land
   (b) Physical capital stock
   (c) Money capital
   (d) Both (a) and (b)
   (e) Both (b) and (c)

3. In collateral based lending, which types of clients are mostly able to secure financing from commercial banks?
   (a) Small scale start-ups who want to borrow to setup business
   (b) Large scale corporations with business history
   (c) Entrepreneurs with a budding business idea who lack resources
   (d) Social entrepreneurs investing in a project of high social significance

4. Which factors will lead to a rightward shift in saving surplus units supply curve of investible funds in Islamic capital markets?
   (a) Increase in Sharpe ratio
   (b) Greater patience in the consumers
   (c) Lower loss aversion
   (d) All of the above

5. Which factors will lead to a downward shift in saving deficient units demand curve for investible funds in Islamic capital markets?
   (a) Lower capital requirement
   (b) Shorter duration of the investment
   (c) Higher Sharpe ratio
   (d) All of the above

Self-Assessment Questions

1. What is the user cost of capital in mainstream economics?
2. What is the rationale of interest charged and stipulated on money capital in conventional economics?
3. Critically evaluate the rationale of interest charged and stipulated on money capital in conventional economics.
4. Illustrate numerically how interest-based leverage increases the prices of goods in the goods market by adding as an additional operating cost in product costing?
5. If producers increase the prices in proportion to the additional cost incurred in obtaining interest-based leverage, is it fair to say that the eventual cost of interest is paid by the consumers?
6. Illustrate the flow of funds and equilibrium in the Islamic capital markets.
7. Identify the factors determining a change in savings supply and investment demand in the Islamic capital markets.
8. Discuss the economic role of Islamic banking in facilitating investments and financing needs for the short term.
9. Illustrate the Islamic economic framework through commodity and monetary flow of funds in goods and resource markets involving households, producers and Islamic banks.
10. Discuss how Islamic banks facilitate real economic activity in the purchase of assets in the goods and resource markets.

Appendix A.1: Effects of *Zakat* on Wealth Redistribution

This appendix provides an illustration of how the institution of *Zakat* in an Islamic economy encourages investment and provides a disincentive for hoarding wealth. For a particular individual, net *Zakat* wealth at a point in time is given by Equation (A.1):

$$A_t = (1 - \text{ROZ}) * (A_{t-1} + Y_t - C_t) \tag{A.1}$$

Here, Y_t represents the income of an individual in period t. A_{t-1} represents the total value of endowments carried forward from the last period. C_t represents the consumption expenditure in time period t. ROZ represents the rate of *Zakat*, which is 2.5% on surplus wealth.

Further expansion of Equation (A.1) yields

$$A_t = A_{t-1} + Y_t - C_t - \text{ROZ}\left(A_{t-1} + Y_t - C_t\right) \tag{A.2}$$

Applying the 2.5% value of ROZ in Equation (A.2) yields

$$A_t = A_{t-1} + Y_t - C_t - 0.025\left(A_{t-1} + Y_t - C_t\right)$$

$$A_t = 0.975 A_{t-1} + 0.975 Y_t - 0.975 C_t$$

If the equation is expanded iteratively forward, it becomes

$$A_{t+1} = A_t + Y_{t+1} - C_{t+1} - 0.025\left(A_t + Y_{t+1} - C_{t+1}\right)$$

$$A_{t+1} = 0.975 A_t + 0.975 Y_{t+1} - 0.975 C_{t+1}$$

$$A_{t+1} = 0.975\left(0.975 A_{t-1} + 0.975 Y_t - 0.975 C_t\right) + 0.975\left(Y_{t+1} - C_{t+1}\right)$$

$$A_{t+1} = 0.950625\left(A_{t-1} + Y_{t-1} - C_{t+1}\right) + 0.975\left(Y_{t+1} - C_{t+1}\right) \tag{A.3}$$

The wealth function will reduce A_{t-1} in the subsequent time period. The increase in wealth only depends on enhancing Y_t or reducing C_t. This shows that only labour income or financial income which involves productive enterprise and risk taking along with moderation in consumption can enhance the wealth.

PART II

Theory and Application of Islamic Banking Products

Chapter 3

Product Structures in Islamic Banking

3.1 Introduction

The key aspects which underpin the core of Islamic banking and finance philosophy and operations include the following five essential features:

(1) Avoid interest, major uncertainty in contracts, and gambling.
(2) Participative and risk-sharing based financial intermediation.
(3) Avoid distributive inequity.
(4) Prohibition of unethical businesses and practices.
(5) Finance real assets or asset-backed enterprises.

Islamic banking is not based on the concept of lending money for interest. In Islamic banking, money is not lent. Islamic principles do not consider money as a tradable commodity since money does not have any intrinsic value of its own. Financing products in Islamic banking provide finance to clients who have a genuine need for purchasing an asset for personal or commercial use.

Islamic banking provides finance to the clients for the purchase of assets using either lease based modes of finance like *Ijarah* or Diminishing *Musharakah* or trade-based modes of finance like *Murabaha*, *Salam*, or *Istisna*. Islamic principles allow profit on trade and rent on the provision of usufruct of an asset in ownership. Hence, Islamic banking earns a legitimate source of income in the form of profit on trade or rental income from the lease of assets.

On the deposits side, Islamic banks do not give stipulated interest to the depositors. When Islamic banks take deposits from the general public,

43

the underlying contract is not that of a *Qard* (loan), except in the current account. In return-generating investment accounts, the depositors invest money and share in actual profits based on a pre-agreed profit-sharing ratio. Hence, the element of interest is not present in Islamic banking in either deposit mobilization or while providing finance to the different consumers and corporate clients. Table 3.1 compares the features of an Islamic bank vis-à-vis a conventional bank.

Table 3.1.   Comparative analysis of Islamic and conventional banks.

Islamic Banks	Conventional Banks
Depositors in Islamic banks bear the risk of the enterprise.	Conventional banks provide guaranteed returns to depositors without any regard to their own profitability.
Islamic banks take deposits as debt for non-remunerative accounts and as an investment in remunerative accounts.	Conventional banks take all deposits as debt, whether it is for remunerative or non-remunerative accounts.
Based on the profit-sharing ratio and the performance of financing assets, the profit amount can be variable in Islamic investment accounts.	Depositors in conventional banks get guaranteed returns no matter how the loan portfolio of bank performs.
Islamic banks work under the surveillance of the Shari'ah Supervisory Boards.	No governing framework for ensuring ethical compliance beyond the secular law of the land.
Islamic banks provide sale-based, equity-based, and lease-based financing where a real asset is sold or leased.	Conventional banks provide money on a loan basis for all short-term and long-term finance needs.
Islamic banks do not provide financing for the purchase of *Haram* goods, such as dealing with casinos, sellers of alcoholic drinks, sellers of drugs, and sellers of weapons.	Conventional banks provide loans for all purposes which are considered legal in a jurisdiction.
The income for Islamic banks comes in the form of profit on sale of asset or rent on lease of asset.	Conventional banks get stipulated interest on a money loan.
In order to earn a profit on sale and rent of asset, Islamic banks take ownership and risk related to the asset until a sale to the client is made in sale-based financing and until the asset is provided for use to the client in lease-based financing.	Conventional banks do not take ownership and risk related to the asset. They provide loans and earn interest on them.

3.2 Asset Side of Islamic Bank: Financing and Advances

After looking at the comparative features of an Islamic bank as compared to a conventional bank, it is easier to appreciate the difference between the two systems of banking. Due to these differences as discussed in Table 3.1, the balance sheet of an Islamic bank has visible differences as compared to the balance sheet of a conventional bank. Table 3.2 illustrates the typical balance sheet structure of an Islamic bank.

This section explains one important asset class for an Islamic bank, i.e. Islamic financing assets. From the perspective of a bank, assets among other things include the financing and advances made by the bank for earning profits. Some of the important and often used financing products of Islamic banks are discussed in this chapter. Figure 3.1 shows a schematic diagram of some of the different modes of financing available in the Islamic banking system.

3.2.1 *Trade based modes of financing*

3.2.1.1 *Murabaha*

Murabaha is a sale transaction. On the contrary, *Murabaha* Muajjal is a deferred payment sale. *Murabaha* as a mode of finance is used in trade

Table 3.2.   Balance sheet of an Islamic bank.

Assets	Liabilities and Equity
Short-Term Assets	**Liabilities**
Cash and balances with treasury banks	Demand deposits
Balances with other banks	Investment deposits
Short-term investments	Special investment deposits
Short-term Islamic financing assets	Bills payable
Other short-term assets	Other liabilities
Long-Term Assets	**Equity**
Long-term investments	Share capital
Long-term Islamic financing assets	Reserves
Other long-term assets	Retained earnings
Total Assets	**Total Liabilities and Equity**

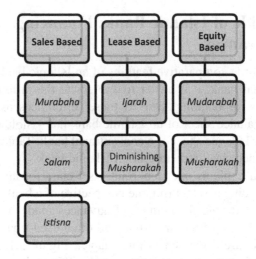

Figure 3.1.   Some widely used Islamic modes of financing.

financing, working capital financing, and small and medium enterprise financing for the short-term period. If a customer wants to buy an asset for which he does not have the capacity to pay immediately, then a *Murabaha* contract could be used to provide short-term financing. The general process flow of *Murabaha* is as follows:

An Islamic bank and the client sign a *Murabaha* finance agreement and an agency agreement. According to the agency agreement, the customer purchases goods from the supplier on the bank's behalf as an agent of the bank. The customer also undertakes to purchase the asset from the bank. It is a one-sided promise and undertaking by the customer. Then, the bank pays the price of the asset to the supplier and obtains a title and physical/constructive possession of the asset through its agent. The customer then signs a declaration that he has purchased the goods on the bank's behalf and now he is willing to purchase the asset from the bank. After the offer and acceptance, the sale is executed and the customer pays the agreed price to the bank. In the sale agreement, the payment date is set keeping in view the customer's need.

The following example shows how *Murabaha* works in Islamic banking for the purchase of raw materials. The various steps in such a *Murabaha* transaction would generally be carried out in the following way as also demonstrated in Figure 3.2.

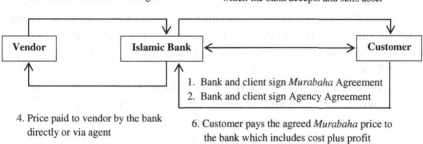

3. Bank buys asset and vendor transfers asset to the bank or bank's agent

5. Customer offers to buy asset from the bank which the bank accepts and sells asset

1. Bank and client sign *Murabaha* Agreement
2. Bank and client sign Agency Agreement

4. Price paid to vendor by the bank directly or via agent

6. Customer pays the agreed *Murabaha* price to the bank which includes cost plus profit

Figure 3.2. *Murabaha* process flow.

(1) The Islamic bank and the client sign a *Murabaha* finance agreement and an agency agreement.
(2) The customer undertakes to purchase the raw material from the bank. It is a one-sided promise and undertaking.
(3) According to the agency agreement, the customer purchases raw material from the supplier on the bank's behalf. The bank pays the supplier and obtains the title and physical/constructive possession of the raw materials.
(4) The customer signs a declaration that he has purchased the raw materials on the bank's behalf and now he is willing to purchase the raw materials from the bank.
(5) After offer and acceptance, the sale is executed, and the customer pays the agreed price to the bank.

Let us take an illustrative example. Ahmed runs a bakery and wants to purchase a heavy-duty oven. The oven costs $1 million in spot payment. Ahmed does not have money now, so he wants to obtain financing. But, he expects to be able to pay the amount in a short period of time. An Islamic bank agrees to finance the asset purchase. This financing need can be met using the mode of *Murabaha*.

In executing *Murabaha*, sometimes, the client is asked to buy the asset acting as an agent to the bank because he has more knowledge about the product and better relationships with the supplier to obtain the assets at a competitive price and in a timely and appropriate manner. However, the roles of the client as an agent and an eventual buyer remain distinct in the *Murabaha* transaction. Islamic banks prefer to pay the suppliers directly, which enhances their involvement as well as ensures that the financing amount is used for the particular objective for which it was provided.

Rollover of debt, i.e. rescheduling, in *Murabaha* is not allowed. It implies that if the *Murabaha* price is to be paid after three months from the date of the transaction, then it cannot be altered if the payment is made after six months from the date of transaction. A price once agreed cannot be altered as any increase in price due to a delay in payment would constitute *Riba*.

To maintain financial discipline, it is important to have a deterrent against wilful and unjustified delays in payment. In practice, the customer is asked to sign a unilateral undertaking in which he unilaterally promises to pay to charity an amount of money if he delays payments without any justifiable reason. Nonetheless, this promise remains unilateral and the Islamic bank does not take the charity amount received from the customer as its income. The reason why the Islamic bank is allowed to receive and administer the charity amount on late payment is that it will ensure that the client pays to charity and does not avoid it. Hence, this payment to charity serves as a deterrent to discourage late payment, but it is not meant to compensate the bank. Having such a deterrent would encourage timely payments, which will protect the depositors from losing their investments.

It is also important that the goods cannot be sold if they are consumed already. Hence, the sequence of steps in *Murabaha* is important for it to be a valid contract. It is also necessary that the price is stipulated clearly in the *Murabaha* contract. In *Murabaha*, the seller discloses the cost. *Murabaha* price is the sum of the disclosed cost-plus profit for the seller.

Lastly, all rules of sale pertaining to Islamic principles of trade must be followed, which implies that the subject matter in *Murabaha* must be (a) *Halal*, (b) existing, (c) valuable and, (d) remaining in ownership, possession and risk of the bank when the bank wants to sell the asset to the client. If the asset does not exist or the bank does not have ownership and possession of the asset, then the *Murabaha* transaction cannot be executed. The sale price must be determined without any ambiguity and the sale must be unconditional. To ensure possession, either physical or constructive possession can be taken.

3.2.1.2 *Salam*

Salam is a sale transaction in which delivery of the subject matter is deferred, while payment in a *Salam* transaction for the subject matter is immediate. A *Salam* contract can only be done for commodities whose characteristics can be specified. Goods that are traded using the *Salam* contract must be specified and quantified in a manner that no ambiguity or uncertainty is left in the contract. It is also necessary that the *Salam* contract does not involve partial payment. Full, immediate payment is necessary for the validity of the *Salam* contract.

Salam is used in financing goods and services that are not ready for spot sale and will have to be delivered later. In *Salam*, payment is on spot basis, but the delivery is deferred. Thus, *Salam* is used in special cases to facilitate transactions. Islamic principles of sale do not allow selling of a commodity whose possession is not with the seller at the time of sale, but *Salam* is an exception to this rule along with another sale contract which is known as *Istisna*.

In current practice, *Salam* is used to provide financing in the agriculture sector. For instance, if a farmer needs to grow a crop and needs financing to buy fertilizers, pesticides, and seeds, then he can be provided with financing by an Islamic bank using *Salam*. First, the bank will buy the crop from the farmer in specified quantity, quality, and standards. The bank will pay the price for the purchased crop on the spot. Nonetheless, in a *Salam* contract, the seller of the crop in this case has the chance to provide the subject matter of sale (crop) at a specified future date.

Then, the Islamic bank will resell the crop to another potential buyer at a higher price by entering into another *Salam* contract. Since it is a *Salam* contract, the Islamic bank will deliver the crop at a specified future date but will receive the payment on the spot. On the maturity date, it is vital that the seller in the *Salam* contract deliver the crops. In practice, the Islamic bank generally supplies the same crop to the buyer in a parallel *Salam* which it receives from the farmer who obtained finance from the bank originally. However, in case the delivery dates do not match or the same crop cannot be supplied to the buyer in a parallel *Salam* contract by the Islamic bank, then the Islamic bank will still have to supply the crops as specified in the parallel *Salam* contract on the delivery date. For this purpose, the Islamic bank might have to purchase new crops in the specified form from the market to settle the delivery obligation in the parallel *Salam* contract. Figure 3.3 illustrates the various steps in the *Salam* transaction.

In a parallel *Salam* contract, it is necessary that the client in the parallel *Salam* contract must not be the same client or his associates as in the first *Salam* contract.

Let us take an illustrative example to explain the use of *Salam*. Faheem is an entrepreneur with specialization in bio-technology. He sells high-quality cotton. He is facing a working capital shortfall to continue production. He has purchase orders from customers, but limited capital to

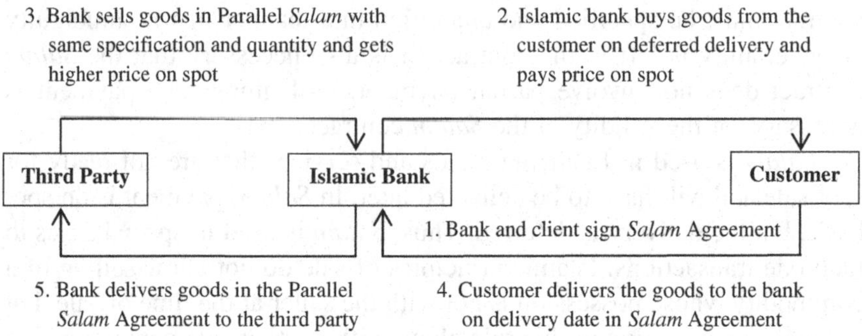

3. Bank sells goods in Parallel *Salam* with
   same specification and quantity and gets
   higher price on spot

2. Islamic bank buys goods from the
   customer on deferred delivery and
   pays price on spot

| Third Party | | Islamic Bank | | Customer |

1. Bank and client sign *Salam* Agreement

5. Bank delivers goods in the Parallel
   Salam Agreement to the third party

4. Customer delivers the goods to the bank
   on delivery date in *Salam* Agreement

Figure 3.3.   *Salam* process flow.

undertake and pay the production cost. He contacts an Islamic bank for working capital financing for his venture. This financing need can be fulfilled by structuring the transaction on the basis of *Salam*.

3.2.1.3 *Istisna*

Istisna is a sale transaction in which the subject matter needs to be manufactured. In an *Istisna* transaction, delivery of the subject matter is deferred due to the fact that the subject matter needs to be manufactured and does not exist at the time of entering into an *Istisna* transaction. Payment in *Istisna* can be immediate and can be deferred and can also be paid in instalments. In *Salam*, payment is on the spot in full, but the delivery is deferred. In *Istisna*, there is no restriction on time of payment. However, unlike in *Salam*, *Istisna* can only be done for goods which need to be manufactured.

It is used in financing goods that are not yet ready for sale and will have to be manufactured. Examples include architectural services or construction services. *Istisna* can be used for financing the construction of houses, plants, railway tracks, bridges, underpasses, dams, roads, and highways, for instance. It is an order to a producer to manufacture a specific commodity or asset for the purchaser. It can be used in pre-shipment export financing and is usable in all other situations where goods have to be manufactured before transfer of ownership and possession. The price can be paid in instalments or via a single payment in advance or after delivery. Execution of *Istisna* would involve the following steps as also illustrated in Figure 3.4.

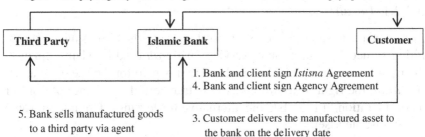

Figure 3.4. *Istisna* process flow.

(1) The Islamic bank and the client sign an *Istisna* agreement whereby the Islamic bank orders the client to produce certain goods.
(2) The client manufactures the goods as per the order specification.
(3) The Islamic bank appoints the client as its agent to stock the goods at its premises on the bank's behalf.
(4) The Islamic bank orders the client to sell the manufactured goods (owned by the bank) to a third party.
(5) The client sells the goods to a third party on the bank's behalf.
(6) The client pays the proceeds of the sale to the Islamic bank.
(7) The Islamic bank pays agency fees to the client for the services rendered by the client as the bank's agent.

It is necessary that the latest delivery date is specified by which date, the goods will be ready for delivery after manufacturing. Since the cost of the finished good or asset cannot be perfectly known in advance, the price of raw material and other costs can be adjusted in the final *Istisna* price if there is actual fluctuation in prices.

Let us take an illustrative example to explain the use of *Istisna* in practice. Ubaid is an architect who serves clients in interior designing of their apartments on a one-off basis. He got a big breakthrough with an offer from a well-known builder to construct false ceilings and wooden cabinets in a residential apartment building. He has expertise, but no capital to undertake the project. The builder will start to receive bookings after completion of 30% of the work and cannot pay Ubaid the whole amount now. But, the builder undertakes to buy the assets from Ubaid upon delivery. So, Ubaid contacts an Islamic bank for financing. This financing need can be fulfilled by structuring the transaction on the basis of *Istisna*.

3.2.2 *Lease-based modes of financing*

3.2.2.1 *Ijarah*

Ijarah means to sell usufruct of an asset on rent. The term is also used for hiring someone to do a job or service. In *Ijarah* used in Islamic finance, the right to use an asset is obtained and rent is paid for the use of an asset. In *Ijarah*, the right of use of an asset is transferred to another person for a consideration. It is an Islamic alternative for leasing a tangible movable or immovable asset.

The lease period begins when the asset is delivered by the lessor in a usable condition to the lessee. The bank (lessor) bears the ownership-related costs and the customer (lessee) bears the usage-related costs. Insurance, import duty, installation, other taxes and delivery charges are paid by the bank, added in its cost, and taken into account when quoting rentals to the customer at the time of entering into the *Ijarah* agreement.

If the asset is destroyed or becomes unusable, the bank stops taking rent and does not charge rent for that period. This is one of the distinct features of *Ijarah* which makes it different from a conventional finance lease.

Penalty for late payment is charged for maintaining financial discipline and is paid to charity. The rationale for this has been discussed earlier. Unlike conventional banks, an Islamic bank cannot take such penalties on late payment as income. Such financial penalties can only be used as a deterrent against a wilful delay in payment obligations by the client.

The asset remains in the ownership and risk of the bank until the bank sells the asset to the customer in a separate agreement. Unlike in a conventional finance lease, the asset's risk is borne by the bank during the whole period of the lease.

Ijarah is commonly used in the leasing of movable assets like a car. If *Ijarah* is used in car financing, the financing arrangement would follow these steps as also illustrated in Figure 3.5.

(1) The customer approaches the bank for obtaining a vehicle on lease. The customer undertakes to enter into a lease agreement with the bank and pay rent for the use of the vehicle during the lease period.
(2) The bank buys the vehicle and gets ownership and possession of the vehicle.
(3) The bank pays the price of the vehicle to the vendor directly.

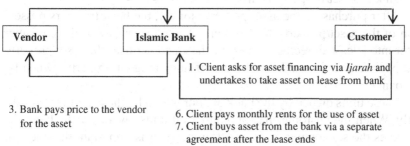

2. Islamic bank purchases the asset from the vendor and takes ownership and possession

4. Bank delivers the asset in usable form to client
5. Bank undertakes to sell asset after lease ends

1. Client asks for asset financing via *Ijarah* and undertakes to take asset on lease from bank

3. Bank pays price to the vendor for the asset

6. Client pays monthly rents for the use of asset
7. Client buys asset from the bank via a separate agreement after the lease ends

Figure 3.5. *Ijarah* process flow.

(4) The lease agreement is signed whereby the bank provides the vehicle on lease and the customer starts using the vehicle and pays rent for each period.

(5) At the end of the lease period, the customer can purchase the vehicle from the bank by way of a separate purchase agreement.

Let us take an illustrative example of Ahmed again who wants to start a bakery business. Ahmed wants to purchase a heavy-duty oven for the bakery. The oven costs $1 million in spot payment. Ahmed does not have money now, so he wants to obtain financing. He expects to be able to pay the amount over a long period of time. So, he is looking for a long-term finance option. The Islamic bank agrees to finance the asset purchase using the *Ijarah* mode of financing. This financing need can be structured using the mode of *Ijarah*.

3.2.2.2 *Diminishing Musharakah*

Diminishing *Musharakah* is also a suitable mode of long term finance in Islamic banking. It is generally used to finance long-term fixed assets for a longer duration in corporate and consumer financing. In consumer financing, it is also the most common structure used in offering house financing products by Islamic banks.

In Diminishing *Musharakah*, the customer approaches the bank for the joint purchase of an asset/property. Designated valuation agencies are consulted for the valuation of the asset/property. The seller of the property is paid by the bank from its own funds as well as the payment received from the customer for the joint purchase of asset/property. The share of the bank in asset/property is divided into units.

After purchasing the asset/property jointly, the bank transfers possession of the asset/property to the client. Then, the bank and the customer enter into a lease agreement whereby the customer uses the asset/property and pays rent to the bank for the use of units in asset/property owned by the bank.

These units owned by the bank are purchased by the customer periodically. When the customer has purchased all units owned by the bank, he becomes the sole owner of the asset/property. It is important that the risk of damage to the asset/property is borne by the bank and the customer, according to the stake in the asset/property at the time of the disaster.

The financing arrangement is referred to as "Diminishing *Musharakah*" because the ownership stake of the tenant increases and that of the bank decreases with the passage of time as the client purchases the ownership share in the asset/property owned by the bank.

Table 3.3 compares conventional mortgage and Diminishing *Musharakah*.

In corporate finance, Diminishing *Musharakah* can be used to purchase an immovable asset like heavy industrial equipment. Financing of such assets through Diminishing *Musharakah* would involve the following steps as also illustrated in Figure 3.6.

Table 3.3.   Comparison of Diminishing *Musharakah* with mortgage.

Features	Conventional Mortgage	Diminishing *Musharakah*
How the bank earns	Interest on the principal amount lent	Rent for use of the asset in ownership and risk
Nature of instalment	Interest + Principal repayment	Rent + Sale of units
Pre-payment penalty	The client pays pre-payment penalty on paying loan before the maturity	Only sale of units at a higher price
In subsequent years	Interest amount decreases with a diminishing principal amount of loan outstanding	Rent payment decreases as more units are owned by the client and hence the client pays rent for a smaller number of units
In subsequent years	Principal repayment increases	More units are purchased by the client

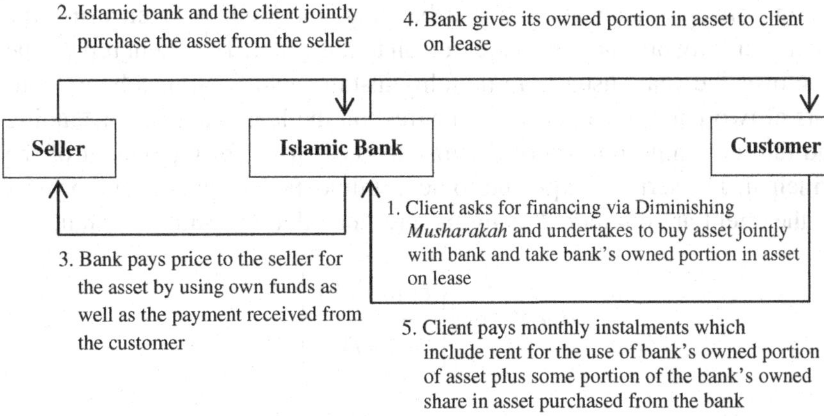

2. Islamic bank and the client jointly purchase the asset from the seller

4. Bank gives its owned portion in asset to client on lease

| Seller | Islamic Bank | Customer |

3. Bank pays price to the seller for the asset by using own funds as well as the payment received from the customer

1. Client asks for financing via Diminishing *Musharakah* and undertakes to buy asset jointly with bank and take bank's owned portion in asset on lease

5. Client pays monthly instalments which include rent for the use of bank's owned portion of asset plus some portion of the bank's owned share in asset purchased from the bank

Figure 3.6. Diminishing *Musharakah* process flow.

(1) The customer approaches the bank for the joint purchase of heavy industrial equipment.

(2) The seller of the industrial equipment is paid by the bank. The share of the bank in the industrial equipment is divided into units.

(3) The bank provides a portion of equipment it owns on lease to the client who can use the equipment in its production facility.

(4) The customer starts using the equipment and pays periodic instalments, which include rent for the use of the bank's units as well as the price of the bank's units purchased by the customer from the bank.

(5) The units owned by the bank are purchased by the customer periodically with each instalment. When the customer has purchased all the units, he becomes the sole owner of the industrial equipment.

In consumer finance, Diminishing *Musharakah* is a useful mode of financing for real estate. Buying a house and an automobile requires substantial resources, which most people are not able to generate only through their regular monthly incomes. Hence, people have two options. One option is that people could postpone their purchase until they accumulate enough amount to enhance the budget. The second option is to obtain financing from a financial institution. Postponing in the case of the house would require more time to accumulate resources and, with soaring prices, owning a house during one's lifetime might remain elusive for most people. Therefore, finance from financial institutions is the option most people take.

In conventional interest-based banking, the bank after ensuring the client's creditworthiness provides a loan to the client. The client repays the loan over the years usually in monthly instalments. Each instalment consists of two parts. One part is for interest on the loan balance outstanding and the remaining portion of the instalment is used for repayment of the principal. The series of equal periodic instalments to be paid over the years by the client are computed using the present value of annuity formula.

$$PVA = A\left[\frac{(1+i)^n - 1}{i(1+i)^n}\right]$$

(3.1)

where, *PVA* represents loan amount required and approved ($), *A* represents amount of instalment to be paid every period ($), *i* represents rate of interest (%), and *n* represents number of years for which loan is approved.

On the contrary, in Diminishing *Musharakah*, the bank and the client enter into the joint purchase of a house. The share of the bank in the house is divided into units. The bank provides its share in house on lease to the client. The client uses the house and pays rent for the use of units of the house in the bank's ownership. These units are purchased by the client with every instalment. The client becomes the sole owner of the house after he has purchased all the units. In every instalment amount paid to the Islamic bank, there are two parts. One part is the rent paid for the use of house units in the bank's ownership. The other portion is used to buy units owned by the bank.

A numerical example will further explain this product structure. Table 3.4 presents the details. The formulas used to compute the results are listed in Equation (3.2) through Equation (3.6):

$$u = n \times m$$ (3.2)

$$p_u = AFN/u$$ (3.3)

$$R_m = (r/m) \times p_u$$ (3.4)

$$TR_m = R_m \times u_o$$ (3.5)

$$A = TR_m + p_u$$ (3.6)

where, *u* represents number of units in bank's ownership, *n* represents duration of lease period, *m* represents number of instalment payments in a year, p_u represents per unit price of the house ($), *r* represents rental rate

Table 3.4. Rental computations in Islamic mortgage.

Expected Rentals — House

Financing amount of asset required ($)	4,000,000
Rental rate (%)	15
Tenure of lease (years)	10
Number of units	120
Unit price ($)	33,333
Rent per unit per month ($)	417
Total starting rent ($)	83,373

Table 3.5. Payment schedule in Islamic mortgage.

Month	Monthly Rent	Per Unit Price	Monthly Payment	Balance Units	Balance Unit Value
0	—	—	—	120	4,000,000
1	50,040	33,333	83,373	119	3,966,627
2	49,623	33,333	82,956	118	3,933,294
3	49,206	33,333	82,539	117	3,899,961
4	48,789	33,333	82,122	116	3,866,628
5	48,372	33,333	81,705	115	3,833,295
...	...	...	...	...	...
116	2,085	33,333	35,418	4	133,332
117	1,668	33,333	35,001	3	99,999
118	1,251	33,333	34,584	2	66,666
119	834	33,333	34,167	1	33,333
120	417	33,333	33,750	0	0

per annum (%), AFN represents financing required for house purchase ($), R_m represents per unit monthly rent ($), TR_m represents total monthly rent ($), u_o represents outstanding units in bank's ownership and A represents total monthly instalment amount ($).

Table 3.5 presents the extract of a payment schedule. It can be seen that monthly payments are declining with the decrease in rents. It is because the units in ownership of the bank decrease with each additional unit purchased by the client every month. The monthly interest payment in a conventional loan amortization schedule is replaced by monthly rent. Plus, the principal repayment in a conventional loan amortization schedule is replaced by unit price.

3.2.3 *Equity-based modes of financing*

3.2.3.1 *Musharakah*

Musharakah literally means sharing. In the context of contemporary business and trade, it refers to a joint enterprise in which all the partners share the profit or loss of the joint venture. Profit is shared based on the pre-agreed profit-sharing ratio. On the contrary, the loss is shared as per the capital contribution ratio.

In *Musharakah*, all partners work and share the profit or loss of their joint enterprise. There is no distinction between a working partner and an investing partner. The contract of *Musharakah* is imbued with the spirit of risk sharing rather than risk shifting or risk avoidance. No partner has a fixed share in profit unlike the case in lending on interest where the lender gets a stipulated return on the amount lent irrespective of whether the borrower earns a profit or loss from that loan. Thus, from the viewpoint of distributive justice and income distribution, *Musharakah* is one of the ideal modes of financing to achieve inclusivity, economic mobility, and equitable distribution of income. Figure 3.7 illustrates the structure of a *Musharakah* between the Islamic bank and the client.

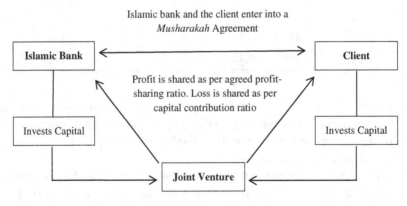

Figure 3.7. *Musharakah* structure.

Let us take an illustrative example. Ali wants to open a furniture business. He has taken courses in interior designing. He is looking for initial seed capital. He has served some clients in his neighborhood. With a portfolio of his successful business transactions with clients and his educational qualifications, he contacts an Islamic bank for an initial investment in a production facility and showroom. Ali would invest his own savings in the business too. This financing need can be structured using the mode of *Musharakah*.

3.2.3.2 *Mudarabah*

Mudarabah is a partnership in which there are two partners, i.e. *Rabb-ul-Maal* and *Mudarib*. *Rabb-ul-Maal* is the investing partner who contributes capital to the partnership. *Mudarib* is the working partner who contributes by rendering services in the partnership. *Mudarabah* is another type of equity-based mode of financing.

In *Mudarabah*, there is a clear distinction of roles for the partners. It is a kind of partnership where one partner invests capital in a joint enterprise. The investment solely comes from the first partner who is called *Rabb-ul-Maal*, while the management and work are the exclusive responsibility of the other, who is called *Mudarib*.

Profit is shared based on the pre-agreed profit-sharing ratio. On the contrary, the loss is shared as per the capital contribution ratio. Since only the *Rabb-ul-Maal* invests capital, the loss is solely borne by the *Rabb-ul-Maal*, except when there is explicit negligence by the *Mudarib*, which causes the loss. In case of loss in normal situations, the *Rabb-ul-Maal* loses the return on capital and bears the loss, while the *Mudarib* loses the effort contributed to the enterprise. Figure 3.8 illustrates the structure of a *Mudarabah* between the Islamic bank and the client.

Let us take the illustrative example of Ali opening a furniture showroom again. Ali wants to open a furniture business. He has taken courses in interior designing. He is looking for initial seed capital. He has served some clients in his neighborhood. With a portfolio of his successful business transactions with clients and his educational qualifications, he contacts an Islamic bank for an initial investment in the production facility and showroom. Ali does not have any capital to start the furniture business. This financing need can be structured using the mode of *Mudarabah*.

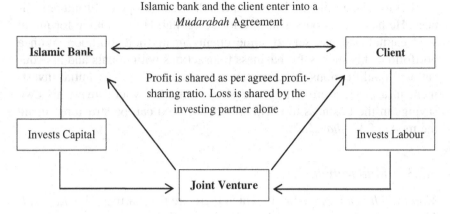

Figure 3.8.   *Mudarabah* structure.

In the application of *Mudarabah*, the scope of investment can be made broad or narrow as per the mutual agreement. In an unrestricted *Mudarabah* (i.e. *Mudarabah Ghair Muqayyada*), the investment can be made flexibly in any permissible enterprise. On the contrary, in a restricted *Mudarabah* (i.e. *Mudarabah Muqayyada*), the investment can only be made in a particular permissible enterprise on which both partners agree.

The difference in *Mudarabah* and *Musharakah* is that in *Musharakah*, all the partners work and share the profit or loss of their joint enterprise. There is no distinction between a working partner and an investing partner, unlike in *Mudarabah*.

Like *Musharakah*, *Mudarabah* is also an inclusive mode of financing, facilitating artisans, innovators, architects, designers, and those with skills to obtain financing and then earn the profit share in the joint enterprise. Thus, from the viewpoint of distributive justice and income distribution, *Mudarabah* is one step better than *Musharakah* to achieve inclusivity, economic mobility, and equitable distribution of income by providing finance to a completely capital-deficient but skilful person. In *Mudarabah*, *Rabb-ul-Maal* does not have a fixed share in profit unlike the case in lending on interest where the lender gets a stipulated return on the amount lent irrespective of whether the borrower earns a profit or loss from that loan.

3.3 Liabilities: Deposits

From the perspective of the bank, liabilities include the deposits placed with the bank by the depositors. The two main categories of deposits are checking accounts and non-checking accounts. In the checking accounts, the depositors can withdraw their deposits on demand without any restriction from the bank at any time. In the non-checking accounts, the deposits are placed for a certain duration during which they cannot be withdrawn. Usually, deposits in non-checking accounts are placed with the motive of investment.

In banking, some accounts are remunerative, and some are non-remunerative. Remunerative accounts pay some financial return to the depositors. On the contrary, non-remunerative accounts usually do not provide a financial return to the depositors.

3.3.1 *Non-remunerative accounts*

The current account is an example of a non-return generating checking account. The customer can deposit and withdraw funds in the current account through checks or other methods at any time.

In Islamic banking, the funds deposited in the current account are regarded as *Qard* (interest-free loan). The repayment of *Qard* is obligatory for the borrower, but the lender is not entitled to any stipulated increase over the amount of principal lent to the borrower. Hence, it is a non-compensatory contract in Islamic jurisprudence.

One alternate option which could have been considered is to use the mode of *Amanah* (safekeeping) in deposit mobilization. However, in *Amanah*, the repayment is not guaranteed in case of loss or theft other than due to negligence of the *Ameen* (safe keeper). Furthermore, in *Amanah*, the funds cannot be used by the *Ameen* personally. Therefore, in order to provide guarantee of repayment to the client and to be able to utilize the funds in investment, Islamic banks use the mode of *Qard* in deposit mobilization for non-return-generating checking accounts.

If the bank wants to offer a checking account that also allows some unilateral profit sharing, then a *Wadiah* (safekeeping) structure can also be used. In a *Wadiah* structure, the bank may gift any part of the profit it earns from the deposited funds. However, the profit cannot be stipulated, and the bank is never obliged or expected to pay any stipulated and predetermined return.

3.3.2 *Remunerative accounts*

Return-generating accounts can be invested with no or some restrictions on withdrawal. A savings account is an example of a return generating checking account with minimal restriction on withdrawal. Term deposits or fixed deposit accounts are return-generating investments where the depositor is restricted from withdrawals for some time. For instance, a one-year term deposit account would restrict withdrawals for one year. In current practice of Islamic banking, the structure of *Mudarabah* is used to offer remunerative or return-generating deposit schemes. The deposited money by all depositors is pooled into a fund and invested in offering various financing products to the clients. The bank acts as *Mudarib*, i.e. fund manager, and the depositors act as *Rabb-ul-Maal*, i.e. investors.

The pooled funds are only invested in *Shari'ah* compliant financing assets. The vertical distribution of profits between the bank and the depositors as a category is done on the basis of the pre-agreed profit-sharing ratio. The horizontal distribution of profits among the different types of depositors is done on the basis of a weightage mechanism.

The depositors are large in numbers and vary with respect to the amount of investment and the tenure of their investment. In the horizontal distribution of profits among the depositors, the weightage mechanism is used to allow the opportunity for greater ex-post profit distribution to depositors who have kept investment in the deposit pool for a longer tenure. However, the actual profit distribution is strictly dependent on the actual profits earned. The horizontal distribution between depositors is done based on the weightage mechanism after vertical distribution between *Mudarib* and *Rabb-ul-Maal* (as a category) has taken place.

The weightage is assigned to each category of investment that is stated to the depositor at the start of the partnership period. Profit is declared at the start of the month for the previous month based on the weightage previously announced. Profit is paid out of the actual income.

Table 3.6 gives an illustration of how the profit is distributed in the horizontal profit distribution process among the depositors. Let us suppose that the total investment deposits of $10,000 are invested in the asset pool. At year-end, the income from financing assets turns out to be $1,000. Table 3.6 describes how the total profit will be distributed among the different categories of depositors. The first column shows the categories of remunerative deposits starting from the savings accounts, which are checking accounts without any restriction on withdrawal. Then, as we move down, there are other deposits with greater restrictions on withdrawal, such as fixed deposits of one month, three months, six months, and one year. The second column gives the amount of deposits in each

Table 3.6.   Profit distribution in Islamic banking.

Deposit Category	Deposit ($)	Weightage	Weighted Average Deposit ($)	Profit ($)	Rate (%)
Savings	1,500	0.1	150	28.3	1.9
TD-1 month	500	0.3	150	28.3	5.7
TD-3 months	1,500	0.5	750	141.5	9.4
TD-6 months	3,000	0.6	1,800	339.6	11.3
TD-1 year	3,500	0.7	2,450	462.3	13.2
Total	10,000		5,300	1,000	

category of deposits. The third column assigns weightage to each category of deposits. These weights are pre-agreed at the beginning of investment in the asset pool. The fourth column computes the product of columns two and three to get the weighted average deposits in each category. The fifth column computes the profit allocation to each category of deposits as per the formula in Equation (3.7). The last column computes the holding period return on investment for each category of deposits as per the formula in Equation (3.8).

$$\text{Profit} = \frac{\text{Weighted Average Investment}}{\text{Total Weighted Average Investment}} \times \text{Total Income} \quad (3.7)$$

$$\text{Profit Rate} = \frac{\text{Profit}}{\text{Total Investment Deposit}} \quad (3.8)$$

For the savings account, the total profit turns out to be $28.3 through the following calculation:

$$\text{Profit} = \frac{150 \times 1,000}{5,300} \quad (3.9)$$

Finally, for the savings account, the total return on investment turns out to be 1.89% through the following calculation:

$$\text{Profit Rate} = \frac{28.3}{1,500} \times 100 \quad (3.10)$$

Self-Assessment Quiz

1. If depositors want capital protection, which mode can be used to accept their deposits?
   (a) *Mudarabah*
   (b) *Musharakah*
   (c) *Amanah* or *Qard*
   (d) None of the above

2. If a financial institution is willing to provide capital protection, but also wants to use the funds deposited by the customer, which mode is then used?
   (a) *Mudarabah*
   (b) *Musharakah*
   (c) *Amanah*
   (d) *Qard*

3. If the leased asset becomes unusable and the repair time takes three months, what will be the ruling about rentals for these three months?
   (a) No rentals charged
   (b) Rentals booked, but paid later
   (c) Rentals booked and charged on a normal basis
   (d) None of the above

4. In which contract of Islamic modes of financing is it mandatory to disclose the cost to the client?
   (a) *Murabaha*
   (b) *Musawamah*
   (c) *Ijarah*
   (d) None of the above

5. In *Murabaha*, before declaration it is necessary:
   (a) Not to consume the asset
   (b) To pay the bank *Murabaha* price
   (c) For the bank to take physical possession
   (d) None of the above

6. *Murabaha* price can include costs like:
   (a) Asset-related costs
   (b) Documentary costs
   (c) Regulatory levies
   (d) All of the above

7. Which of the following will make *Murabaha* invalid?
   (a) Price not agreed
   (b) Price not fully paid
   (c) Supplier not paid directly by the bank
   (d) None of the above

8. Which of the following is not allowed in *Murabaha*?
   (a) Automatic rollover of loans
   (b) Re-pricing of the asset after sale
   (c) Penalty on late payments taken as profit
   (d) All of the above

9. In *Salam*,
   (a) Delivery is deferred, payment is on spot
   (b) Payment is deferred, delivery is on spot
   (c) Both are on spot
   (d) Both are deferred

10. Why *Salam* is considered an exceptional sale?
    (a) Sale executed without the existence of asset
    (b) The asset exists but is not delivered
    (c) Both payment and delivery are deferred
    (d) None of the above

Self-Assessment Questions

1. List the five key aspects of Islamic finance principles.
2. Illustrate the process flow and steps of obtaining inventory on a short-term financing basis through *Murabaha*.
3. Illustrate the process flow and steps of obtaining industrial machinery on a long-term financing basis through *Ijarah*.
4. Illustrate the process flow and steps of obtaining working capital finance through *Salam* for a corporate entity specializing in the production of sugar.
5. Illustrate the process flow and steps of obtaining intermediate-term finance in instalments through *Istisna* for a corporate entity specializing in the construction of buildings.
6. Differentiate between a conventional mortgage and home finance through Diminishing *Musharakah*.

7. Describe key differences between *Ijarah*-based lease finance and conventional finance lease.
8. Differentiate between key features of *Musharakah* and *Mudarabah* in capital contribution and loss sharing.
9. Why is *Qard* used in mobilizing non-return-generating deposits, whereas *Mudarabah* is used in return-generating deposits?
10. What are the vertical and horizontal distributions of profits in Islamic banking? How does the weightage mechanism work in horizontal distribution of profits?

Chapter 4

Economics of Islamic Banking Product Structures

4.1 Introduction

The question of compliance of Islamic banking with the principles of Islamic law can be answered from the analysis of sources of Islamic law, which primarily include *Qur'an* and the way of the Prophet Muhammad (pbuh).

On the contrary, the question of distinction of Islamic banking vis-à-vis conventional banking with regards to its commercial, economic, and social impact is a separate question that can be answered from empirical evidence and methodological approaches of social sciences.

Nonetheless, it is of vital significance to understand the key difference between these two questions and methodological approaches. First, the two questions are different in scope. Second, the tools of analysis and inference are also different while answering these two questions. It is quite plausible that a prohibited form of trade, enterprise, or financial intermediation has some merits as well but is prohibited due to its negative effects on one's psychology, personality, social cohesion, and distributive justice. Furthermore, it is also quite plausible that a permissible form of trade, enterprise, or financial intermediation brings with it some challenges but is useful for its positive effects on promoting participative relationships, minimizing the stimulus of selfishness and greed, and avoiding social and economic distortions in terms of crises, inequality of income, and loss of one's social, economic, and even political freedoms in the case of multilateral finance between countries.

In this chapter, the answer to the second question is discussed. This chapter seeks to analyse the economics of Islamic banking product structures. It evaluates how Islamic banking product structures enable inter-temporal finance between the saving-surplus and saving-deficient units without involving interest.

4.2 Real Sector-Based Enterprise in Islamic Banking

Islamic banking has some distinct economic differences over the interest-based financial intermediation. Islamic banking as a form of financial intermediation offers tremendous potential in reinforcing links between finance and the real economy.

Islamic banks can only earn income from trade of assets or by providing the usufruct of real assets. This ensures that their profits are linked with real assets in the economy. They cannot simply lend money and earn compound interest on it.

For instance, consider a corporate customer who purchases a real asset on *Murabaha* financing basis at $11,000. The spot price of the asset on cash payment is $9,000. Islamic bank purchases the asset in spot market and pays the price. Islamic bank takes the ownership and constructive possession of the asset. Until the asset is sold to the client, Islamic bank bears the risks related to the real assets. In order to bring efficiency, transparency and cost competitiveness, Islamic bank engages customer as agent to purchase the real asset on bank's behalf and take constructive possession of the asset. In order to reduce its own risk, Islamic bank takes insurance cover for the asset. Islamic bank would charge a price that will enable it to earn profits after deducting all direct and indirect costs which arise in the form of price, insurance, installation, transportation and taxes, for instance. Let us suppose that the insurance, installation, transportation, taxes, duties and documentation related costs sum up to $1,000. Thus, the total investment by bank is $10,000 (Present Value or PV).

If the transaction goes as per plan, Islamic bank would earn a profit of $1,000, which is 10% return on its invested funds. If the customer delays payment for 3 years or 5 years, then the Islamic bank can only charge price of $11,000. In case, the payment of $11,000 (Future Value or FV) is received after 3 years, the return on investment r would turn out to be 3.22% as illustrated below.

$$FV = PV(1+r)^n \tag{4.1}$$

$$\frac{FV}{PV} = (1+r)^n \tag{4.2}$$

$$\frac{11,000}{10,000} = (1+r)^3 \tag{4.3}$$

$$1.1^{1/3} = (1+r)^{3\times 1/3} \tag{4.4}$$

$$r = 1.0322 - 1 = 3.22\% \tag{4.5}$$

In case, the payment of $11,000 (Future Value or FV) is received after 5 years, the return on investment "r" would turn out to be 1.92% as illustrated below.

$$\frac{11,000}{10,000} = (1+r)^5 \tag{4.6}$$

$$1.1^{1/5} = (1+r)^{5\times 1/5} \tag{4.7}$$

$$r = 1.019 - 1 = 1.92\% \tag{4.8}$$

On the other hand, the conventional bank would earn compounded interest on delayed payment at the market interest rate of 10%. Islamic bank would receive the *Murabaha* price of $11,000 no matter whether the price is received after 1 year, 2 years, 3 years, 4 years or 5 years. In contrast, conventional bank would charge interest on its outstanding loan amount as long as the payment is not made. Conventional bank would get $11,000 if payment is received after 1 year. If payment is delayed, then conventional bank will get $12,100, $13,310, $14,641 and $16,105 if payment is received after 2, 3, 4 or 5 years, respectively.

In the conventional mainstream finance, some financial securities incentivize risk creation than just risk sharing. Investment banks survive on issuing new securities. Increased securitization means increased business and returns to them. The proliferation of securities like credit default swaps (CDS) provides a cushion as well as incentive for excessive risk taking by financial asset creators like banks. A high level of debt in the conventional interest-based financial architecture is one of the prime causes of financial crises.[1,2]

In contrast, the balance sheet of Islamic banks is capable of absorbing financial shocks. Islamic banks are not obliged to give a fixed return to their depositors and general creditors. The creditors, shareholders, and depositors share and participate in the bank's business. Therefore, in case, there is a shock on the asset side with an increase in non-performing financing assets, Islamic banks will be able to share this loss with their depositors and shareholders.

Furthermore, Islamic banks cannot roll over loans in trade-based financing contracts. Therefore, the packaging and repackaging of loans and then issuing more and more debt securities on the backing of these non-performing loans cannot legally happen in Islamic banks. Islamic banks are obliged to have the backing of assets in all their investments. Hence, the Islamic bank's losses even theoretically cannot go beyond the value of the real asset in any given financing contract.

Most capital-intensive businesses require the purchase of industrial machinery and equipment. With the advancement in technology, it is necessary to invest in physical capital goods from time to time in order to remain competitive and efficient. Islamic banking enables infrastructure investments and expansion in productive capacity for the businesses through the provision of trade- and lease-based finance of real assets rather than loaning out money on interest. This checks financial leverage.

Asset-backed financing is also conducive to public finance where the requirement for financing is huge and the duration of financing is also long term. The realization of sustainable development goals (SDGs) depends on the availability of funds, infrastructure, inclusive growth, creation of jobs, "environment-friendly" technological advancements, and

---

[1]Buiter, W. H. and Rahbari, E. (2015). "Why Economists (and Economies) Should Love Islamic Finance". *Journal of King Abdulaziz University: Islamic Economics*, 28(1), 139–162.

[2]Mian, A. and Sufi, A. (2015). *House of Debt: How They (and You) Caused the Great Recession, and How We Can Prevent It from Happening Again*. Chicago: University of Chicago Press.

business processes reengineering. All of this is not going to be possible without the availability of funds. By some estimates, around $3.5 trillion to $5 trillion is needed every year to make desirable progress on SDGs. At the global level, investment in infrastructure is estimated to be $100 trillion over the next two decades.[3]

As per Islamic Development Bank, innovative Islamic financial instruments, especially for infrastructure development such as *Sukuk*, can be used to mobilize resources to finance water and sanitation projects (SDG-6), sustainable and affordable energy projects (SDG-7) and build resilient infrastructure (SDG-9) and shelter (SDG-11).[4]

In the Middle East, there is immense potential to use solar energy alongside oil. Lack of financing is one of the major obstacles for the minimal use of renewable energy in developing countries. Financial markets of developing countries are often underdeveloped and are unable to efficiently channel funds to produce renewable energy. In this scenario, Islamic banks can mitigate the information asymmetries which cause the problem of moral hazard and adverse selection. Since the financing provided by Islamic banks is purely for the purchase of real assets, it cannot be misused or mishandled.

As per the World Bank, developing countries spend about $1 trillion a year on infrastructure. An additional $1–$1.5 trillion will be needed through 2020 in areas such as water projects like dams, desalination plants, power projects, and transportation projects. Asian Development Bank estimates that emerging Asian economies alone will require $8 trillion over the next decade to satisfy the growing demand in the areas of energy, water, and transportation.

As part of its commitment to the SDGs, the Islamic Development Bank has announced it will increase its funding of SDG-related activities from $80 billion recorded during the MDGs to $150 billion over the next 15 years (2016–2030). With resilient growth, effective risk mitigation, and participative modes of financial products, Islamic banking promises to play a significant role, especially in the Muslim world.

---

[3] Ahmed, H., Mohieldin, M. *et al.* (2015). *On the Sustainable Development Goals and the Role of Islamic Finance.* Policy Research Working Paper, World Bank, No. WPS7266.
[4] Islamic Development Bank (2015). *The Role of Islamic Finance in Achieving Sustainable Development Goals.* Published by Islamic Development Bank.

4.3   Economics of Islamic Banking Product Structures

4.3.1   *Economic benefits of Mudarabah and Musharakah*

Equity financing is closest to the spirit and ideals of Islam where the risk of the enterprise is shared among the partners. Thus, every partner's payoffs are linked with the outcome of the enterprise. Since there is no financial cost of funds, the residual profit is shared among the partners equitably through a mutually agreed profit-sharing ratio. In the costing for products and services in *Mudarabah-* and *Musharakah*-funded enterprise, interest does not feature, and hence, the prices are not increased in anticipation of bearing the cost of interest.

From the perspective of income distribution and social co-operative behaviour, *Mudarabah* and *Musharakah* are ideal modes of financing since payoffs for all parties are linked with the productive sector of the economy. Consequently, markets do not have to produce speculative surplus output just to service exorbitant amounts of debt. Thus, more penetration of this mode of financing could stabilize business cycles and avoid crises that are quite common in contemporary interest-based financial markets.

4.3.2   *Economic benefits of Ijarah and diminishing Musharakah*

In the olden days, the production was primarily restricted to agriculture and industry where manual labour was employed more prominently than the capital. After the onset of the industrial revolution, the use of technology has enabled a rise in productivity. Most of the industrial machines nowadays have long lives as well as high cost. Employing advanced industrial equipment can ensure long-term benefits in reducing costs, improving efficiency, and gaining a competitive edge. However, often it is difficult to pay the full cost of such capital goods upfront.

Lease-based financing ensures that businesses can employ capital goods without having to pay the full cost of machinery upfront. In *Ijarah*, the usufruct of an asset is transferred for the consideration of rent. Once the lease period ends, the client has the option of purchasing the asset. This mode of financing ensures that investments in technology and capital goods are not hampered just due to the cash flow mismatch. This enables the firm to expand, achieve efficiency and economies of scale, and improve its asset turnover ratios. *Ijarah* can facilitate both the corporate clients as well as individual clients who want to purchase a fixed asset like car, motorcycle, and consumer appliances, for instance.

If the cost of equipment is high and the duration of the desired lease term is of longer duration, then Diminishing *Musharakah* is also a useful mode of financing which ensures that the share of the asset owned by the financier is purchased by the client from time to time. This ensures self-discipline on the part of the client as well as avoids a large balloon payment at the end of the lease term to purchase the asset or property. Diminishing *Musharakah* is a useful contract embedding parallel lease and purchase of equipment or real estate whose cost is high and the client desires the lease term to be longer for ease in payments to the financier. This is also useful in situations where the market price of the asset or property usually increases, such as constructed houses in urban areas. By purchasing the share of asset owned by the financier from time to time rather than all at end, the client is able to avoid the rise in market prices.

4.3.3 *Economic analysis of Murabaha*

There is often a need for short-term financing for the acquisition of an asset. Hence, it is not possible to issue new equity every time when financing is needed for the short term and when retained earnings are not enough for the purchase of fixed assets. In such a scenario, *Murabaha* serves the short-term financing needs of businesses, especially those small and medium enterprises which find it expensive to bear high floatation costs in funding their needs through financial markets.

Businesses would like to earn more operating income from a given level of fixed assets. Bulk inventory and asset purchases at the very start of the production cycle raise inventory maintenance costs and may result in underemployment of assets. It may dampen liquidity and turnover ratios and hence affect the stock price of companies. Since, not all assets can be acquired from paid-up capital right away, it is desirable to use short-term bank financing than long-term equity financing in some cases. Equity financing may not be appropriate in running projects in which projects and income sources cannot be easily segregated. In such a case, *Murabaha* is an easy-to-use, short-term financing solution.

Often, the investors with the bank (the deposit holders) are risk averse and want consistent returns. With equity financing, the operating cycle of some enterprises may be lengthy and this may not bring consistent cash flows required by such investors right away. In that case, *Murabaha* financing is beneficial for investors and enables the bank to generate income from the sale of real assets in trade finance. *Murabaha* enables the financing of raw materials as well as finished goods. This improves supply chain management and reduces bottlenecks caused due to cash flow problems or mismanagement.

In capital markets, share *Murabaha* can improve liquidity in equity markets and hence enable efficiency and stability in markets. From the risk perspective, *Murabaha* financing keeps the Islamic financial system liquid and less prone to risk due to the backing with real assets.

4.3.4 *Economic analysis of Istisna and Salam*

The cash conversion cycle typically involves cash inflows at the end once the products are sold and the payments are received. In manufacturing, firms often have a need for working capital financing. *Istisna* allows firms to finance the cost of manufacturing an asset. Instead of losing customers due to inability to continue manufacturing with shortage of funds, firms can access financing from Islamic banks to effectively run their operations.

Furthermore, keeping a large inventory is costly and risky from the financial and operational perspectives. Thus, engineering and construction companies can source funds to fulfil construction and manufacturing contracts as and when there is a purchase order. The deposit holders of the bank are also able to share in the profits arising from large-scale mega construction projects, such as building bridges, roads, highways, dams, railway tracks, airports, residential apartments, and shopping malls, for instance. Financing the construction of these long-term fixed assets fosters capital formation in the economy through the private sector. Furthermore, financing public projects through this method enables the provision of public goods. Such investments in infrastructure are also positively linked with economic activities and employment generation.

On the contrary, *Salam* enables the financing of raw materials for the production of standardized products. This reduces the supply chain bottlenecks caused due to cash flow problems. It can also be used in financing overhead costs and other supplies. This is quite useful for small producers and traders facing a shortage of funds during the production stage in the cash conversion cycle.

4.4 Combining Values with Catalytic Instruments for Effective Social Change

Despite exemplary growth since the Second World War in the middle of the twentieth century, the world is still facing serious food insecurity, hunger, poverty, inequities, climate change, loss of biodiversity, and waste and existential threat to life on this planet for future generations due to the damage caused by humans through waste, pollution, and showing inaction for corrective measures.

According to the World Health Organization, over 820 million people are suffering from hunger in 2019 despite consistent rise in per capita food production ever since the 1970s. As per Oxfam, 26 people together own the same amount of wealth as the combined wealth of 3.8 billion people who make up the poorest half of humanity. The redistribution of resources through taxation is ineffective. According to Oxfam, only 4 cents in a dollar of tax revenue come from wealth tax. Even progressive income taxation has not been able to check the rising inequities both in the developed and in the developing countries.

The rich people and countries having enough economic muscle to invest in green technology and infrastructure are doing very little. In fact, Oxfam reports that around 50% of all carbon emissions are emitted by the richest 10% of the world's population.

Tied aids and debt servicing on money debt result in more money flowing out of poor countries than comes in as aid. Ending poverty and hunger does not require insurmountable financial resources. But the lack of political will and greed leaves much of the population in South Asia and Africa to face poverty despite the consistent increase in the overall value of Gross World Product. It is estimated that $600 million daily is needed to feed every poor person, yet about $2.75 billion value of food is wasted every day, according to the Food and Agriculture Organization.

Interest-based financial intermediation provides a risk-less means for the wealthy and rich to continue wealth accumulation and avoid wealth taxes through various means of parking wealth in parts of the world in different forms. The 26 wealthiest people in the world own $1.4 trillion, according to Oxfam. Imagine that a 10% interest on it can give them a risk-free increase in wealth of $140 billion, just enough to feed all the poor people for eight months of the year alone.

While reflecting on these facts, one can comprehend that a value system which idealizes and gives absolute liberty for pursuing self-interest is

Table 4.1.   *Maqasid-e-Shari'ah* and sustainable development.

Maqasid-e-Shari'ah	**Implications in Policy Design and Approach**
Spirituality (*Hifdh al-Deen*)	Belief and value system emphasize moderation, responsibility, and justice.
Physiology (*Hifdh al-Nafs*)	Emphasis on hunger, malnourishment, stunting, cleanliness, and sanitation.
Intellect (*Hifdh al-Aqal*)	Emphasis on human capital, including education and innovation.
Sustainability (*Hifdh al-Nasl*)	Emphasis on resource conservation, biodiversity, and ecosystem.
Economy (*Hifdh al-Maal*)	Emphasis on employment, need fulfilment, economic opportunities, and equitable wealth distribution.

unable to help create social change by looking beyond one's personal interest and affairs in life. Also, in a society with high income and wealth inequality, policymaking under democracy struggles to reflect the will of the people and working for the common good of all.

Looking at the current financial system, we see that banks lend money on interest to those who have collateral. The poor are targeted to save with the bank, but are excluded when it comes to obtaining finance. Money mainly flows from a large number of small savers to a small number of big corporates and upper class people. This can cause a rise in inequities in the society. Hence, there is need for an economic framework that brings moderation, responsibility, conservation, dignity of life, empathy, sharing, equitable distribution, and justice in society.

The values governing policy in the Islamic social framework take into account *Maqasid-al-Shari'ah* (objectives of Islamic law). These embody the objectives, aims, and spirit of Islamic faith and its principles and rules. It can be seen from Table 4.1 that these objectives can play an effective role and provide impetus towards responsible behaviour through inculcating the right ethical values.

4.5 Economic Potential of Islamic Banking

According to a World Bank study, there is a high degree of financial exclusion among Muslims. Part of the reason is the lack of availability of Islamic banking in many jurisdictions. Muslims willing to avoid interest that is prevalent in conventional banking voluntarily exclude themselves from most banking products and services. Therefore, an increased penetration of Islamic finance can enhance financial inclusion. Inclusive finance can assist people to achieve income smoothing, consumption smoothing, higher social mobility, and financial stability.

In a lot of populous Muslim-majority countries, the savings ratio is very low. Part of the reason why savings culture is weak is that people do not want to invest in interest-based investment options. Thus, a greater penetration of Islamic savings products can allow Muslim investors to earn *Halal* return on their investments. This will boost the savings rate and allow the savings–investment gap to reduce. This will also have a positive effect on stability in the current account balance in the external sector as well as lead to enhanced capital formation in the economy for fuelling economic growth and productivity.

Furthermore, development spending in most of the Muslim-majority developing countries is quite low. Part of the reason is low tax revenues and high cost of debt servicing, which eat up as much as half of the total tax revenues. Islamic banks can finance the governments for the purchase of infrastructure that can be used in development projects. Innovative Islamic financial instruments, especially for infrastructure development such as *Sukuk*, can be used to mobilize resources to finance water and sanitation projects, sustainable and affordable energy, and build resilient infrastructure including residential buildings.

Islamic finance products are not only interest-free alternatives for the financial needs of the contemporary Muslim communities wanting to avoid interest, but the products are generating increased appeal primarily because of their financial and economic merits. That is why the Islamic banking industry is growing at a rate twice as much as the conventional banking system.

In the middle of the financial and economic crisis of 2007–2010 and even afterwards, the Islamic banking and finance industry has witnessed significant growth in double digits. The two most important problems identified in the great financial crisis of 2007–2009 were (i) de-linking of financial sector growth and activities with the real sector of the economy and (ii) perverse incentives. Islamic finance principles through asset-backed financing are able to ensure adequate risk management.

In financing provided by international development finance institutions and multilateral financing between governments, the *Sukuk* structure can be effectively utilized for developing real estate infrastructure, high-cost equipment, and facilities. The recent success in the use of *Sukuk* by even the non-Muslim-majority countries provides credence to the view that Islamic finance is broad in its appeal and scope to different clients as well as to their different needs. If development finance is structured using Islamic finance structures, then the necessary mobilization of funds can be ensured to obtain finance for meeting sustainable development goals. This could be vital for underdeveloped Muslim-majority countries.

Asset-backed financing is also conducive to public finance where the requirement for financing is huge and the duration of financing is also long term. Table 4.2 outlines the 17 goals that are part of the sustainable development agenda. It also illustrates how Islamic values, institutions, and instruments can help in contributing toward achieving each of these sustainable development goals.

Islamic values would play a role in shaping preferences and attitudes toward avoiding waste and ensuring recycling and responsible use of resources. Islamic finance would allow investments in technology that can foster efficiency in the use of finite resources and allowing the use of renewable resources in the production processes. Finally, Islamic social finance through *Qard-e-Hasan*, *Zakat*, and *Waqf* would ensure that the resources flow even to those who are not able to earn income for meeting their needs from the resource markets due to lack of skills and inadequate health and education. The ban on interest and selling of debt on premium would allow the liquidity in the financial system to be utilized in the real economy.

Islamic finance principles and institutions also have the potential to induce inclusive growth in the economy. Table 4.3 lists how Islamic modes of financing can stimulate various components of aggregate demand in the economy. An increase in aggregate demand can spur the growth. Since the benefits of enterprise through Islamic finance are shared mutually and are derived from activities in the real sector of the economy, the distributional effects of such financing modes and mechanisms are also qualitatively different and more egalitarian. In contrast, conventional banks can park and invest their major chunk of liquidity with banks and financial institutions in the money market and earn money on money by investing in money-based financial securities.

In economic growth literature, several models have been developed mathematically and tested empirically. Some of the well-known models

Table 4.2.   Use of Islamic finance in sustainable development goals.

Sustainable Development Goals	Methods of Intervention in Islamic Economic Framework
GOAL 1: No poverty	*Zakat, Waqf, Qard-e-Hasan, Mudarabah, Salam.*
GOAL 2: Zero hunger	*Zakat, Waqf, Qard-e-Hasan.*
GOAL 3: Good health and well-being	*Waqf, Takaful, Qard-e-Hasan.*
GOAL 4: Quality education	*Waqf, Takaful, Qard-e-Hasan.*
GOAL 5: Gender equality	Islamic socio-ethical values providing property rights to women, financial sustenance in a marital relationship, and freedom to engage in any *Halal* business or financing contract.
GOAL 6: Clean water and sanitation	*Ijarah Sukuk, Istisna Sukuk, Waqf.*
GOAL 7: Affordable and clean energy	*Ijarah Sukuk, Istisna Sukuk.*
GOAL 8: Decent work and economic growth	Islamic trade-based (*Murabaha, Salam, Istisna*), lease-based (*Ijarah, Musharakah Mutanaqisa*), and
GOAL 9: Industry, innovation, and infrastructure	participation-based modes of financing (*Mudarabah, Musharakah*).
GOAL 10: Reduced inequality	*Zakat, Waqf, Qard-e-Hasan, Mudarabah, Musharakah*
GOAL 11: Sustainable cities and communities	*Takaful* and using Islamic trade-based (*Murabaha, Salam, Istisna*), lease-based (*Ijarah, Musharakah Mutanaqisa*), and participation-based modes of financing (*Mudarabah, Musharakah*).
GOAL 12: Responsible consumption and production	Islamic socio-ethical values encouraging moderation, conservation, and avoiding wastefulness.
GOAL 13: Climate action	Islamic socio-ethical values. Financing through markets via *Sukuk* or via intermediaries by using Islamic trade- and lease-based modes of financing.
GOAL 14: Life below water	Islamic socio-ethical values encouraging cleanliness and discouraging wastefulness.
GOAL 15: Life on land	Islamic socio-ethical values encouraging conservation, moderation, and avoiding wastefulness and harm to other living beings in the ecosystem.
GOAL 16: Peace and justice strong institutions	Islamic socio-ethical values prioritizing justice, rule of law, banning harm to other's property, life and honour, and penalizing offenses.
GOAL 17: Partnerships to achieve the goal	*Ta'awwun Al-al Birr* (cooperation in goodness) and promote *Maslaha* (welfare).

Table 4.3.   Aggregate demand stimulants in Islamic finance.

Components of Aggregate Demand	Islamic Modes of Financing Used
Consumption	• *Murabaha* and *Musawamah* for short-term financing. • *Ijarah* for long-term durable goods finance.
Investment	• *Murabaha* and *Salam* for short-term financing. • *Ijarah*, diminishing *Musharakah* for long-term financing. • *Sukuk* based on the above structures if financial markets are approached.
Government expenditure	• *Sukuk* based on *Ijarah, Istisna, Mudarabah*, and *Musharakah* structure.
Net exports	• *Murabaha, Salam*, and *Istisna* for raw materials finance and *Ijarah* and diminishing *Musharakah* for long-term fixed assets finance.

include Harrod[5]–Domer[6] Model, Solow's[7] Growth Model, and Endogenous Growth Model by Romer.[8] In these models, the emphasis is laid on increase in savings, investment, human capital, technological advances, and social infrastructure.

In discussing the Islamic perspective on the insights of these models, it is important to know that savings that result in investment contribute to growth. Thus, it is investment that leads to growth. Islamic principles allow individuals to invest savings directly in the real economy. Such investments lead to increase in capital formation and productivity. Islamic finance does not give any chance for idle savings to earn any return from the production process. In fact, by levying *Zakat* on idle savings, Islamic finance principles encourage circulation of idle resources to productive uses. Thus, in an Islamic economic framework, there is expected to be

---

[5] Harrod, R. F. (1939). "An Essay in Dynamic Theory", *The Economic Journal*, *49*(193), 14–33.

[6] Domar, E. (1946). "Capital Expansion, Rate of Growth, and Employment", *Econometrica*, *14*(2), 137–47.

[7] Solow, R. M. (1956). "A Contribution to the Theory of Economic Growth", *Quarterly Journal of Economics*, *70*(1), 65–94.

[8] Romer, P. M. (1994). "The Origins of Endogenous Growth", *Journal of Economic Perspectives*, *8*(1), 3–22.

higher levels of savings and Islamic finance would channel these savings directly in the real economy since there is no mechanism to earn money on money through the lending of money in an Islamic framework. Also, the equity-based modes of financing like *Mudarabah* encourage investment in ideas by providing capital support to enterprising individuals with budding business ideas.

On the contrary, human capital development is also necessary for inclusive growth. Those poor people who are unable to generate income in the market economy due to a shortage of funds can be financed through equity-based modes of financing to ensure inclusivity and socio-economic mobility. In classical and neoclassical growth theory, it is argued that inequality is necessary to kick-start economic growth. In the Lewis model,[9] the capitalist class is expected to instigate economic growth through production in modern manufacturing sector. Kuznets argues that economic growth will trickle down to the masses after sustainable economic growth is achieved.[10] However, even sustained economic growth does not result in equitable distribution of income as the recent evidence suggests.[11]

Inclusive finance requires provision of capital on the basis of equity rather than exorbitantly expensive interest-based microfinance. The interest-based microfinance only raises the cost of capital for the lack of availability of collateral. Hence, it does not result in inclusivity, and thus, regions that have higher penetration of microfinance still have higher rates of poverty. Whatever decrease in poverty has occurred, it is due to the increase in economic growth rates, such as in China and Bangladesh, for instance.

Islamic equity-based modes of financing like *Mudarabah* and *Musharakah* ensure that ideas and human capital are provided with financial capital on a profit- and loss-sharing basis so that these ideas and human capital have a greater chance of achieving socio-economic mobility. This is unlike the case in interest-based microfinance, where the cost of debt is higher and the repayment terms are of shorter duration.

---

[9]Lewis, W. A. (1954). "Economic Development with Unlimited Supplies of Labour", *The Manchester School*, 22(2), 139–191.

[10]Kuznets, S. (1955). "Economic Growth and Income Inequality", *The American Economic Review*, 45(1), 1–28.

[11]Piketty, T. (2014). *Capital in the Twenty-first Century*. New York: Harvard University Press.

Lastly, the values of cooperation (*Ta'awun*) and brotherhood (*Akhuwwa*) together with accountability (*Hisba*) give a boost to social capital. Islamic social finance through *Zakat* and *Waqf* caters to the development needs indigenously through redistribution of resources from the haves to the have-nots without having to resort to interest-based debts.

4.6   Islamic Banks as Intermediaries: Idealism versus Realism

Islamic banks are commercial financial institutions. Their primary objective is to provide *Shari'ah*-compliant financing and investment solutions to the saving-deficient and saving-surplus units in compliance with *Shari'ah* principles. Since Islamic banks are commercial institutions, they are also responsible for safeguarding the interest of shareholders and depositors who provide investment capital to the bank. They are expected to provide *Halal* returns in terms of profits to the shareholders and depositors. Thus, they would be expected to invest in commercially viable contracts in order to earn *Halal* profits for their major stakeholders, i.e. shareholders and depositors.

Nonetheless, since Islam prohibits *Riba*, Islamic banks are also perceived to make a distinct mark in their economic impact. Early thinkers in Islamic finance literature built high expectations from Islamic banks to contribute to egalitarian income distribution and inclusive financial products and to achieve a reduction in poverty.

However, in economics terminology, Islamic banks operate in a market where the leading firm or the group of firms practicing interest-based conventional banking hold scale and regulatory advantage. Islamic banks as new entrants with small market share and facing regulatory disadvantages cannot be price-setters and cost leaders in the beginning. Thus, what they can realistically achieve in the short term is to be competitive, liquid, and solvent and then penetrate slowly in the market to increase their share and efficiency without compromising the principles and boundaries of Islamic rules of trade and lease in which they engage as financial intermediaries.

This difference in idealist vision and ground realities in the current scenario has created a gap between the idealists and the realists. The realists have to compete alongside conventional banking within the same legal, governance, and market conditions which at best are only neutral to Islamic banking, if not unfavourable in some respects.

Thus, the practical approach which realists take is to gradually penetrate the market by remaining competitive to gain market share. Besides Islamic banks there are Islamic microfinance institutions, crowdfunding institutions, and *Waqf* institutions which cater to the financial needs of those clients who cannot afford the price or rents of assets which Islamic banks charge as commercial financial institutions. If Islamic banks subsidize the price and rents for the clients who cannot afford, then they will earn lesser returns and the shareholders and depositors will be worse off. However, the idealist scholars take the view that Islamic banking has to strive towards making a distinctive socio-economic impact in society. They also opine that since interest-based banking is primarily criticized in economic terms for its exclusive focus on the richer segments of the society and thus creating asymmetric access to funds and concentration of wealth, the Islamic banks need to be different. Islamic banks need to focus more on equity-based modes of financing, which ensure inclusivity of both richer and poorer segments of society in access to funds and thereby lead to a much more egalitarian distribution of income. A brief review of both perspectives is provided below.

In the critical evaluation, Mehmet Asutay concludes that Islamic banking fails to fulfill the required needs of the (*Maqasid*) higher objective of *Shari'ah*.[12] Muhammad Akram Laldin and Hafas Furqani argue that fulfilling minimal *Shari'ah* legal compliance in product structuring is insufficient to make progress towards the circulation of wealth, transparency, and distributive justice.[13] In contemporary discourse about Islamic finance, it is widely noted that the Islamic finance industry remains broadly delinked from the real economy and, thus, the prosperity of the society.[14] Due to the overemphasis on the form over substance, Wajid Dusuki and Abdulazeem Abozaid argue that Islamic banks are just an exercise in semantics and their functions and operations are no different from conventional banks, except in their use of euphemisms to disguise

---

[12] Asutay, M. (2008). "Islamic Banking and Finance: Social Failure", *New Horizon (October–December 2008)*, 169, 1–4.

[13] Laldin, M. A. and Furqani, H. (2013). "Developing Islamic Finance in the Framework of Maqasid al-*Shari'ah*: Understanding the Ends (Maqasid) and the Means (Wasa'il)", *International Journal of Islamic and Middle Eastern Finance and Management*, 6(4), 278–289.

[14] Ibrahim, A. A., Elatrash, R. J. *et al.* (2014). "Hoarding versus Circulation of Wealth from the Perspective of Maqasid al-*Shari'ah*", *International Journal of Islamic and Middle Eastern Finance and Management*, 7(1), 6–21.

interest and circumvent the many *Shari'ah* prohibitions.[15] Killian Balz thinks that Islamic finance is experiencing a "formalist deadlock" where the industry is more concerned with formal adherence to Islamic law instead of promoting Islamic ethical values.[16] For instance, *Qard-e-Hasan* and *Mudarabah* are useful products for ensuring equitable distribution of income, but they are used against the spirit, whereby the Islamic bank becomes the *Mudarib* and borrower in *Mudarabah* and *Qard-e-Hasan*, contracts, respectively, in the liability-side operations.

In defence, Mohamed Fairooz Abdul Khir explains that mainstream Muslim scholars supporting the Islamic finance movement contend that Islam recognizes the legitimacy of the time value of money in Islamic financial transactions, such as in deferred sale.[17] Tariqullah Khan thinks that critics of practiced Islamic banking do not appreciate how important debt financing is for value creation in an economy and especially for inclusive growth and economic development through making financial services accessible for asset acquisition.[18] Umer Chapra argues that even if debt financing is predominantly used in Islamic banking practice, asset-backed financing does not allow the debt to exceed the growth of the real economy.[19] He argues that the introduction of such a discipline would ensure greater stability as well as efficiency and equity in the financial system.

On the contrary, Islamic economists holding on to the more egalitarian vision like Muhammad Nejatullah Siddiqi argue that the role of debts needs to be drastically reduced and replaced by participatory modes of finance.[20] But, revealing the ground reality, Rasem Kayed observes that

[15] Dusuki, A. W. and Abozaid, A. (2007). "A Critical Appraisal on the Challenges of Realizing Maqasid Al-*Shari'ah* in Islamic Banking and Finance", *IIUM Journal of Economics and Management*, *15*(2), 143–165.

[16] Balz, K. (2008). Sharia Risk? *How Islamic Finance Has Transformed Islamic Contract Law*. Islamic Legal Studies Program, Harvard Law School.

[17] Khir, M. F. A. (2013). "The Concept of the Time Value of Money: A *Shari'ah* Viewpoint", *International Journal of Islamic Banking & Finance*, *3*(2), 1–15.

[18] Khan, T. (2014). "Comment on: Islamic Economics: Where From, Where To?", *Journal of King Abdul Aziz University: Islamic Economics*, *27*(2), 95–103.

[19] Chapra, U. (2007). "The Case Against Interest: Is It Compelling?", *Thunderbird International Business Review*, *49*(2), 161–186.

[20] Siddiqi, M. N. (2014). "Islamic Economics: Where From, Where To?", *Journal of King Abdul Aziz University: Islamic Economics*, *27*(2), 59–68.

the experiences of Islamic banking in various Muslim countries have shown that the profit- and loss-sharing (PLS) model has been marginalized.[21] Muhammad Kabir Hassan and Abdel-Hameed explain that a typical Islamic bank's loan portfolio is heavily biased towards short-term trade financing.[22] Islamic economists like Shamim Ahmed Siddiqui[23] who expect a lot from Islamic banks than just acting as financial brokers like conventional banks think that unless Islamic banking gradually moves away from debt like financing, it cannot claim to be a substantive alternative of the conventional banking system.

On the practical difficulties of moving towards PLS modes, Waqar Masood Khan notes that informational asymmetry and higher monitoring costs hinder the widespread use of equity contracts.[24] Muhammad Mansoor Khan and Muhammad Ishaq Bhatti explain that banks do not find it feasible to enter into the PLS relationship with businesspeople whose majority maintains double sets of accounts for the sake of avoiding exorbitant tax payments.[25] The absence of a just and speedy judicial system also discourages banks from adopting the PLS system. Businesspeople also show a high reluctance to enter into the PLS relationship in order to preserve the privacy of their business operations from outside stakeholders.

Other critics of Islamic banking dismiss the notion that the current models and institutional structure can result in any real and meaningful transformation of the way banks function. Masudul Alam Choudhury unequivocally remarks that Islamic banking is a mainstream enterprise, good for the rich shareholders in the narrow pre-conceived notion of avoidance of financial interest, while not understanding the epistemological

---

[21] Kayed, R. N. (2012). "The Entrepreneurial Role of Profit & Loss Sharing Modes of Finance: Theory & Practice", *International Journal of Islamic and Middle Eastern Finance and Management*, 5(3), 203–228.

[22] Hassan, M. K. and Bashir, A. H. (2003). "Determinants of Islamic Banking Profitability", *ERF Paper*, 10, 3–31.

[23] Siddiqui, S. A. (2007). *Establishing the Need and Suggesting a Strategy to Develop Profit and Loss Sharing Islamic Banking*. In IIU Malaysia Conference on Islamic Banking and Finance at Kuala Lumpur.

[24] Khan, W. M. (1989). "Towards an Interest-Free Islamic Economic System", *Journal of King Abdul Aziz University: Islamic Economics*, 1(1), 3–38.

[25] Khan, M. M. and Bhatti, M. I. (2006). "Why Interest-free Banking and Finance Movement Failed in Pakistan", *Humanomics*, 22(3), 145–161.

meaning underlying this principle.[26] Roszaini Haniffa and Muhammad Hudaib argue that *Maqasid al-Shari'ah* (purposes of the law) have been unduly used to justify the innovation of financial products to compete and converge with conventional banking.[27] Another staunch critic of practiced Islamic finance, Mahmoud El-Gamal observes that Islamic finance as it exists today is a prohibition-driven industry, which attempts to provide Muslims with permissible analogues of conventional financial services and products that are generally deemed impermissible in Islamic jurisprudence.[28] Mahmoud El Gamal contends that growth in Islamic finance is enabled by synthesizing contemporary financial products and services from classical nominate contracts, without regard to the corporate structure of financial institutions.[29]

The realist camp scholars argue that these redistribution objectives will be taken care of by Islamic social finance institutions, which include Islamic microfinance, *Zakat* and *Waqf*, while Islamic banks will continue to serve the short-term finance needs of businesses and middle to high income class urban households and for which mostly the debt-based Islamic modes of financing are the suitable options.

In Malaysia and Indonesia, Islamic microfinance, *Zakat* and *Waqf* institutions have been used as social finance vehicles in the overall Islamic finance architecture very successfully. In Pakistan also, institutions like Akhuwat have shown how *Qard-e-Hasan* can be used to help the downtrodden on a large scale. Mufti Muhammad Taqi Usmani has been a strong proponent for introducing equity-based financing and regards them as more preferable in order to achieve Islamic egalitarian and redistributive objectives even through the Islamic banking institutions. But, he explains that idealism from a financial and development perspective does not

---

[26]Choudhury, M. A. (2012). "The 'Impossibility' Theorems of Islamic Economics", *International Journal of Islamic and Middle Eastern Finance and Management*, 5(3), 179–202.

[27]Haniffa, R. and Hudaib, M. (2010). "Islamic Finance: From Sacred Intentions to Secular Goals?", *Journal of Islamic Accounting and Business Research*, 1(2), 85–91.

[28]El-Gamal, M. A. (2005). "Limits and Dangers of *Shari'ah* Arbitrage", in S. Nazim Ali, *Islamic Finance: Current Legal and Regulatory Issues*, Cambridge, Massachusetts: Islamic Finance Project, Islamic Legal Studies, Harvard Law School, pp. 117–131.

[29]El Gamal, M. A. (2007). "Mutuality As an Antidote to Rent seeking *Shari'ah* Arbitrage in Islamic Finance", *Thunderbird International Business Review*, 49(2), 187–202.

determine legitimacy and illegitimacy of the other alternatives which may lack in contributing significantly to the redistributive ideals, but which nevertheless provide a practical solution to avoid *Riba* and its ramifications. In his book, *Interest Free Banking*, the respected scholar Mufti Muhammad Taqi Usmani has clarified that the criticism on underachievement of the ideal redistributive objective in current practice is different from the status of legitimacy of Islamic banking which by and large has to use Islamic debt-based modes of financing.[30] But, it does not help in improving the chance to use equity financing any better if an unqualified legitimacy is accorded to interest-based borrowing by the borrowers, especially when the large majority of them are the corporate clients and well-to-do professionals.

At the very least, Islamic banks take ownership of the asset for which they provide finance, bear the risks along with mitigating these risks as a custodian of depositors' funds, charge rent after the asset is transferred in usable condition, and charge these rents only until the asset remains in their ownership and is being possessed by the client in usable condition. In conventional debt-based financing, this feature is absent and the interest is charged no matter whether the asset exists and no matter whether it is available in usable condition or not.

Islamic banks do not charge late-payment penalties as income. In practice, it is found that late-payment penalty is seldom charged and it is used in the contract to avoid the very real moral hazard problem and the eventuality of customers willfully defaulting on loans. As a result, the non-performing loan to financing ratio in Islamic banking has remained much lower than conventional banks in many jurisdictions. Hanif argues that Islamic Financial Institutions (IFIs) cannot claim interest on their balances with other banks and mandatory cash reserve maintained with a central bank.[31] Islamic banks cannot invest in interest-based government securities and interest-based bonds. They cannot claim the time value of money from defaulters and they have to bear risks in the sale. Hence, these differences exist in practice between the operations of Islamic and conventional banks.

---

[30] Usmani, M. T. (2007). *Ghair Soodi Bankari* [*Interest Free Banking*]. Karachi: Maktaba Ma'ariful Quran.

[31] Hanif, M. (2014). "Differences and Similarities in Islamic and Conventional Banking", *International Journal of Business and Social Science*, 2(2), 166–175.

4.7 Conclusion

This chapter discussed that there is ample flexibility and enriched product line in Islamic banking and finance to cater to diverse risk preferences. For commercial finance, Islamic banking products can cater to financing needs for capital investments as well as working capital management. The interlinkages between macro economy and Islamic banking operations are direct, transparent, and support stability in the economy. Real sector-based productive enterprise can contribute towards full employment of resources and inclusive growth. Finally, the development finance needs can also be dealt with through Islamic social and commercial financial institutions and instruments.

Self-Assessment Quiz

1. *Mudarabah* has the benefit over other modes of finance in that it:
   (a) Provides finance based on the value of the collateral
   (b) Provides finance based on the creditworthiness of the client to meet repayment obligations
   (c) Provides finance on the business potential of the project
   (d) None of the above

2. If a manufacturing concern is financed purely with *Mudarabah* and *Musharakah*, what potential economic benefits it may have:
   (a) Expansion of access to capital to large-scale as well as small-scale enterprises with good business potential
   (b) The outcome of the productive enterprise will be equitably shared
   (c) There will be no stipulated cost of finance which will add to costing and prices of goods
   (d) All of the above

3. Which of the following features distinguish an Islamic mortgage based on Diminishing *Musharakah* from a conventional mortgage?
   (a) The cost of Islamic mortgage is necessarily lower than conventional mortgage
   (b) Benchmark for pricing is distinct in both types of mortgage
   (c) Instead of interest, rent is charged for the portion of asset/property owned by the financier during the lease period
   (d) Instead of principal loan repayment, the portion of asset/property owned by the financier is purchased in periodic instalments
   (e) Both (c) and (d)

4. For fixed-asset finance, which of the Islamic modes of financing is suitable if the client wishes to obtain long-term finance and also own the asset eventually by paying its price in phased payments.
   (a) *Murabaha*
   (b) *Ijarah*
   (c) Diminishing *Musharakah*
   (d) None of the above

5. What economic criticism is faced by Islamic banks generally?
   (a) The cost of finance and the pattern of cash flows are similar in Islamic and conventional finance
   (b) For the pricing of Islamic finance products, the market benchmark based on interest-based interbank transactions used by conventional banks is also used by Islamic banks by and large
   (c) The distributive effects of Islamic debt-based modes of finance are similar to conventional banking products
   (d) All of the above

Self-Assessment Questions

1. Explain how the balance sheet of Islamic banks is capable of taking financial shocks in a better way as compared to conventional banks.
2. Discuss how *Mudarabah* and *Musharakah* ensure equitable distribution of income in access to finance and in the outcomes of the productive enterprise.
3. Examine how *Ijarah* and Diminishing *Musharakah* facilitate fixed assets finance by enabling asset purchase with flexible rental schedule spread over a longer period.
4. Discuss how *Murabaha* facilitates short-term financing in effective working capital management.
5. In cases where the use of funds is required not necessarily for the purchase of assets, but to meet broader costs, how do *Salam* and *Istisna* help in corporate finance?
6. Identify how *Sukuk* can help in development finance in the purchase of infrastructure for development.
7. Discuss how the use of asset-backed finance and real economic activities involved in Islamic finance contracts mitigate the risk of financial crises.

8. Illustrate how Islamic finance principles, institutions, and instruments can help in meeting each of the 17 UN Sustainable Development Goals (SDGs).
9. Explain how Islamic finance instruments stimulate the components of aggregate demand in the macro economy.
10. Critically evaluate the main arguments of idealist and realist schools in Islamic finance.

PART III

Islamic Capital and Money Markets

Chapter 5

Islamic Equity Investments

5.1 Significance of Financial Investments

Financial investments with financial institutions or in financial markets make the lifetime resources grow in periods when they are not needed for current consumption. Investment decision-making requires a careful analysis of risk and return. Investors desire more returns and less risk. For the same risk levels, they would prefer high return investments. For the same return levels, they would prefer low-risk investments.[1] The objective of financial investments is to achieve the highest returns for a given level of risk or to minimize the risk of achieving a given target level of return. Investors like an increase in returns and dislike increase in risk. As the risk level rises, most risk-averse investors would prefer a proportionately higher increase in returns for the constant increase in risk as illustrated in Figure 5.1.

Risk comes in two forms, i.e. diversifiable and non-diversifiable. The non-diversifiable risk is a systematic risk that cannot be reduced through further diversification. On the contrary, the diversifiable risk is a firm-specific risk. Diversifiable risk can be avoided by forming a carefully selected portfolio comprising financial assets that have less than perfect correlation.[2] Figure 5.2 illustrates this idea that as the number of stocks in the portfolio increases, the unsystematic risk tends to decline and a

---

[1] Markowitz, H. (1952). "Portfolio Selection", *The Journal of Finance*, 7(1), 77–91.
[2] Wagner, W. H. and Lau, S. C. 1971. "The Effect of Diversification on Risk", *Financial Analysts Journal*, 27(6), 48–53.

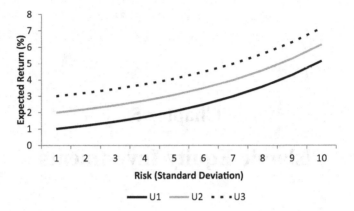

Figure 5.1.   Risk–return preferences in utility curve for investors.

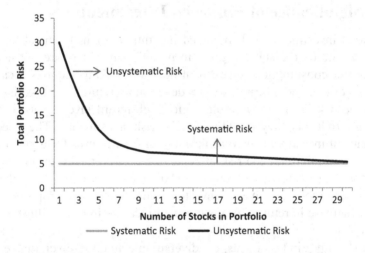

Figure 5.2.   Systematic and unsystematic risk in the portfolio.

well-diversified portfolio only has systematic risk. A risky portfolio of less than perfectly correlated assets always offers better risk–return opportunities than the individual component securities on their own.

In this way, if some stocks move down, others will move up and reduce the overall risk. For instance, in winters, sales of hot beverage may increase while sales of cold desserts may go down. If an investor keeps both types of stocks in his portfolio, it will ensure that some of his stocks do well in summers as well as in winters. However, picking stocks based on such intuitive expectations is not always possible. An investor has to undertake a careful analysis of expected returns, risk, and correlations among hundreds and thousands of securities in local, regional, and even global capital markets. Most investors do not utterly survive on financial investments, and hence, they cannot devote time or possess unique skills to conduct and interpret detailed financial analysis on a continuous basis. What most small investors do is to delegate the investment and portfolio management work to the professional asset management companies or invest in passive portfolios which try to mimic the market portfolio closely.

The financial needs of investors differ with varying degrees of risk appetite. A typical young investor who has just entered the labour force and who is unmarried and who can potentially remain in labour force for a long duration of time would have a long-term investment horizon and he will have more risk appetite. On the contrary, a retired person at old age who has less inclination and chances to enter labour force again and who depends on small amount of pensions and past savings would be willing to take much less risk and want a consistent stream of regular income.[3] Hence, the asset management companies cater to these varying needs of their clients by offering mutual funds of different investment styles. These asset management companies pool investments from individual investors and then make investments from the pool of funds available at their disposal.

According to the modern portfolio theory, investors analyse investment opportunities in terms of return and risk. The expected utility of investors is a decreasing function of risk (risk aversion) and an increasing function of return. Preferences are represented by the indifference curve. An indifference curve represents those risk and return combinations among which the investor is indifferent, i.e. obtains same utility.

In modern portfolio theory, an efficient portfolio has the highest return for a given level of risk, or no other portfolio has a lower risk for a given level of return. Combining the efficient frontier with preferences of investors about risk and return, the equilibrium can be illustrated where the investor chooses an optimal portfolio as illustrated in Figure 5.3. An optimal portfolio on efficient frontier is the one that is tangent to the investor's indifference curve.

---

[3] Bodie, Z., Merton, R. C. *et al.* (1991). "Labour Supply Flexibility and Portfolio Choice in a Lifecycle Model", *Journal of Economic Dynamics and Control*, *16*(3), 427–449.

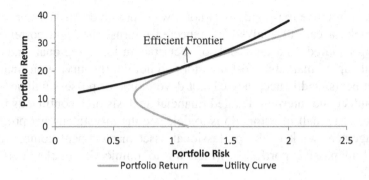

Figure 5.3.   Efficient frontier and investor equilibrium.

The choice of the optimum portfolio of risky assets is independent of the preferences of individual investors. This explains the rationale for the existence of mutual funds.[4]

5.2 The Distinct Character of Islamic Investments

Given the differences in the investment opportunity set, the objective of the investor in the Islamic framework would be no different in seeking an efficient portfolio within the permissible investment universe of assets. The possible choices in the investment opportunity set would not contain interest-based investments or equity securities that are deemed *Shari'ah* non-compliant through a compliance screening process. Muslim investors must comply with the ethical injunctions prescribed for them while making financial investments. As per Islamic principles, the use of *Riba* (interest), *Maysir* (gambling), and *Gharar* (uncertain or contingent payoff contracts) is prohibited. Hence, the Muslim investor who wants to comply with these principles would not be willing to invest in conventional bank deposits, annuities, insurance, and derivatives with contingent payoffs. For Muslim investors with surplus endowments, the available investment avenues would include interest-free bank investments, mutual fund investments, and direct equity investments.

Another difference that comes in Islamic investments is the cost of portfolio revision due to changes in the *Shari'ah*-compliant list of stocks.

---

[4]Merton, R. C. (1972). "An Analytic Derivation of the Efficient Portfolio Frontier", *Journal of Financial and Quantitative Analysis*, 7(4), 1851–1872.

Untimely disinvestment can be costly to Muslim investors. Furthermore, Islamic principles require that all income earned by Islamic investments must be *Halal*, and if some non-*Halal* portion arises in income, then it must be purified. For instance, if a *Shari'ah*-compliant stock invests in conventional bonds and earns 1% of its net income from interest income, then the Islamic funds which have invested in the company and who receive dividends must purify their income. The dividend purification ensures *Shari'ah*-compliant returns for the Muslim investor, but with the caveat that this dividend purification cost is peculiar to Islamic portfolios while conventional portfolios do not have to undertake dividend purification.

The total global Islamic assets under management (AUM) stood at $110 billion by the end of 2017. Table 5.1 shows the share in global Islamic fund assets in some countries. Even some of the non-Muslim-majority countries like the United States of America, Ireland, and Luxembourg have ventured in offering investment funds that are compliant with the principles of Islamic investments.

If one looks at the investment allocation concentration of these Islamic funds, it appears that most of these invest in equities, commodities, and money market instruments like *Sukuk* as can be seen in Table 5.2.

Table 5.1. Global market share in Islamic asset management.

Country	Share in Islamic Fund Assets (2017) (%)
Malaysia	31.7
Ireland	8.6
United States	5.3
Luxembourg	4.8
Indonesia	3.0
Kuwait	2.5
South Africa	2.4
Pakistan	2.3
Saudi Arabia	1.3
Jersey	0.5
Cayman Islands	0.3
UAE	0.3
Others	37.1

Source: Islamic Financial Services Industry Stability Report 2018.

Table 5.2.   Investment allocation in Islamic asset management.

Asset Class	Share (2017) (%)
Equity	42
Money market	26
Commodity	14
Fixed income/*Sukuk*	10
Mixed allocation	7
Real estate	1
Other	0.04

Source: Islamic Financial Services Industry Stability Report 2018.

5.3 *Shari'ah* Compliance Governance Framework for Islamic Investments

To determine the eligibility of a company with regards to *Shari'ah* compliance, two sets of criteria are employed. The first step is the qualitative screening. In this process, the companies are screened on the basis of whether their core business is in conformity with Islamic principles or not. Companies dealing in prohibited goods and services are considered non-eligible for selection in the Islamic index or portfolios. For instance, if a company sells goods and services, such as alcoholic drinks, arms, pork, intoxicants, pornography, or betting, the company is considered *Shari'ah* non-compliant. If a company engages in interest- and gambling-based financial products, such as conventional banking, leasing, and insurance, then the company is rendered non-eligible for selection in the Islamic index or portfolios.

After removing companies with non-compliant business activities, the rest of the companies are examined on certain quantitative indicators. These quantitative indicators are related to leverage, liquidity, the share of revenues derived from non-compliant activities, and dividend purification. All of these are subject to evaluation on an ongoing basis. In Table 5.3, we give a brief summary of the quantitative screens followed in three major indices globally, i.e. Standard and Poor (S&P), Financial Times Stock Exchange (FTSE), and Dow Jones Islamic Market Index (DJIM).

Table 5.3. Screening criteria of global indices.

Quantitative Screens	S&P	FTSE	Dow Jones
Interest-based leverage	Debt to market equity (12 month average) must be lower than 33%.	The debt must be lower than 33% of the total assets.	Debt to market equity (24 month average) must be lower than 33%.
Interest-based liquidity	Accounts receivables to market equity (12 month average) must be lower than 49%. (Cash plus interest-based securities) to market equity (12 month average) must be lower than 33%.	Cash and interest-based investments must be lower than 33% of the total assets. Accounts receivable and cash must be lower than 50% of the total assets.	Cash- and interest-based securities divided by market equity (24 month average) must be lower than 33%. Accounts receivables divided by market equity (24 month average) must be lower than 33%.
Non-compliant revenues	Non-compliant income other than interest income to revenue must be lower than 5%.	Non-compliant income including interest income should not be greater than 5% of the total revenue of the company.	—
Income purification	$Dividends * \dfrac{Non\text{-}compliant\,income}{Total\,revenue}$		

These principles discourage high financial leverage without the backing of real assets. The cap on interest-bearing leverage guards against high financial risk. The cap on interest-based investments encourages the firm to invest in the real economy and productive enterprise. If a company invests in its core operations by procuring raw materials, expanding its production capacity and investing in advanced technological equipment, then it will be able to gain and retain a competitive advantage. The minimum limit on illiquid assets ratio encourages investment in productive capacity. The minimum limit on illiquid assets to total assets ratio together with the condition that minimum price for stock should not be less than the net liquid assets per share guard against the market price to be significantly different from the value of underlying net assets in the business.

5.4 Requirement of Dividend Purification

It is also important for Muslim investors and institutional investors like Islamic funds, *Takaful* companies, and Islamic banks to purify the non-compliant portion of the income from the dividend income received from the stock of a company. If the non-compliant portion of a firm is very small and the core business of the firm is *Halal*, then it is allowed to invest in such a company if it complies with other screening criteria, such as a cap on interest-based leverage and investments.

One such method of dividend purification used in practice is as follows:

$$\text{Income purification} = \text{Dividend} \times \frac{\text{Non-compliant income}}{\text{Total revenue}} \quad (5.1)$$

There are certain issues with this method which are described below:

(1) Non-compliant income is earned and reported independently as part of the net income. Being a common stockholder, one is part-owner in every asset and earning of the company whether it is paid in the form of dividends or retained for reinvestment. This has no relation to the dividend policy.

(2) The company may not pay dividend and still has non-compliant income reported in the income statement.

(3) Total revenue and dividend paid do not necessarily have a proportional relationship. Dividend policy may take into account many factors. Also, the Dividend payout ratio (DPO) is not necessarily constant overtime.

(4) This method does not effectively result in the total purification of non-compliant income. By allowing capital gains to be exempt from purification process, it tilts the preference towards capital gains, and it may result in more speculative short-term activities in equity markets rather than investing meaningfully in a company with long-term horizon in anticipation of the dividend.

Accounting and Auditing Organization for Islamic Financial Institutions (AAOIFI) has given a conservative, but more effective, purification methodology in its *Shari'ah* Standard 21. Clause 3/4/6/4 reads as follows:

"The figure, whose elimination is obligatory on the person dealing in shares, is arrived at by dividing the total prohibited income of the corporation whose shares are traded by the number of shares of the corporation; thus, the figure specific to each share is obtained. Thereafter, the result is multiplied by the number of shares owned by the dealer — individual, institution, fund or another — and the result is what is to be eliminated as an obligation".

In this methodology, stock dividend and stock splits which change the number of shares outstanding are not potential problems as long as the effect is proportionally felt in stock price at least in the most immediate instance. But, even if it is not proportional and is different, there is no way that it systematically benefits or costs the investor. In addition to that, the most important thing is that it ensures total income purification in all cases and does not leave this matter contingent on dividend policy and particular reporting standards followed to prepare financial statements.

5.5 Empirical Literature on Performance of Islamic Passive Indices

Muslim investors apply both Islamic ethical and financial criteria when evaluating investments in order to ensure that the securities selected are consistent with their value system and beliefs. Here, we give a brief review of empirical literature that looks at the comparative performance of Islamic indices vis-à-vis conventional market indices.

Studies suggest that the screening criteria adopted to eliminate *Shari'ah*-non-compliant companies results in a subset of a sufficient number of companies for effective diversification and hence does not affect the performance of the Islamic index in relation to the broad equity market adversely.[5] However, in fixed-income portfolios, Islamic investors face

---

[5]Hakim, S. and Rashidian, M. (2002). *Risk and Return of Islamic Stock Market Indexes.* In 9th Economic Research Forum Annual Conference in Sharjah, UAE, pp. 26–28.

lack of fixed-income securities due to the limited availability of *Sukuk*. Hence, they face challenges in diversification.[6]

Some empirical studies attempt to see the potential impact that Islamic ethical restrictions may have on investment performance by comparing the performance characteristics of Islamic and conventional indices. Results show that the expected returns of Islamic portfolios are higher than the expected returns of conventional unrestricted portfolios.[7]

During the financial crisis of 2007–2009, Islamic portfolios proved to be less volatile even in an emerging market, such as India, where the Islamic indices outperformed conventional unrestricted indices both on return as well as in volatility.[8] Some regional studies show that the financial crisis impacted volatility in three Gulf Cooperation Council (GCC) markets (Kuwait, Bahrain, and the UAE), while the impact on the remaining markets (Saudi Arabia, Oman, and Qatar) and the Islamic index was insignificant.[9]

It is empirically observed that the Dow Jones Islamic Market Index is the least susceptible to global contagion effects.[10] In a study for Indonesia, it is found that there is no significant difference in performance between Islamic and conventional market index, but the Islamic index is less volatile than conventional indices generally.[11]

---

[6]Rana, M. E. and Akhter, W. (2015). "Performance of Islamic and Conventional Stock Indices: Empirical Evidence from an Emerging Economy", *Financial Innovation*, *1*(1), 15.

[7]Hassan, A. (2005). "Evaluating the Performance of Managed Funds: The Cases of Equity, Ethical Funds & Islamic Index". PhD Thesis, Durham University.

[8]Beik, I. S. and Wardana, W. (2011). "The Relationship between Jakarta Islamic Index & Other Selected Markets: Evidence from Impulse Response Function". *Majalah Ekonomi*, *21*(1), 100–109.

[9]Miniaoui, H., Sayani, H. *et al.* (2015). "The Impact of Financial Crisis on Islamic and Conventional Indices of the GCC Countries", *Journal of Applied Business Research*, *31*(2), 357–370.

[10]Akbar, Z. and Barkely, D. (2015). "The Performance of Islamic Equity Indexes Global Capital Markets", *Journal of Islamic Economics, Banking and Finance*, *11*(1), 71–92.

[11]Pranata, N. and Nurzanah, N. (2016). "Conventional and Islamic Indices in Indonesia: A Comparison on Performance, Volatility, and the Determinants". *Indonesian Capital Market Review*, *7*(2), 113–127.

Results from some cross-country studies reveal that there is no significant statistical difference in risk-adjusted returns between Islamic and conventional stock market indices during the pre-crisis period.[12] Studies confirm that there is no significant difference in the returns of Islamic and conventional market indices in emerging and developed markets, such as Malaysia, United Kingdom, and the USA.[13] Other studies also show that there is no significant difference in mean returns between Islamic and conventional indices, except for Italy and Australia.[14]

What do these results imply for the faith-conscious, ethical, and impact investors. The results suggest that Muslim investors can pursue Islamic capital market investments in conformity with their religious beliefs without sacrificing financial performance. Global evidence from cross-country studies suggests that Islamic indices perform better than conventional ones during crisis periods because of their lower volatility and systematic risk. Findings reveal that Islamic indices outperformed their conventional counterparts during crisis periods, but results are inconclusive for the non-crisis periods.[15] This could be due to the conservative nature of *Shari'ah*-compliant investments offering investors a superior investment alternative during the crisis. Studying the volatilities and correlations of Islamic indices suggests that there is a low moving correlation between the conventional and Islamic indices. The results substantiate that during the crisis, Islamic indices provide insulation from the downward spiral in asset prices.[16] This might be because of the higher extent of real

[12]Albaity, M. and Ahmad, R. (2008). "Performance of *Shari'ah* & Composite Indices: Evidence from Bursa Malaysia", *Asian Academy of Management Journal of Accounting & Finance*, 4(1), 23–43.

[13]Albaity, M. and Ahmad, R. (2011). "Return Performance, Leverage Effect, and Volatility Spill over in Islamic Stock Indices: Evidence from DJIMI, FTSEGII and KLSI", *Investment Management and Financial Innovations*, 8(3), 161–171.

[14]Abbes, M. B. (2012). "Risk and Return of Islamic and Conventional Indices", *International Journal of Euro-Mediterranean Studies*, 5(1), 1–23.

[15]Ho, C. S. F., Rahman, N. A. A. *et al.* (2014). "Performance of Global Islamic versus Conventional Share Indices: International Evidence", *Pacific-Basin Finance Journal*, 28, 110–121.

[16]Rizvi, S. A. R. and Arshad, S. (2014). "An Empirical Study of Islamic Equity As a Better Alternative during Crisis Using Multivariate GARCH DCC", *Islamic Economic Studies*, 22(1), 159–184.

and tangible assets on the balance sheet whose value does not tumble as swiftly or abruptly as the price of the non-real asset-backed financial securities.

Furthermore, studies attempting to use multi-factor asset pricing models like the Carhart model to analyse the comparative performance of Islamic and conventional market returns do not identify significant differences in the performance of the Islamic index compared to that of the conventional market.[17]

5.6 Comparative Performance of Islamic and Conventional Indices

This section provides some recent evidence on the comparative performance of Islamic and conventional market indices. In Table 5.4, we give a summary of annualized daily returns, annualized standard deviation and coefficient of variation statistics for five Islamic and five conventional indices. We select the following five indices groups: Developed, Global, Emerging, S&P 500, and S&P Europe for both Islamic and conventional indices.

We find that for the overall period, Islamic indices outperformed conventional market indices in terms of annualized returns, except for emerging markets. Apart from Europe, Islamic indices did not have a lower coefficient of variation in the great financial crisis of 2007–2010. Likewise, Islamic indices did not have a lower annualized standard deviation of returns in the great financial crisis of 2007–2010 except in S&P 500 and S&P Europe. However, Islamic indices had a lower standard deviation and coefficient of variation in the post-crisis period of 2011–2016. This shows that Islamic indices recovered well and more than the conventional market indices after the great financial crisis of 2007–2010. In the overall period of 2007–2016, we find that Islamic indices have a lower coefficient of variation and hence higher reward to variability ratio. This suggests that Islamic indices are superior to conventional market indices adjusting for variability in returns.

---

[17]Dhai, R. (2015). "A Comparison of the Performance of the FTSE South Africa Islamic Index to the Conventional Market (JSE) in South Africa", *South African Journal of Accounting Research*, 29(2), 101–114.

Table 5.4.   Returns and volatility of Islamic and conventional indices.

Measures/Groups	Annualized Return (%)			Annualized S.D. (%)			Coefficient of Variation		
	07–16	07–10	11–16	07–16	07–10	11–16	07–16	07–10	11–16
Islamic									
S&P Developed Shari'ah	6.2	1.7	8.5	17.4	23.5	13.4	2.8	14.3	1.6
S&P Global Shari'ah	5.7	1.6	7.8	17.2	23.4	13.1	3.0	14.4	1.7
S&P Emerging Shari'ah	1.4	2.4	0.9	20.0	28.2	14.3	14.8	11.9	16.8
S&P 500 Shari'ah	9.9	6.4	12.1	19.7	25.4	14.9	2.0	4.0	1.2
S&P Europe 350 Shari'ah	8.1	4.9	10.0	19.1	23.6	15.6	2.4	4.8	1.6
Conventional									
S&P Developed Index	5.9	1.9	8.4	17.7	22.8	13.5	3.0	11.8	1.6
S&P Global Index	5.7	2.9	7.4	17.5	22.6	13.3	3.1	7.8	1.8
S&P Emerging Index	4.9	13.2	−0.5	20.1	26.0	15.2	4.2	2.0	−29.2
S&P 500 Index	9.1	3.1	12.9	25.6	27.9	24.1	5.4	8.9	4.2
S&P Europe 350 Index	5.5	−0.4	9.3	21.0	25.5	17.4	3.8	−73.7	1.9

5.7 Security Analysis Using Mainstream Asset Pricing Models

Choosing the appropriate financial assets and securities in the portfolio requires security analysis. For analysing securities, different asset pricing models are employed to assess potential investments.

Islamic equity investments can also be analysed using the mainstream asset pricing models after modifications for the choice of risk-free rate of return and choosing an appropriate benchmark market portfolio. Asset pricing models do not suggest any particular rate of return on financial investments. Asset pricing models provide an *ex ante* method of evaluating investment choices for investors.

In the Islamic finance literature, Hazny and Yusof discuss the assumptions of Markowitz's Mean Variance Analysis and Capital Asset Pricing

Model (CAPM) from the *Shari'ah* perspective and conclude that these assumptions are simplistic only for the purpose of facilitating tractable analysis with the given data limitations.[18] Some argue that the principle of *Al Ghunm bil Ghurm* means that returns are justified by taking risks.[19] Moreover, *Al-Kharaj bil Dhaman* entitles profits on corresponding liability to bear losses. These legal maxims in Islamic jurisprudence are quite resonant with the positive *ex ante* relationship between risk and return espoused in modern portfolio theory. Furthermore, it is also possible to have divisible investments in Islamic finance through *Sukuk*, Islamic mutual funds, and *Shari'ah*-compliant common stocks. Thus, the assumption of divisibility, liquidity, and marketability of investments are quite admissible in the Islamic capital markets as well.

Apart from that, the other assumptions which seemingly look contradictory with Islamic principles can be altered for bringing uniformity with Islamic capital market practices and norms. For instance, the risk-free rate can be replaced with the *Sukuk* profit rate or to the benchmark rate with which *Sukuk* profits are related. Zamir Iqbal argues that the assumption of short selling might be solved by assuming complete markets.[20] In recent developments in Islamic capital markets, *Murabaha, Salam*, and *Bai Arboun* products have facilitated liquidity in the market for efficient price adjustments.

Salam is a transaction whereby an asset is sold at the spot with deferred delivery, but in which the full price of the asset is paid at spot. *Arboun* is a type of sale which is executed using down payment or advance money with the condition that if the buyer accepts to complete the sale by taking the object of sale, then the down payment will be treated as part of the selling price. *Murabaha* is a sale in which the assets are purchased at spot, but sold for a higher price later.

In conventional finance, the interest rate on sovereign debt serves as a proxy for risk-free rate.[21] Hanif suggests that the inflation rate can be

---

[18] Hazny, M. H. and Yusof, A. Y. (2012). *Revisiting Markowitz's Mean Variance Analysis: A Review from Shari'ah Perspective*. International Conference on Statistics in Science, Business and Engineering (ICSSBE), Langkawi, 2012, pp. 1–6.

[19] Rosly, S. (2005). *Critical Issues on Islamic Banking and Financial Markets*. Kuala Lumpur: Dinamas Publishing.

[20] Iqbal, Z. (2002). "Portfolio Choices and Asset Pricing in Islamic Framework", in Ahmed, H., *Theoretical Foundations of Islamic Economics*, pp. 167–189.

[21] Askari, H., Iqbal, Z. and Mirakhor, A. (2009). *New Issues in Islamic Finance and Economics: Progress and Challenges*, Singapore: John Wiley & Sons (Asia).

included in place of the risk-free rate in Islamic security analysis.[22] Nonetheless, Muhammad Ayub argues that in the light of the Fiqh Academy of the OIC ruling, the indexation of a lent amount of money to the cost of living indicators is inappropriate.[23]

Some scholars suggest use of *Zakat* rate in place of the risk-free rate. As per this proposal, investors would demand at least 2.5% return to keep intact their net value of the investment after payment of *Zakat*.

In corporate finance, *Zakat* could also be used as a proxy for risk-free return on the premise that once the capital is invested and converted into a means of production, i.e. physical capital stock, then at least the implied minimum return equals savings on *Zakat*. For long-term indirect investment in stocks purchased with the intention of earning dividend income, the savings on *Zakat* would not equal 2.5%. Rather, if the mainstream method on the estimation of *Zakat* on stocks is followed, then the savings in *Zakat* would equal

$$ZSR = 2.5\% \left(\frac{\text{Capital} - \text{Net current assets}}{\text{Capital}} \right) \tag{5.2}$$

For illustration, suppose a firm has total assets equalling $100,000 divided between $30,000 of current assets and $70,000 of fixed assets. Against these assets, the firm has liabilities of $40,000 and equity of $60,000. The liabilities are divided into $10,000 worth of current liabilities and the rest is long-term liabilities. The face value of each of the shares is $10. Suppose that an investor has purchased 100 shares of the firm. The total investment equals $1,000. In this case, the *Zakat* Savings Rate (ZSR) would be 1.67%. No matter what the level of profit of investing liquid assets as physical capital stock in a business undertaking directly or indirectly through part-ownership in corporations is, this much savings in *Zakat* would accrue as reflected in Equation (5.2).

This rate can replace the risk-free cost of capital in corporate finance valuations in areas of capital budgeting, project valuation, asset pricing, security analysis, and portfolio management.

---

[22] Hanif, M. (2011). "Risk and Return under *Shari'ah* Framework: An Attempt to Develop *Shari'ah* Compliant Asset Pricing Model (SCAPM)", *Pakistan Journal of Commerce and Social Sciences*, 5(2), 283–292.

[23] Ayub, M. (2007). *Understanding Islamic Finance*. England: Wiley.

Nonetheless, a problem with such a proposal is that there is no actual security that is paying this much return, i.e. 2.5%. It can be used as a proxy if financial investments are made exempted from *Zakat*. Then, it would lead to an automatic saving in *Zakat*. This view has been taken by some scholars like Muhammad Akram Khan,[24] who opines that *Ushr* is levied on income and not on means of production. Hence, investment in financial securities like stocks is a means of financing and contributing to the purchase of assets by the firm. Thus, as per his proposal, investment in stocks can be exempted from *Zakat*, and it should be levied on income from investment in stocks, such as dividend and capital gain.

In searching for a better alternative for risk-free rate in Islamic capital markets, the return offered by the government on its sovereign *Sukuk* could be a suitable choice. Financial claims to the government have the highest security in terms of default risk. For market competitiveness, the *ex post* return on *Sukuk* and interest-based Treasury securities can be closely linked; however, the underlying structure of the transaction is different in both. Treasury bills involve loaning of money on interest. On the contrary, the government pays rent on the assets which are owned by investors in the commonly used *Ijarah Sukuk* structure. Investors owning a proportionate share of the assets get periodic returns in the form of rents. In fact, *Sukuk* is safer than Treasury bills for investors since investors have recourse to the real assets underlying the *Sukuk*.

Commenting on other alternative asset pricing models, some argue that asset pricing models that do not require a risk-free rate of return can be used as well, such as Zero-beta CAPM.[25] On the contrary, the multi-factor models which use internal factors of the company to explain *ex post* returns are empirical models based on facts without strong assumptions. The choice of factors in multi-factor models depends on the observed relationships between internal factors of the company and the *ex post* realized returns on stocks. These include factors like size, book value to market value, past pattern of returns on the stock, liquidity, leverage, and

---

[24] Khan, M. A. (2005). "Comments on A. Azim Islahi & M. Obaidullah: Zakat on Stocks: Some Unsettled Issues", *Journal of King Abdul Aziz University: Islamic Economics*, *18*(1), 41–42.

[25] Hakim, S. A., Hamid, Z. et al. (2016). "Capital Asset Pricing Model and Pricing of Islamic Financial Instruments", *Journal of King Abdul Aziz University: Islamic Economics*, *29*(1), 21–39.

finally, the profitability of the firm. Islamic investments follow the risk-sharing philosophy which entails that investments must be evaluated based on their internal strength. Such multi-factor models are also quite close in spirit with the Islamic investment norms.

Hence, from the *Shari'ah* perspective, it can be seen that the mainstream asset pricing models can be used for security analysis in Islamic equity investments with some modifications. Nonetheless, the choice of which asset pricing models to choose would depend on the empirical performance of these asset pricing models in practice.

5.8 Conclusion

This chapter introduced the investment norms in Islamic equity investments and screening methodology employed in different jurisdictions to evaluate *Shari'ah* compliance of stocks. Furthermore, this chapter provided a review of the empirical literature on the performance of Islamic equity investments and also provided some recent post-crisis evidence on the comparative performance of Islamic and conventional market indices during 2008–2016. Islamic indices were found to be competitive on returns and had less volatility as compared to the conventional indices. Finally, the chapter also discussed the modifications required to perform security analysis for Islamic equity investments using mainstream asset pricing models.

Self-Assessment Quiz

1. In Islamic mutual funds, the relationship between investors and Asset Management Company is based on:
   (a) *Mudarabah*
   (b) *Musharakah*
   (c) *Wakalah*
   (d) None of the above

2. In *Wakalah* used in Islamic funds investment, the fund management receives its remuneration in which form:
   (a) Fixed fee for management
   (b) Share in profit
   (c) Share in dividends received
   (d) None of the above

3. In Islamic mutual funds, the fund management company is responsible:
   (a) To place the funds in *Shari'ah*-compliant options
   (b) To bear losses on investments
   (c) To provide capital protection guarantee to investors
   (d) None of the above

4. The "income purification" process removes the "prohibited income" from:
   (a) Dividends
   (b) Capital gains
   (c) Interest income
   (d) None of the above

5. If the nature of the business is not compliant with *Shari'ah*, then stocks of such a company:
   (a) Cannot be taken in the Islamic portfolio
   (b) Can be taken in Islamic portfolio if the quantitative screening criteria are fulfilled
   (c) Can be taken in the Islamic portfolio if no dividends are paid
   (d) None of the above

Self-Assessment Questions

1. List the trading strategies and contracts which are not permissible as per Islamic investment principles.
2. Contrast the main features of screening criteria for *Shari'ah* Compliance followed by FTSE, S&P500, and Dow Jones.
3. Does the empirical evidence generally support that Islamic investments are well-performing as compared to conventional investments in times of crisis? If yes, what could be the reasons for that?
4. Can the mainstream asset pricing models be used in the security analysis of *Shari'ah*-compliant stocks? What adjustments need to be made if any in their use?
5. What is the choice of a risk-free asset if any in Islamic investments?
6. Why is dividend purification necessary for Islamic investments?
7. Why do the interest-bearing debt, interest-based investments, and non-compliant portion of income need to be smaller in a *Shari'ah*-compliant stock?

8. Does the modern portfolio theory apply to *Shari'ah*-compliant investments if the investment universe is filtered to include only *Shari'ah*-compliant stocks and when trading strategies avoid the Islamic prohibitions?
9. Modern portfolio theory states that there is a positive relationship between the expected return and risk. Do Islamic principles have affinity with this postulate of modern portfolio theory?
10. In place of shorting and financial derivatives, what liquidity management instruments are there in Islamic investments to facilitate intertemporal investments for hedging and managing genuine liquidity needs?

Chapter 6

Sukuk in Islamic Capital Markets

6.1 Introduction

Sukuk is a financial security which is employed by the issuer to obtain asset-backed financing from the financial markets. Investors purchase the *Sukuk* securities, by virtue of which they become the joint owners of the assets that underlie the *Sukuk* structure. The returns earned on the *Sukuk* are passed on to the investors. In its functional nature, *Sukuk* is a substitute to conventional interest-bearing coupon bonds. Accounting and Auditing Organization for Islamic Financial Institutions (AAOIFI) defines *Sukuk* as follows:

> *Certificates of equal value representing undivided shares in the owner-ship of tangible assets, usufructs and services or (in the ownership of) the assets of particular projects or special investment activity.*

As per Thomson Reuters Report on Islamic Finance published in 2018, total outstanding *Sukuk* value has reached $426 billion in 2017 from $260 billion in 2012 with an impressive compound annual growth rate of 9%. There were as many as 2,590 outstanding *Sukuk* in 2017. Table 6.1 shows the major structures that have been followed in the issuance of *Sukuk* in 2017. Lease, agency, and equity-based structures are more common along with the hybrid structure.

In the sovereign issues by the governments, even non-Muslim-majority countries like United Kingdom and Hong Kong in the past have taken interest in using *Sukuk* for their financing needs. Table 6.2 gives the

Table 6.1. *Sukuk* structures in 2017.

Sukuk Structure	Share in 2017 (%)
Hybrid	30.3
Murabaha	27.7
Ijarah	22.3
Wakalah	15.9
Musharakah	2.5
Mudarabah	1.2
Salam	0.1

Source: Islamic Finance Services Industry Report 2018.

Table 6.2. Share of top 10 countries in sovereign *Sukuk* issuance in 2017.

Country	Sovereign (%)
Saudi Arabia	38.8
Malaysia	32.9
Indonesia	6.7
Qatar	5.5
Oman	3.3
Turkey	3.2
Bahrain	3.00
UAE	2.2
Pakistan	2.2
Hong Kong	1.3

Source: Islamic Finance Services Industry Report 2018.

share of top 10 countries with sovereign *Sukuk* issues in 2017. It can be seen that the sovereign *Sukuk* market is dominated by countries in the Gulf Cooperation Council (GCC) region and by Malaysia and Indonesia in the South East Asian region.

In the corporate *Sukuk* market, the major share rests with Malaysia as illustrated in Table 6.3. In the corporate *Sukuk* market in 2017, Malaysia appears to be more active than the countries in GCC partly because of higher taxation and recession witnessed in GCC.

Table 6.3. Share of countries in corporate *Sukuk* issuance in 2017.

Country	Corporate (%)
Malaysia	60.6
UAE	12.9
Turkey	7.2
Qatar	5.2
Kuwait	4.8
Saudi Arabia	3.2
Indonesia	2.8
Bahrain	2.5
Oman	0.7

Source: Islamic Finance Services Industry Report 2018.

6.2 *Sukuk* Structures

In what follows, the widely used *Sukuk* structures in practice are briefly explained and illustrated.

6.2.1 *Ijarah Sukuk*

A typical *Ijarah Sukuk* would be structured like this. For example, if a manufacturer needs industrial machinery, it will issue *Sukuk* that can be purchased by institutional and/or retail investors. From the proceeds of the *Sukuk*, the industrial equipment is purchased and is leased to the manufacturer. During the period of the lease, the manufacturer will pay rents and that will generate a regular income stream for the *Sukuk* holders who had invested in the *Sukuk*. After the lease period is over, the manufacturer will purchase the asset in a separate contract, and this will enable the *Sukuk* holders to be able to redeem their investments.

A special purpose vehicle (SPV) is usually established for the issuance of *Sukuk* certificates. The entity requiring finance will sell the asset to the SPV. The SPV will issue *Sukuk* to the investors. *Sukuk* represents the part ownership of the *Sukuk* holder in the assets. By purchasing *Sukuk* certificates, the *Sukuk* holders would become part owners of the assets. The SPV

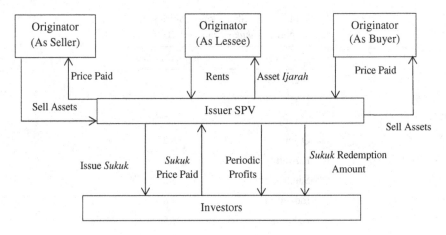

Figure 6.1.   *Ijarah Sukuk* structure.

will use the *Sukuk* proceeds to pay the price of assets purchased from the entity requiring finance. Then, the SPV would provide the asset on lease basis to the entity requiring finance by using *Ijarah* mode of financing. The rent received by the SPV from the lease of assets will be distributed among the *Sukuk* holders who own the asset. The maturity of *Sukuk* and the lease term would usually be the same. At the end of the lease period, the SPV will sell the asset to the entity requiring finance on behalf of *Sukuk* holders and the sale proceeds will be distributed among the *Sukuk* holders. The cash flows at the end would usually enable the *Sukuk* holders to recoup their original investments with income arising as rents during the lease period. Figure 6.1 gives the structure of *Ijarah Sukuk*.

6.2.2 *Istisna Sukuk*

This *Sukuk* is employed when the underlying assets require the manufacturing process. The structure would follow these steps. First, an SPV issues *Sukuk*, which represent undivided ownership in an underlying asset. The investors subscribe the *Sukuk* and pay the proceeds to the SPV. Then, the Originator requiring finance enters into an *Istisna* arrangement with SPV. As per this agreement, the Originator agrees to manufacture or construct certain assets and undertakes to deliver those assets at a future date. SPV pays the price of assets in phased payments against certain milestones to Originator.

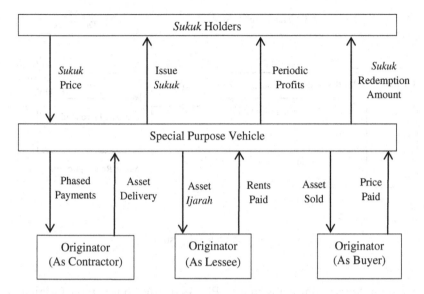

Figure 6.2.   *Istisna Sukuk* structure.

The SPV undertakes to lease the assets to Originator under a forward lease arrangement (known as *Ijarah Mawsufah fi-Zimmah*) for the duration which is usually identical to the maturity of the *Sukuk*. Then, Originator (as Lessee) makes payments of advance rentals prior to the delivery of the assets and actual rentals following the delivery of the assets. In turn, SPV distributes the rents received from the Originator as profit on *Sukuk*. At the end of the lease term, on behalf of the *Sukuk* holders, the SPV will sell assets to the Originator at the agreed exercise price. The proceeds of the sale will then be distributed by the SPV to the *Sukuk* holders. Forward leasing is permitted by some scholars on the condition that advance rentals have to be refunded in full if the assets are never actually delivered for leasing. Figure 6.2 gives the structure of *Istisna Sukuk*.

6.2.3 *Salam Sukuk*

This *Sukuk* structure is used when the underlying asset does not exist at the time of sale. The structure of *Salam Sukuk* involves these steps. An SPV issues the *Sukuk* and the investors subscribe and pay the *Sukuk* price. Here, the *Salam Sukuk* represents undivided ownership in an underlying asset that is going to be purchased. Then, the Originator requiring finance

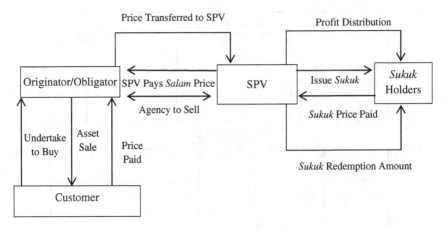

Figure 6.3.   *Salam Sukuk* structure.

enters into *Salam* contract with the SPV. As per the contract, the Originator agrees to sell, and the SPV agrees to purchase the *Salam* assets on immediate payment and deferred delivery terms.

Then, the SPV appoints the Originator as its agent to sell the *Salam* assets on behalf of the SPV. The SPV pays the sale price in advance to the Originator as consideration for its purchase of the *Salam* assets. The Originator then delivers *Salam* assets to the SPV as per the *Salam* contract.

Then, the SPV delivers the *Salam* assets back to the Originator as an agent to sell the same on behalf of the SPV and pay the relevant sale price to the SPV. SPV makes profit distribution payments to the investors using the sale price it receives from the Originator as agent. Figure 6.3 gives the structure of *Salam Sukuk*.

6.2.4 *Wakalah Sukuk*

This *Sukuk* structure is used when there is a need for investment management of assets. The structure of *Wakalah Sukuk* involves these steps. The SPV issues the *Sukuk*, which represent undivided ownership in the *Wakalah* assets. The investors purchase the *Sukuk* in return for a price paid to the SPV. Then, the SPV enters into a *Wakalah* agreement with the entity requiring funds. The *Wakeel* agrees to invest the *Sukuk* proceeds on behalf of the SPV in the *Wakalah* asset, i.e. a portfolio of investments. Then, the *Sukuk* proceeds are used by SPV to purchase the selected *Wakalah* assets.

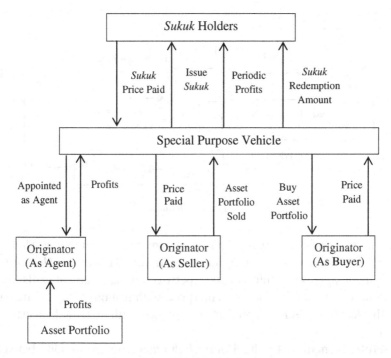

Figure 6.4. *Wakalah Sukuk* structure.

The *Wakalah* assets will be held and managed by the *Wakeel*, on behalf of the SPV for the duration of the *Sukuk* in order to generate an expected profit. Over time, the *Wakalah* assets will generate a profit, which will be held by the *Wakeel* on behalf of the SPV. The profit earned on *Wakalah* assets will be used by the SPV to share the profits with the *Sukuk* holders. Any profit in excess will be paid to the *Wakeel* as an incentive fee. At the maturity date, the SPV will sell the *Wakalah* assets at an exercise price that is eventually passed on to the *Sukuk* investors. Figure 6.4 gives the structure of *Wakalah Sukuk*.

6.2.5 *Mudarabah Sukuk*

This *Sukuk* structure is used when there is a need for obtaining financing on an equity basis rather than debt. In this *Sukuk* structure, the Originator requiring funds does not invest capital of its own. The structure of *Mudarabah Sukuk* involves these steps. The SPV issues *Sukuk* which the investors subscribe and pay the proceeds to the SPV. Then, the SPV and

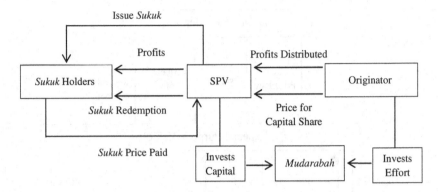

Figure 6.5.   *Mudarabah Sukuk* structure.

Originator enter into a *Mudarabah* agreement with Originator as *Mudarib* and SPV as *Rabb-ul-Maal*. Originator, as *Mudarib* under the *Mudarabah* Agreement, agrees to contribute its expertise and management skills to the *Shari'ah*-compliant *Mudarabah* enterprise with responsibility for managing the *Rabb-ul-Maal*'s capital in accordance with specified investment parameters.

Profits generated by the *Mudarabah* enterprise are divided between the SPV (as *Rabb-ul-Maal*) and Originator (as *Mudarib*) in accordance with the profit-sharing ratios set out in the *Mudarabah* agreement.

When the SPV receives the *Mudarabah* profits, it will pass it on to the *Sukuk* investors. On maturity of the *Mudarabah Sukuk*, the *Mudarabah* enterprise would be dissolved in accordance with the terms of the *Mudarabah* agreement. The Originator will buy the *Mudarabah* equity capital of SPV at market value so that the proceeds can be used by the SPV to service the outstanding amounts due to the investors. The investors would be entitled to a return comprising their pro rata share of the market value of the liquidated *Mudarabah* capital. Figure 6.5 gives the structure of *Mudarabah Sukuk*.

6.2.6 *Musharakah Sukuk*

Like *Mudarabah Sukuk*, this *Sukuk* structure is used when there is a need for obtaining financing on an equity basis rather than debt. In this *Sukuk* structure, the Originator requiring funds also needs a capital of its own to invest in *Musharakah*. The structure of *Musharakah Sukuk* involves these steps.

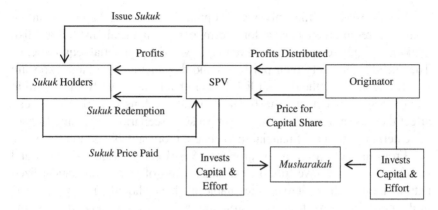

Figure 6.6. *Musharakah Sukuk* structure.

The SPV issues *Sukuk* which the investors subscribe and pay the price to the SPV for the purchase of *Musharakah Sukuk* certificates. Then, the SPV enters into a *Musharakah* agreement with the Originator. The SPV contributes the proceeds from the issuance of the *Sukuk* into the *Musharakah* and is allocated a number of units in the *Musharakah* in proportion to its capital contribution. On each periodic distribution date, the SPV shall receive a pre-agreed percentage share of the expected profits generated by the *Musharakah* assets. In case the *Musharakah* assets generate a loss, the SPV shall share that loss in proportion with its capital contribution to the *Musharakah*. Upon receiving its profit share, the SPV will share the profits with the *Sukuk* holders. At maturity, the SPV will sell the *Musharakah* assets at the applicable exercise price to the Originator. Upon receiving the price for the *Musharakah* assets sold to the Originator, the SPV will pay the *Sukuk* price to the investors to process redemption. Figure 6.6 gives the structure of *Musharakah Sukuk*.

6.3 Economic Function of *Sukuk*

Sukuk is a viable financing mechanism to access funds on a long-term basis for the purchase of long-term fixed assets. By way of issuing *Sukuk*, the issuer obtains the required amount of financing from a wide range of retail and institutional investors who are looking for *Halal*, but stable, source of regular incomes.

Often, *Sukuk* is the only viable option for meeting large amount of financing requirements on a long-term basis. Financial institutions like banks are highly regulated and have to follow strict prudential requirements. They need to diversify their portfolios and they cannot take large exposure to one client. Since the deposit liabilities in banks are usually short term in nature, banks cannot provide finance for a very long period since it can affect their asset liability management. In such scenarios, accessing financing externally from the financial markets is a more suitable option for firms.

From the point of view of investors, *Sukuk* can provide consistent and regular incomes to investors over a long period of time. The standardized nature of *Sukuk* allows it to be marketable and hence liquid. Thus, with *Sukuk* in the portfolios, investors can restructure their portfolios depending on the market performance and their own liquidity needs. Investors will be able to bypass unnecessary intermediation and will save transaction costs and be able to have direct access to the more profitable investment opportunity.

For the Islamic banking industry, an increase in *Sukuk* issuance can increase the investment choices for Islamic banks and also enable them to have a wider market of firms looking for expansionary investment in long-term fixed assets. In public finance, sovereign *Ijarah Sukuk* issued by the governments is structured in such a way that it allows the government to mobilize funds for public projects. The *Sukuk* holders are also able to earn *Shari'ah*-compliant income. It also facilitates Islamic banks to manage their liquidity as well as meet statutory liquidity requirements stipulated by the central banks.

Through the issuance of more *Sukuk*, the investment class assets universe will expand and it will enable the Islamic-conscious individual and institutional investors to effectively diversify their portfolios. Treasuries of Islamic banks will also have an expanded set of investment avenues. It will increase the liquidity of these *Sukuk* and generate wider interest among all investors in the economy to consider investing in these investment vehicles.

Self-Assessment Quiz

1. If the *Ijarah* asset owned by *Sukuk* holders is destroyed due to some reason, who will bear the risk?
   (a) Originator
   (b) Special purpose vehicle

(c) *Sukuk* holders

(d) None of the above

2. Which type of *Sukuk* is suitable if the originator wants to obtain finance not necessarily to buy a new asset, but to meet the overall costs involved in the productive enterprise?

(a) *Murabaha Sukuk*

(b) *Ijarah Sukuk*

(c) *Musharakah Sukuk*

(d) None of the above

3. Which type of *Sukuk* is suitable if the originator wants to obtain long-term finance for the purchase of a fixed asset and own it eventually?

(a) *Murabaha Sukuk*

(b) *Ijarah Sukuk*

(c) *Musharakah Sukuk*

(d) None of the above

4. In conventional bonds, bondholders receive the par value of the bond at maturity to recoup their original investment. In *Sukuk*, original investment is recouped by *Sukuk* holder at maturity through

(a) Purchasing new *Sukuk*, i.e. selling proportionate ownership in the asset

(b) Selling *Sukuk*, i.e. proportionate ownership in the asset back to the originator

(c) Earning mark-up on investment benchmarked with an interbank benchmark rate

(d) None of the above

5. In *Salam Sukuk*, which of the following is true?

(a) SPV purchases the *Salam* assets on immediate payment and deferred delivery terms

(b) SPV purchases the *Salam* assets on deferred payment and spot delivery terms

(c) SPV purchases the *Salam* assets on spot payment and spot delivery terms

(d) SPV purchases the *Salam* assets on deferred payment and deferred delivery terms

Self-Assessment Questions

1. Define *Sukuk* and explain its concept and typical structure.
2. Identify situations where *Sukuk* can be used in corporate finance.
3. Identify situations where *Sukuk* can be used in public finance.
4. What are the key differences in meeting financing needs through financial institutions and financial markets?
5. Illustrate the process flow and steps of obtaining industrial machinery on a long-term financing basis through *Ijarah Sukuk* in financial markets.
6. Illustrate the process flow and steps of obtaining working capital finance through *Salam Sukuk* for a corporate entity specializing in the production of cotton.
7. Illustrate the process flow and steps of obtaining intermediate-term finance in instalments through *Istisna* for a corporate entity specializing in the construction of shopping malls.
8. Differentiate between a conventional bond and a typical *Sukuk*.
9. How *Sukuk* helps in liquidity management for Islamic banks and Islamic mutual funds?
10. Differentiate between asset-backed securities in conventional finance and the structure of a typical *Sukuk*?

Chapter 7

Islamic Money Market

7.1 Introduction

The money market is vital for liquidity management, especially for financial institutions like banks. In order to manage the liquidity requirement, both in terms of shortage of liquidity as well as when there is surplus liquidity, there is need for liquid instruments of a variety of maturities to ensure efficient liquidity management. For Islamic banks, this is even more crucial since they have various regulations to follow including *Shari'ah* compliance regulations. This chapter discusses money market instruments and traditional derivative instruments from the lens of Islamic rules of finance. Then, this chapter also delves into describing the distinct money market instruments available for money market operations in Islamic finance. Finally, the chapter also highlights the hindrances faced in liquidity management by Islamic banks in particular to manage short-term liquidity needs.

7.2 Issues with Conventional Money Market Instruments

7.2.1 *Treasury bills*

Treasury bills are zero-coupon instruments issued by the government and sold through the central bank via auctions. Treasury bills are short-term instruments and are issued with maturities ranging from one month to one year. Holder of a Treasury bill is not entitled to any coupon or interest payment.

However, having zero-coupon payment or no explicit interest payment does not make this instrument *Halal*. To compensate the buyer of the instruments, these bills are sold at a discount from par value. At maturity, the buyer, who is a financier to the government, is entitled to receive the face value of the Treasury bill. Since it involves an exchange of money with money with a time difference, any difference in counter value is *Riba*. When the buyer of Treasury bill pays discounted price to the issuer, the discounted price of the Treasury bill is the money loaned to the government. If, at maturity, the buyer receives more than what it loaned out, the excess is the increase. Any pre-determined and stipulated excess in a loan transaction is *Riba*. Hence, due to the involvement of *Riba*, this instrument is not permissible as per Islamic principles.

7.2.2 *Repo and reverse repo*

A repurchase agreement, also known as a repo is a form of short-term borrowing, mainly in government securities. The financial institution sells the underlying security to investors and buys them back shortly afterwards, at a slightly higher price.

Repo or repurchase agreements are not compliant with Islamic principles due to the involvement of *Riba* in the underlying instrument of sale as well as due to the buyback nature of the contract.

7.2.3 *Corporate bonds*

Bonds are long-term instruments to source debt finance in capital markets from individual and institutional investors without the involvement of a financial intermediary. The firm requiring large sum of money on a long-term basis will fund its debt requirements by selling bonds. To increase wide participation from investors to fund the long-term funds requirement, the price of bond is kept at a reasonably lower level. Bondholders purchase the bonds at the face value. Bondholders are the lenders to the corporations. The firm which issues bond stipulates to pay coupon payment periodically on a semi-annual or annual basis. These coupon payments are interest on the principal amount of loan, which is equal to the face value of the bond. Upon maturity of the bond, the issuer firm repurchases the bond to allow redemption.

From the Islamic point of view, a bond is an instrument to source money on long-term basis. Coupon payments are simply *Riba*. Hence, interest-based bonds or coupon-based bonds are not permissible as per Islamic principles. Thus, any investment in such instruments on short-term or long-term basis is also not permissible.

7.2.4 *Certificate of deposits*

A certificate of deposit is like a conventional deposit scheme offered by conventional banks. The difference here is that these certificates have short-term maturity and a relatively larger sum of deposit. In order to incentivize large scale investments in these instruments by financial institutions, a relatively higher rate of interest is paid as compared to the interest rate paid to the depositors.

Conventional banks have only one contract, i.e. loaning of money on interest. These deposits also carry an increase over the principal amount of deposit. The excess over the principal amount of loan is *Riba*. Hence, these instruments are also non-compliant with Islamic principles.

7.2.5 *Commercial paper*

Commercial paper is an unsecured, short-term debt instrument issued by a corporation. Commercial paper is usually issued at a discount from face value. It is like a Treasury bill in structure with the difference that here the issuer is a private firm rather than the government. The yield or interest rate on commercial paper is higher than the Treasury bill. It is because of the credit rating quality of the issuer. Since the government can print money, it has zero default risk on domestic debt. However, a privately held firm has a non-zero default risk. Hence, to source funds, it has to offer a higher rate of interest to attract investors.

From the Islamic perspective, commercial papers or commercial bills are not permissible due to the involvement of *Riba*. An intertemporal exchange of money at different time intervals is a loan transaction. Any excess over the amount lent is *Riba*. Since *Riba* is not allowed, it is impermissible to issue as well as invest in this instrument.

7.3 Islamic View on Conventional Derivatives

7.3.1 *Forward contract*

A forward contract is a private agreement between two parties giving the buyer an obligation to purchase an asset (and the seller an obligation to sell an asset) at a set price at a future point in time.

Islamic principles of sale require that first the seller shall have ownership and possession of the asset which it wants to sell. Second, the sale shall be executed on a spot basis. The delivery of the asset can be deferred. Hence, sale of a good through e-commerce is allowed where price is paid on spot, but delivery is deferred. Likewise, if delivery is on spot basis, but the price is paid later on, then this credit sale is also allowed. However, in the case of such credit sale, the sale is executed now at a contractually agreed price and the delivery is on spot basis. Time of payment is the only difference between cash and credit sale.

In a forward contract, the sale is not executed on spot basis. Rather, parties have a bilateral obligation to buy and sell the asset at a future date depending on who decides to go long (buy) and who takes a short position (sell). Such future sales are not permissible in the Islamic rules of trade.

7.3.2 *Futures contract*

A futures contract is a legal agreement to buy or sell a particular commodity, asset, or financial security at a pre-determined price at a specified time in the future. The difference between a forward and a futures contract is that futures contracts are (i) standardized, (ii) traded on exchange, and (iii) settled usually on a cash basis. It implies that usually the physical delivery of the commodity, metal, or crop is not taken and the parties just settle the transaction through netting, i.e. cash settlement of financial obligations between the parties.

Let us take an illustrative example. A kilogram of wheat is currently priced at \$1. Suppose an investor goes long in a futures contract for the purchase of 100 kilograms of wheat at a future date, which is one week from now. The price of wheat in a futures contract is \$1 per kilogram. The investor is going long (buy stance) in the futures contract in order to hedge against increase in the price of wheat. If the price of wheat increases to \$1.1 per kilogram, the investor will bag return of \$10 from the counterparty. The underlying asset, i.e. wheat, does not change hands. Only the net payoffs are settled in cash.

From the Islamic perspective, this transaction is not permissible since it breaches the requirements of a valid sale in Islamic rules of trade. It is impermissible for the same reason due to which the forward contract is not allowed. The only difference in futures contract is that it is standardized, exchange traded, and cash settled.

7.3.3 *Options*

An option is a contract that gives the buyer the right, but not the obligation, to buy or sell an underlying asset or instrument at a specified strike price prior to or on a specified date, depending on the form of the option. In an American option contract, the option can be exercised at any time before or at the maturity date. In a European option contract, the option can be exercised at the maturity date only. Call options give option to buy. On the contrary, put options give option to sell.

The call option writer is the counterparty which sells call option for a call price. Call option writer has the obligation to sell the asset if the call option buyer decides to exercise the option.

The put option writer is the counterparty which sells put option for a put price. Put option writer has the obligation to buy the underlying asset if the put option buyer decides to exercise the option.

From the Islamic perspective, an option is not a valuable subject matter and an asset to be traded. Thus, it is impermissible to sell options for a put or call price. The put and call price are not permissible as "consideration" for the provision of merely an option. It is different from a sale transaction where an advance payment is made to mitigate the risk of the buyer backing away from the contract. In options, the sale may or may not be executed, and at the time of entering in option, no sale of underlying asset takes place. Thus, contingent sales for future dates are not consistent with Islamic rules of valid sale.

7.3.4 *Swaps*

A swap is a derivative contract through which two parties exchange the cash flows or liabilities from two different financial instruments. The most common kind of swap is an interest rate swap.

In an interest rate swap, the parties exchange cash flows based on a notional principal amount (this amount is not actually exchanged) in order to hedge against interest rate risk or to speculate. For example, imagine

ABC firm has just issued $1 million in five-year bonds with a variable annual interest rate defined as the London Interbank Offered Rate (LIBOR) plus 2%. Also, assume that LIBOR is at 2.5% and ABC management is worrying about a possible rise in interest rate.

The management team finds another company, XYZ that is willing to pay ABC an annual rate of LIBOR plus 2% on a notional principal of $1 million for five years. In other words, XYZ will fund ABC's interest payments on its latest bond issue. In exchange, ABC pays XYZ a fixed annual rate of 5% on a notional value of $1 million for five years. ABC benefits from the swap if rates rise significantly over the next five years. XYZ benefits if rates fall, stay flat, or rise only gradually.

From the Islamic perspective, the sale of debt with debt is not allowed at different values. Only debt assignment is permissible at the principal amount without any excess or discount. Thus, interest rate swaps are going to be impermissible due to multiple reasons, i.e. including the element of *Riba* (interest), *Gharar* (uncertainty), and sale of debt at different values.

7.4 Instruments for Liquidity Management in Islamic Finance

7.4.1 *Ijarah Sukuk*

Ijarah Sukuk and other *Sukuk* issues by government and corporations are an alternative of treasury and corporate bonds, respectively. These *Sukuk* can be traded in the secondary market as well. Thus, Islamic financial institutions like banks and mutual funds can invest in *Sukuk* to earn return from the underlying assets. In *Ijarah Sukuk*, the *Sukuk* holders earn a return based on rents coming from Lessee (issuer) for the use of assets jointly owned by the *Sukuk* holders. The details of the various types of *Sukuk* and their structures have been explained in Chapter 6.

7.4.2 *Shari'ah-compliant stocks*

Shari'ah-compliant stocks are stocks of companies whose core business is *Halal*. For instance, the stocks of conventional leasing, insurance, and banking companies operating on the basis of *Riba*, *Maysir*, and *Gharar* are not permissible. Likewise, investment in the stocks of companies that sell goods and services which are not allowed to be used and consumed under Islamic principles is also not allowed. For instance, investment in the stocks of companies selling liquor, pork, lottery, and forms of entertainment which are not permitted under Islamic moral code and etiquette is also not allowed.

When the first filter on the permissibility of core business is passed, the remaining stocks are screened for compliance with certain financial ratios which put a cap on interest-based leverage, interest-based investment, and non-compliant portion of income. These screening principles had been explained in Chapter 5.

7.4.3 *Interbank pool management*

The need for acquiring funds from the interbank market arises usually due to the following reasons, i.e. (i) withdrawals by existing depositors, (ii) new financing requirement, and (iii) meeting liquidity requirements or shortage.

In interbank pool management, the funds from financial institutions can be pooled by using the underlying contract of *Musharakah* or *Mudarabah*. If the mode of *Mudarabah* is used, then an Islamic bank requiring capital would invite some other financial institution to invest in a special pool. The funds invested in the pool will be used to purchase Islamic financing assets. Usually, the tenure of the financial institutions pool is less than or equal to the tenure of the financing assets in the pool. The return on these Islamic financing assets will be distributed as per the profit-sharing ratio agreed between the *Rabb-ul-Maal* (financier bank or financial institution) and *Mudarib* (an Islamic bank). In this mechanism, Islamic bank cannot be *Rabb-ul-Maal* if the funds are invested in interest-based financing assets.

The funds can also be pooled using *Musharakah* contract. The difference in both contracts will be in the investment allocation. In *Musharakah*, the investment in *Shari'ah*-compliant Islamic financing assets will be made by both financial institutions. The profit or return from the underlying *Shari'ah*-compliant financing assets will be distributed as per the profit-sharing ratio. Loss, if any, will be borne by counterparties according to their capital contribution ratio. In the case of *Musharakah*, the profit-sharing ratio of the sleeping partner (the financial institution) cannot be greater than the ratio of its investment share in the pool.

7.4.4 *Commodity Murabaha*

Commodity *Murabaha* is also used in liquidity management. It allows Islamic banks to manage short-term liquidity through trading of highly liquid commodities in the market. The process flow of the transaction is as follows:

(1) The Islamic Financial Institution (IFI) purchases commodities from Broker A in the commodity market on cash basis.
(2) Ownership of the identified commodity will then be transferred to IFI.
(3) Thereafter, the IFI sells the commodity to the counterparty on deferred price, i.e. (cost price plus profit margin). In interbank transactions, the counterparty will be the bank requiring short-term finance.
(4) The ownership of the commodity will be transferred to the counterparty.
(5) The counterparty will then sell the commodity to Broker B on a cash basis in the commodity market.
(6) Finally, the ownership of the identified commodity will be transferred to Broker B.

Figure 7.1 illustrates the structure of commodity *Murabaha*. In practice, the counterparty will appoint the bank as his agent to sell the commodity to Broker B on a cash basis in the commodity market.

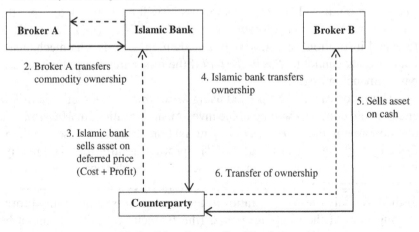

Figure 7.1.   Commodity *Murabaha*.

7.4.5 *Alternatives of derivative instruments*

In place of forward and futures sale, Islamic rules of trade allow *Salam* and *Istisna*. *Salam* is a sale contract where the delivery of the subject matter of sale is deferred, but the price of the subject matter is paid in full. For instance, if an entrepreneur having specialization in biotechnology sells high-quality cotton and faces working capital shortfall to continue production, the contract of *Salam* can be used to provide working capital financing. The cotton will be sold for spot payment, whereas the delivery will be deferred. The entrepreneur will be able to use the *Salam* price to continue production and deliver the subject matter of sale in *Salam* contract on delivery date. Islamic banks providing finance through *Salam* can offset their position by selling the assets in a separate *Salam* contract to any third party other than the original entrepreneur or its associate.

In place of options, some experts propose the use of *Bai Arboun*. It is a type of sale which is executed using down payment or advance money with the condition that if the buyer accepts to complete the sale by taking the object of sale, then the down payment will be treated as part of the selling price (*thaman*). Otherwise, if the buyer chooses to rescind the sale, the advance money will be forfeited. In this sense, this sale comes with an option (*khiyar*) to rescind the contract by forgoing the down payment as a penalty on the refraining buyer. Thus, it is a sale with a non-refundable down payment.

Furthermore, in place of interest rate swaps, the lease contracts can be priced using a variable-rate benchmark with a cap and floor. This can allow Islamic banks to mitigate the risk of wide fluctuations in the benchmark rate. With asset-backed financing, Islamic banks have recourse to the assets and can easily avoid the use of credit default swaps. Avoiding the use of credit default swap also makes an economic sense since such derivatives encourage imprudent financing operations and compromise on credit risk checks and protocols.

Finally, in order to hedge currency risk, Islamic banks cannot enter into a forward sale/purchase agreement. However, they can enter into a promise to sell/purchase agreement in order to sell/purchase foreign currencies in the future. The important point which makes it different from the traditional forward contract is that Islamic bank only makes a unilateral promise/undertaking. Hence, there is no bilateral obligation and future sale. At current date, there is only a unilateral promise/undertaking by one party without executing the sale.

7.5 Issues in Liquidity Management in Islamic Finance

There are various risks faced by Islamic banks in liquidity management due to the (i) absence of an Islamic interbank market, (ii) lack of *Shari'ah*-compliant alternatives for liquidity management, both at the interbank and central bank level, (iii) absence of liquid Islamic *Sukuk* both in short- and long-term maturities, and (iv) absence of Islamic discount window at the central bank level for Islamic financial institutions.

In liquidity management, banks often have surplus liquidity as well as a shortage of liquidity. The problem becomes more pressing as there are lesser alternatives for managing liquidity shortage for Islamic banks. An Islamic bank can take investment from any financial institution and invest it in *Shari'ah*-compliant financing assets. However, it cannot invest its surplus liquidity on equity financing basis with conventional banks since they are operating on the basis of interest-based loans in all their operations including lending and deposit mobilization.

7.6 A Possible Alternate Money Market Instrument

Time value of money is the basis of interest. As per Islamic principles, the time value of money is the problem for the investor to avoid keeping his money idle and to avoid forgoing the use of money that may bring positive value to his investment. However, it does not mean that the investor can demand an arbitrary increase as the cost of using money without taking the market and price risk of a productive enterprise. As per Islamic principles, the person who owns money has to undertake the risk of productive enterprise by becoming self-entrepreneur or an investing entrepreneur as equity partner in others' businesses to have any justifiable compensation out of the production process.

In the contemporary monetary system, interest-based Treasury bills are not Islamic since they involve *Riba*, which is prohibited in Islam. Islamic principles prohibit a pre-determined interest rate but permit variable returns in commercial undertakings based on equity participation, trade, and other economic activities.[1] As a substitute to T-bills, the

---

[1] Choudhry, N. and Mirakhor, A. (1997). "Indirect Instruments of Monetary Control in an Islamic Financial System", *Islamic Economic Studies*, 4(2), 27–65.

governments can issue Treasury *Sukuk Ijarah* Bills to source funds. This instrument can also be used in open market operations. In place of reverse repo and repo, ready buy deferred sale can be used to inject and mop up funds. If the commercial banks want to deposit funds with the central bank, they will buy Treasury *Sukuk Ijarah* Bills at a lower price on spot and sell at a higher price in future. Likewise, if they want to access funds from the central bank, they will sell Treasury *Sukuk Ijarah* Bills at a lower price on spot and buy at a higher price in future. The difference in price will be the financial cost to the party that is obtaining funds and return to the counterparty that is providing funds. The imputed rate of return will be higher on reverse repo than on repo. A unilateral undertaking will separate the two legs of the transaction. To ensure that it is not an outright buyback transaction, it is important to ensure proper identification of *Ijarah* asset, transfer of ownership, constructive possession, and prior valid offer and acceptance to execute the sale of *Ijarah* assets.

In outright open market operations where the objective is to buy and hold the treasury securities till maturity, *Murabaha Sukuk* can also be used where there is no need for the secondary market and for multiple sales between counterparties during the life of the security.

The question arises as to what should be the profit rate benchmark. To solve this issue, the government can setup a trading corporation that trades in commodities like food crops and petroleum products. In some countries, such a trading corporation already exists and the governments procure goods through these trading corporations to achieve the objective of smooth supply, exports of surplus and imports of shortage, protect the small growers, and regulate prices. In these trading operations, the government can set prices to reflect its target profit rate. This target profit rate can become a benchmark for issuing Treasury *Sukuk Ijarah* Bills and affect the other rates of returns in Islamic short-term debt financing instruments. Nonetheless, this instrument shall be used domestically in national currency and the investment shall not be open to foreign investors. It is because if the national infrastructure is used as a subject matter in these Treasury *Sukuk Ijarah* Bills, any default might result in the transfer of significant national wealth if the Treasury *Sukuk Ijarah* Bills are not denominated in national currency and are open to foreign investors.

Open market operations would involve injecting and mopping up funds. This will be achieved through purchasing and selling Treasury *Sukuk Ijarah* Bills. Credit controls can utilize *Qard-e-Hasan* ratio (for cash reserve ratio) and sovereign investment ratio (for statutory liquidity ratio) where investments are made in Treasury *Sukuk Ijarah* Bills or composite equity certificate as suggested in Islamic finance literature.[2]

Capital rationing is useful to avoid the free-rider problem as long as an artificial and rigid scarcity of capital can be avoided. In pricing capital in intertemporal transfer of funds, Mannan recommends the use of accounting price of capital which will neither add to the cost of production nor form part of the profits, but instead will be used to appraise projects.[3] In corporate finance, the weighted average profit rate in commodity trade operations of the government could be used in valuation models to provide a quantitative mechanism to rank investment alternatives. In project valuation, this benchmark rate could be used to find "estimated intrinsic value" of cash flows.

From the perspective of rules governing Islamic finance, this proposal would be appropriate since it is using a real sector-oriented profit rate benchmark rather than an interest-based benchmark. In equity-based asset market in Islamic economy, saving deficient partner will not be obliged to provide the returns based on these valuations. However, the investor, i.e. saving surplus partner can use this indicative valuation to rank investment alternatives.

It will provide a quantitative mechanism to rank investment alternatives. In the actual distribution of income between investors and firms using equity modes of financing, profit-sharing ratio (PSR) would be used and agreed upon at time (t) and applied to the actual operating profit earned in time period ($t + 1$).

In ranking projects, a project with the highest net present value would be most preferable for investment. So, the investor could prefer to enter into that contract with even a slightly lower profit-sharing ratio. A project with the lowest net present value is least preferable for investment, so the investor could prefer to enter into that contract only with a slightly higher profit-sharing ratio. Ranking would be facilitated by using a profit rate as a benchmark in financial valuation models. This process of bargaining will lead to equilibrium in Islamic investible funds market as shown in Chapter 2. Furthermore, the instrument "Treasury *Sukuk*

---

[2]Zangeneh, H. and Salam, A. (1993). "Central Banking in an Interest Free Banking System", *Journal of King Abdulaziz University: Islamic Economics*, 5, 25–36.

[3]Mannan, A. M. (1982). *Interest Free Islamic Economy — A Comparative Policy Approach. International Centre for Research in Islamic Economics*. Jeddah: Kind Abdul Aziz University Press.

Ijarah Bills" will also enable effective conduct of monetary policy, liquidity management in Islamic interbank market, and distinct pricing of Islamic banking financing products with a close link to the real economy.

7.7 Conclusion

This chapter explained the money market from an Islamic perspective. It discussed why some of the conventional money market instruments are incongruent with Islamic rules of trade and commerce. It also discussed the issues with conventional derivatives due to which they become unusable in Islamic finance. Then, the chapter also described the Islamic instruments which can be used in the money market. The chapter also highlighted the problems which Islamic banks face when it comes to short-term liquidity management.

Self-Assessment Quiz

1. T-bills are not allowed in Islamic finance due to
   (a) Exchange of money at different time periods at different counter values
   (b) It is allowed because it does not carry an extra interest payment explicitly
   (c) Due to *Gharar* and *Maysir*
   (d) None of the above

2. Forward contracts are not allowed in Islamic finance because
   (a) There is no asset involved
   (b) It is allowed if the subject matter to use is *Halal*
   (c) It includes a bilateral obligation for a future sale
   (d) None of the above

3. Options are not allowed in Islamic finance due to
   (a) Options are not a valid subject matter of sale to allow consideration as put and call price
   (b) Uncertainty and contingency in a sale
   (c) It is allowed if the subject matter to use is *Halal*
   (d) Both a and b

4. Which of the following is an Islamic alternative of forward contract?
   (a) *Salam*
   (b) *Ijarah*
   (c) *Bai Arboun*
   (d) None of the above

5. Which of the following is an Islamic alternative of T-bills where the risk of default is least?
   (a) Sovereign *Ijarah Sukuk*
   (b) T-bill is allowed because it does not carry an extra interest payment explicitly
   (c) Below Investment Grade Corporate *Ijarah Sukuk*
   (d) None of the above

Self-Assessment Questions

1. Why T-bills are not allowed for investment in Islamic finance?
2. Why corporate bonds are not allowed for investment in Islamic finance?
3. What is the reason for the impermissibility of forward and future contracts in Islamic finance?
4. Identify and explain the Islamic alternative of forward contract?
5. Identify and explain the Islamic alternative of options contract?
6. Describe the structure and application of commodity *Murabaha* in interbank transactions?
7. Describe the structure and application of institutional investment accounts using pool management under *Mudarabah*?
8. Describe the structure and application of institutional investment accounts using pool management under *Musharakah*?
9. What are the important things and rules which Islamic financial institutions need to follow if they want to invest in stocks?
10. What is the alternative of hedging currency movements in Islamic finance?
11. Discuss how the open market operations can be conducted by a central bank in the Islamic finance framework.
12. Explain the hurdles faced by Islamic banks in liquidity management when they have surplus liquidity and when they have a shortage of liquidity.

PART IV

Risk Management in Islamic Finance

Chapter 8

Takaful

8.1 Rationale for Having Insurance

Risk and uncertainty are a fact and part of life. Adverse events can and do occur. The human response to adverse events naturally is one of displeasure. Most people are averse to risk. They tend to avoid risk if possible. Empirical evidence also finds support for this tendency in most cases. If offered a certain payoff as against another payoff which has the same expected value, but uncertainty surrounding it, then most people would prefer a certain payoff as against a payoff that has the same expected value of the former choice, but with the probability that the actual value of payoff may turn out to be lower as well. For instance, consider two offers.

(1) A salary of $1,000 per month with certainty.
(2) An alternative offer of $500 of salary per month if the unit sales are below 100 units per month and $1,500 of salary if unit sales are above 100 units per month where both outcomes have 50% chance of occurrence.

What would most people do? They will prefer offer (a) over offer (b). It is because of risk aversion. Insurance companies exist in order to allow people to insure against adverse circumstances. Figure 8.1 illustrates typical risk aversion behaviour. As the wealth increases, the utility or satisfaction derived from an additional unit of wealth increases at a diminishing rate. For gain in wealth, the utility curve is concave, i.e. flatter. For loss in wealth, the utility curve is convex, i.e. steeper. It implies that the same

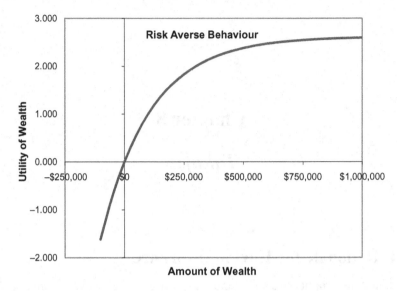

Figure 8.1.   Utility function of a risk-averse person.

amount of gain in wealth and the same amount of decrease in wealth will have a different reaction from a typical risk-averse person. Gain in wealth by $100 will not increase utility or satisfaction as much as the loss in utility or satisfaction from a $100 decrease in wealth. This phenomenon is known as loss aversion and was noted by Nobel Laureate Daniel Kahneman.[1]

A question arises that Islamic principles encourage *Tawakkul*, i.e. trusting Allah for all that happens. However, this trust is not supposed to be without making efforts that are humanly possible to achieve an economic end. For instance, Islam encourages pursuit of earning livelihood through trade and commerce. *Rizq*, i.e. livelihood, is provided by Allah by His will. Nonetheless, it still requires humans to make an effort to earn that.

Likewise, Allah guards against adversity and Muslims are encouraged to seek protection from Allah to guard against adversity. However, this does not imply that people should not make an effort to guard against an adverse outcome. In one narration, Prophet Muhammad (pbuh) asked a

---

[1] Kahneman, D. and Tversky, A. (2013). *Prospect Theory: An Analysis of Decision Under Risk. In Handbook of the Fundamentals of Financial Decision Making: Part I*, pp. 99–127. Singapore: World Scientific Publishing Company.

person who had left his camel unattended whether he has tied the camel or not. The person said: "I put my trust in Allah". Prophet (pbuh) then asked him to tie the camel first and then put trust in Allah.[2]

Islam regards spending on one's dependents as a charity if done with the intention to please Allah.[3] Prophet Muhammad (pbuh) said that the greatest reward for what you spend is on your spending on the family.[4] Islamic principles are not averse to financial planning, precautionary savings, and leaving enough wealth for the dependent family members. Prophet Muhammad (pbuh) said: *It is better for you to leave your inheritors wealthy than to leave them poor begging others* . . . [5] In another *Hadith*, Prophet Muhammad (pbuh) said: *As for one who is the guardian of an orphan who has wealth, then let him do business with it and not leave it until it becomes consumed by charity.*[6]

Therefore, it is clear that financial planning to mitigate risk and uncertainty against adverse circumstances and future needs is permissible. It is permissible to protect oneself from the adverse consequences of pure risks. Pure risks are risks that are there in routine part of life and commercial undertakings, such as risk of theft, fire, storms, floods, earthquake, pest attacks in the crop fields, and so on. They are different from the risk in a gambling activity since the risk in gambling is willingly and consciously taken up by the person involved in gambling. If gambling is avoided, there is no compulsion to take impure risks in gambling since they are not part of the routine course of life and trade. The next question which arises is how to achieve insurance against pure risks.

8.2 What is Wrong with Conventional Insurance?

Insurance is based on the concept of law of large numbers. If one out of 100 cars can suffer an accident in a locality in a given year, then one solution is that everyone tries to self-insure by keeping reserves for meeting the post-accident expenses. However, if each person shares a particular contribution towards mutual insurance, then everyone in that locality can

---

[2] *Jamai-at-Tirmidhi*, Chapter on Day of Judgement, Vol 4, Hadith Number 2517.

[3] *Sahih Muslim*, Vol 3, Book of Zakah, Hadith Number 2322.

[4] *Sahih Muslim*, Vol 3, Book of Zakah, Hadith Number 2311.

[5] *Sahih Bukhari*, Vol 5, Book of Al-Maghazi, Hadith Number 4409.

[6] *Jamai-at-Tirmidhi*, Vol 2, Chapters on Zakah, Hadith Number 641.

achieve the aim of insurance from pure risks with minimal contribution. For instance, if the average cost of accident is $2,000, then if each of the 100 individuals in that locality shares $20 contributions towards mutual insurance, then everyone can achieve the aim of insurance from pure risks. Apparently, there is nothing wrong with the idea of mutual insurance. However, any arrangement of insurance needs to comply with Islamic principles and teachings and also avoid the prohibited elements in the product and operations.

The conventional insurance companies provide products and services which mitigate risk against adverse events. A large number of people pay premium amounts to the insurance company, which in turn guarantees compensation to the insured clients if they suffer from an insured risk. However, conventional insurance is not permissible due to the involvement of *Riba* (interest), *Gharar* (uncertainty), and *Maysir* (gambling).

Riba exists in conventional insurance since the premiums received from the policyholders are invested in interest-based investment options, i.e. corporate bonds, treasury bonds, and interest-based fixed deposits, for instance. These investments and the return on these investments are impermissible.

Gharar in insurance contracts pertains to "deliverability" of subject matter, i.e. uncertainty as to:

- Whether the insured will get the compensation promised?
- How much amount the insured will get?
- When will the compensation be paid?

Thus, it involves an element of uncertainty in the subject matter of the insurance contract, which renders it void under Islamic law.

On the other hand, *Maysir* exists in an insurance contract since the payment by the insurance company is contingent on a future event that has not occurred. The policyholder contributes a small amount of premium in the hope to gain a larger sum. The policyholder loses the money paid for the premium when the event that has been insured for does not occur. That is why the structures of conventional insurance policies become similar to gambling.

The policyholder may never have any claims and therefore never receive any "consideration" for the payments made. This is akin to gambling wherein any of the two parties involved may win a sum of money from the other, but one of them is destined for loss depending on the happening of an uncertain future event.

It is quite possible that the policyholder may have only paid a single premium and becomes worthy of huge amounts to compensate him for the loss that has occurred. On the contrary, the policyholder may pay premiums for several years without having obtained any valuable "consideration" in return. That is why, the Fiqh Council of World Muslim League (1398/1978) resolution and The Fiqh Council of Organization of Islamic Conference (1405/1985) in Jeddah resolved that conventional insurance as presently practiced is impermissible.

8.3 *Takaful*: The Islamic Alternative

The Islamic alternative to conventional insurance is *Takaful*. It is based on mutual cooperation and joint responsibility. Cooperative insurance (*Takaful*) is permissible and is consistent with *Shari'ah* principles. *Takaful* provides risk protection in accordance with *Shari'ah* based on the principles of *Ta'awwun* (mutual assistance).

The premiums paid in *Takaful* are unilateral payments on the basis of *Tabarru* (donation). This makes the relationship different from a bilateral monetary exchange where the payments from both parties are stipulated.

Operationally, *Takaful* refers to participants mutually contributing to the same fund with the purpose of having mutual indemnity in the case of peril or loss. Unlike insurance companies, whose investment income may contain *Riba*, *Takaful* companies invest funds in property, Islamic investment schemes, *Shari'ah*-compliant stocks and other *Shari'ah*-approved securities like *Sukuk*. *Takaful* also aims to provide compensation against possible losses, yet the crucial difference lies in the way that this is done. In *Takaful*, not only the element of *Riba* (interest), *Maysir* (gambling), and *Gharar* (uncertainty) are avoided but it is also ensured that all other Islamic principles are complied with. It is ensured through a *Shari'ah* Supervisory Board at the level of each *Takaful* company. In a nutshell, the fundamental differences between a conventional insurance company and *Takaful* are summarized in Table 8.1.

In global Islamic finance assets, the share of *Takaful* is 2%. With a Compound Annual Growth Rate (CAGR) of 6%, *Takaful* assets have grown from $31 billion to $46 billion in 2017 as compared to 2012. In 47 countries, there are 322 *Takaful* operators working globally. These 322 *Takaful* operators are classified into Composite (113), General (112), Life (76), and *Re-Takaful* (21). Table 8.2 shows the penetration of *Takaful* in key regions by focusing on gross *Takaful* contributions. It can be seen that

Table 8.1.   Distinction between conventional insurance and *Takaful*.

Issue	Conventional Insurance	*Takaful*
Basis	Risk transfer	Co-operative risk sharing
Laws	Law of land	Law of land and *Shari'ah*
Prohibited elements	*Riba, Gharar, Maysir*	No *Riba, Gharar, Maysir*
Ownership	Shareholders	Participants
Management status	Company management	Operator
Form of contract	Intertemporal exchange of money with money	The relationship is based on *Wakalah* or *Mudarabah* with *Tabarru* (contributions)
Investments	Include interest based	Exclude all prohibited investments which are based on *Riba, Maysir, Qimar, Gharar* or any *Haram* element
Surplus	Shareholders' account	Participants' account

Table 8.2.   Regional statistics on *Takaful* contributions.

Regions	Gross *Takaful* Contributions ($ Million)
GCC	15,000
Other MENA Countries	9,516
Southeast Asia Pacific	2,818
South Asia	706
Africa	492

Source: Islamic Financial Services Industry Stability Report 2018.

Arab countries have the greatest volume followed by East Asia, South Asia, and Africa.

There are two major types of *Takaful* products. General *Takaful* plans are intended to meet the insurance needs of people and corporate bodies in connection to materialistic loss or damage done due to any catastrophic condition. Family *Takaful* plans are intended for broader needs which include long-term saving plans for meeting future financial needs, such as marriage, educational needs, and health needs, for instance.

If we look at the composition of *Takaful* contributions in Table 8.3, a major chunk of *Takaful* contributions are with general *Takaful*. On the contrary, the share of family *Takaful* is less except in Southeast Asia.

Table 8.3. Share of general and family *Takaful*.

Regions	Share of General and Family *Takaful* (%)	
	General	Family
GCC	92.5	7.5
Other MENA Countries	85.6	14.3
Southeast Asia Pacific	25.5	74.5
South Asia	42	58
Africa	63	37

Source: Islamic Financial Services Industry Stability Report 2018.

Takaful is an important institution in the Islamic finance ecosystem. The growth in *Takaful* is also connected with growth in related Islamic financial institutions, such as Islamic commercial banks. Since Islamic banks are delegated monitors of faith-conscious risk-averse investors, they tend to insure the underlying assets for which they provide finance. Hence, increase in Islamic banking financing operations will also generate market opportunities for *Takaful* companies. Likewise, Islamic banks offer jointly marketed *Takaful* products which allow the *Takaful* companies to leverage the physical outreach of Islamic commercial banks. On the contrary, growth in *Takaful* contributions would enhance the institutional liquidity in Islamic capital markets with investment of *Takaful* contributions in *Sukuk*, *Shari'ah*-compliant stocks, and Islamic mutual funds.

On the other hand, *Re-Takaful* is a mechanism for the *Takaful* operator to insure from the large and widespread risks which can be difficult to guard against for small scale *Takaful* companies unless re-insurance is taken. *Re-Takaful* ensures the stability of *Takaful* companies and the entire industry in the event of large number of claims received by the *Takaful* operator. *Takaful* operator can spread its risks based on different criteria such as location and class of insured assets. This would enable the *Takaful* operator to stabilise frequency of claims overtime and would therefore be able to hedge against possible insolvency or incapability to meet a large number of *Takaful* claims.

8.4 *Takaful* Models in Practice

In the *Waqf* model, the *Takaful* Operator acts only as the *Wakeel* of the *Waqf* Fund. If, at the end of the year, there is a surplus in the fund

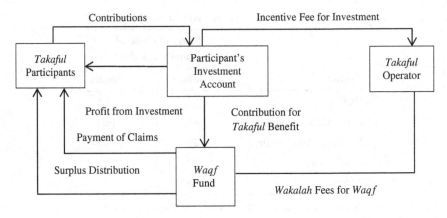

Figure 8.2.   *Takaful Wakalah* model.

(i.e. after adding all its income and deducting all the payments), such surplus will be distributed amongst the participants proportionately after taking into account any claim benefits already availed. Cooperative risk-sharing occurs among participants where a *Takaful* operator earns a fee for services (as a *Wakeel* or Agent). Any surplus or deficit goes to the participants. Under the *Wakalah* model, the operator may also charge a fund management fee and performance incentive fee. A typical *Wakalah*-based *Takaful* model is illustrated in Figure 8.2.

Under the *Mudarabah* model, surplus (or profits) is shared fairly and equitably between the shareholders and the policyholders (i.e. the "Participants"). On the contrary, under the *Wakalah* model, the surplus is returned entirely to the participants. Figure 8.3 describes the structure of *Takaful Mudarabah* model.

8.5 Conclusion

This chapter described the Islamic concept of insurance. Islamic principles allow the concept and aim of mitigating genuine risks like theft and various kinds of damages to the assets due to human or non-human factors, such as natural calamities in the form of floods, earthquake, and fire, for instance. However, the mechanism to mitigate the risk shall avoid prohibited elements like *Riba* (interest), *Gharar* (uncertainty), and *Maysir* (gambling). The Islamic system of insurance, known as *Takaful*, avoids

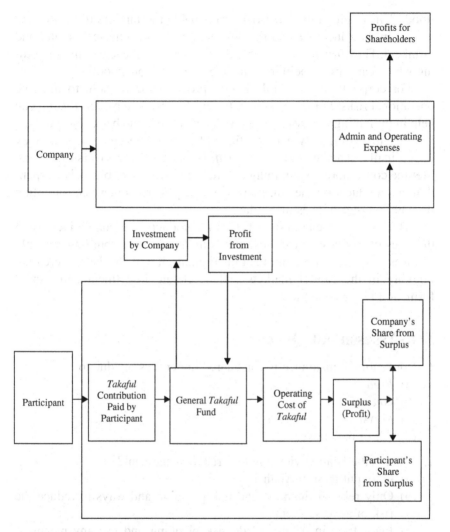

Figure 8.3.   *Takaful Mudarabah* model.

these elements and achieves the economic need of mitigating genuine risks in life.

Muslim majority countries in particular need insurance since the predominant occupation of people in less developed Muslim countries in Africa and South Asia is agriculture. In agriculture, the crops are subject to various types of risks, such as heavy rainfall, fire, pest attacks, and floods. Thus, mitigating such risks can enable the farmers to avoid fluctuation in their incomes and the destruction of their physical capital and farmland. Thus, *Takaful* can enable the farmers to achieve income smoothing which can further help in achieving consumption smoothing.

For corporations, general *Takaful* products allow them to mitigate operational risks. For financial institutions like Islamic banks, *Takaful* can help in mitigating the asset-related risks which Islamic banks have to take in order to legitimately earn profits and rents related to the assets they own. Finally, schemes in family *Takaful* can enable the savers to achieve lifetime consumption smoothing and fund the necessary big-ticket expenditures on education, health, marriage, and post-retirement consumption through long-term investment plans.

Thus, greater penetration of *Takaful* products can enable increasing the rates of savings. Since these funds in *Takaful* contributions can only be invested in *Shari'ah*-compliant instruments, it will also help in creating liquidity in the capital markets and accelerate investment and capital formation in the economy.

Self-Assessment Quiz

1. Conventional insurance is considered impermissible due to
   (a) *Riba*
   (b) *Gharar*
   (c) *Maysir*
   (d) All of the above

2. What is the Islamic viewpoint on risk management?
   (a) Only put trust in Allah
   (b) Only rely on financial and risk planning and ways to reduce the risk of adverse events
   (c) Place trust in Allah and do risk planning and use any means to manage risk
   (d) Place trust in Allah and do risk planning and use *Shari'ah*-compliant means to manage risk

3. In which *Takaful* model, the *Takaful* operator can also claim a share in profits
   (a) *Waqf* model
   (b) *Mudarabah* model
   (c) *Wakalah*
   (d) None of the above

4. In which *Takaful* model, the *Takaful* operator can only claim agency fee
   (a) *Mudarabah* model
   (b) *Wakalah*
   (c) Both (a) and (b)
   (d) None of the above

5. The contributions in *Takaful* are regarded as
   (a) *Qard*
   (b) *Amanah*
   (c) Voluntary donation
   (d) None of the above

Self-Assessment Questions

1. Do Islamic principles allow managing risk and uncertainty?
2. Explain how conventional insurance includes the element of *Riba* directly?
3. Explain how conventional insurance includes the element of *Riba* indirectly?
4. Discuss how conventional insurance includes the element of uncertainty which makes it very much similar to gambling?
5. How the premiums paid to an insurance company are structured in a *Takaful* model?
6. Discuss the structure of *Takaful* based on the *Wakalah-Waqf* model.
7. Discuss the structure of *Takaful* based on the *Mudarabah* model.
8. Name and list the investment instruments and options available to a *Takaful* operator.
9. Differentiate between general and family *Takaful*.
10. Explain how Islamic banks, Islamic capital markets, and Islamic mutual funds are interconnected with *Takaful* operators in the Islamic finance architecture.

Chapter 9

Risk Management in Islamic Banks

9.1 Introduction

Risk management is vital for Islamic banks since Islamic banks are delegated monitors of depositors and shareholders. They are entrusted with the safekeeping of deposits. Depositors provide funds to the Islamic banks on the basis of loan (*Qard*) or investment (*Mudarabah*). Islamic banks are responsible for investing the funds of investors in order to achieve *Halal* returns on investments.

Risk management entails prudence in asset and liability management. It is also necessary for effective oversight to avoid the misuse of funds or taking unsound decisions which prove to be risky. Risk management requires effective control and the use of instruments and contractual covenants to minimize the risk.

Islamic banking is interest-free banking, which makes it necessary for Islamic banks to take an active part in the operations of the business, i.e. share profits as well as losses. Banks including Islamic banks prefer to take minimum risk since they operate as delegated monitors for the relatively risk-averse depositors whose primary concern is safekeeping of deposits and the secondary concern is to earn a stable return with preservation of their investment.

Islamic banks cannot merely lend money to earn interest as interest is prohibited in Islam based on *Qur'anic* injunctions. Islamic banks are obliged to take an active part in the business and share profits as well as losses since interest-based investments and borrowings are not permitted in Islam. Since Islamic banks cannot charge a fixed return, it may seem that Islamic banks face more risk. One may tend to think that Islamic banks will have more volatile returns on their assets as they have to own the asset before they sell or lease it to their clients. Islamic banks also take on subject matter risk which conventional banks do not take.

On the surface, direct participation in trading and lease of assets by taking ownership and possession of the assets may suggest that Islamic banks face greater risk and hence, will have more volatile returns on their financing assets. Islamic banks also have restrictions on using conventional financial derivatives like forwards, futures, options, swaps, and certain trades like short selling.

One would be curious to explore how Islamic banks manage exchange risk when derivative instruments like forwards, futures, and options are not allowed in Islamic banking? How Islamic banks mitigate price risk and operational risk while exposed to price fluctuations in the asset market?

The two broad phases in risk management include (i) identification and quantification of risks and then (ii) applying the risk management tools to minimize the risks from adversely affecting the bank. This chapter discusses how Islamic banks mitigate various types of risks which they face in their operations.

9.2 Governance for Risk Management in Banks

Banks are financial intermediaries between saving-deficient units and saving-surplus units. They take deposits from the general public which have surplus savings and provide financing to the saving-deficient units, be they individuals or firms. The major part of their funding for financing side operations come from the depositors rather than the shareholders. In order to ensure that banks remain solvent and prudent, the Basel Committee on Banking Supervision (BCBS) was established by the central bank governors of the Group of 10 countries in 1974. By 2019, the BCBS comprises 45 members from 28 Jurisdictions, consisting of Central Banks and authorities with responsibility of banking regulation. This committee has come up with three major accords, BASEL I (1998), BASEL II (2004), and BASEL III (2013). Basel III was agreed upon by the members of the Basel Committee on Banking Supervision in November 2010 and was scheduled to be introduced from 2013 until 2015. However, the implementation was extended repeatedly to 31 March 2019 first and then

Table 9.1.   Comparison of BASEL II and BASEL III.

Capital Requirements	BASEL II	BASEL III
Minimum ratio of total capital to risk weighted assets	8.00%	10.50%
Minimum ratio of common equity to risk weighted assets	2.00%	4.50–7.00%
Tier 1 Capital to risk-weighted assets	4.00%	6.00%
Core Tier 1 Capital to risk-weighted assets	2.00%	5.00%
Capital conservation buffers to risk weighted assets	None	2.50%
Leverage ratio	None	3.00%
Countercyclical buffer	None	0–2.50%
Minimum Liquidity Coverage Ratio	None	More than 100%
Minimum Net Stable Funding Ratio	None	More than 100%

again until 1 January 2022. Table 9.1 highlights the key features of BASEL II and BASEL III. The most significant feature which appears from the comparison is that BASEL III requirements are more stringent in order to ensure solvency and liquidity to absorb shocks and losses.

For the purpose of ensuring compliance with BASEL III, Liquidity Coverage Ratio (LCR), Net Stable Funding Ratio (NSFR), and Leverage Ratio (LR) are computed as follows:

$$LCR = \frac{\text{Stock of high-quality liquid assets}}{\text{Total net cast outflows over the next 30 days}} > 100\% \qquad (9.1)$$

$$NSFR = \frac{\text{Amount available of stable funding}}{\text{Required amount of stable funding}} \geq 100\% \qquad (9.2)$$

$$LR = \frac{\text{Tier 1 Capital}}{\text{Total exposure}} \geq 3\% \qquad (9.3)$$

For the purpose of computing Capital Adequacy Ratio (CAR), Islamic Financial Standards Board has defined Common Equity Tier 1 (CET1) Capital, Additional Tier 1 (AT1) Capital and Tier 2 (T2) Capital.

CET1 Capital includes the following:

- Common shares issued by the Islamic financial institutions.
- Stock surplus (share premium) from the issue of common shares.

- Retained earnings.
- Other disclosed reserves and comprehensive income, including interim profit or loss.
- For interim profit or loss, supervisory authorities may seek verification by external auditors or require other review procedures.
- Common shares issued by consolidated subsidiaries of Islamic financial institutions.
- *Minus*: Regulatory adjustments/deductions applicable to CET1.

AT1 Capital includes the following:

- Instruments which have loss absorbency, perpetuity, and which are unsecured and do not create call expectation.
- Premiums received on such instruments which meet AT1.
- Instruments issued by a subsidiary which meet AT1 criteria.
- *Minus*: Regulatory adjustments/deductions applicable to AT1.

Finally, T2 Capital includes the following:

- Instruments issued by Islamic financial institutions which have convertibility, the maturity of at least five years, callable after five years, and which are unsecured.
- General provisions or reserves held against future, presently unidentified losses on financing.
- Any premium paid on issue of T2 capital instruments.
- Instruments or T2 qualifying capital issued by the subsidiary.
- *Minus*: Adjustments/deductions applicable to T2 capital.

For computing CAR, the following formula can be used:

$$CAR = \frac{\text{Tier 1 Capital} + \text{Tier 2 Capital}}{\text{Total Risk} - \text{Weighted Assets}} \tag{9.4}$$

where,

$$\text{Tier 1 Capital} = \text{CET1 Capital} + \text{AT1 Capital} \tag{9.5}$$

$$\text{Total Capital} = \text{Tier 1 Capital} + \text{Tier 2 Capital} \tag{9.6}$$

Table 9.2 provides illustrative data which can be used to determine CAR. Column one gives different types of assets on the balance sheet.

Table 9.2. Numerical illustration of CAR.

Items	Risk Exposure ($)	Weights (%)
Government *Sukuk*	5,000,000	0
Corporate financing	15,000,000	10
SME financing	10,000,000	20
Consumer financing	10,000,000	25
Other non-balance sheet exposures	5,000,000	10

Table 9.3. Computation of RWA.

Items	Risk Exposure ($)	Weights (%)	RWA ($)
Government *Sukuk*	5,000,000	0	0
Corporate financing	15,000,000	10	1,500,000
SME financing	10,000,000	20	2,000,000
Consumer financing	10,000,000	25	2,500,000
Other non-balance sheet exposures	5,000,000	10	500,000
Total			6,500,000

Column two gives the exposure in each of the different asset types. Finally, Column three gives weights to each of the asset types. These weights can be interpreted as the percentage of the value of asset that can be lost when these assets are liquidated. Alternatively, these weights can also be regarded as the percentage of deterioration in value of these assets over time.

Risk-weighted assets (RWA) for each asset type can be computed by multiplying risk exposure in each asset type with the assigned weight with that asset type. Finally, the sum of total RWA for each asset type will be the aggregated value of RWA that can be used in computing the CAR for the bank. Table 9.3 provides the computation of RWA.

Let us suppose, CET1 Capital is $400,000, AT1 Capital is $60,000 and T2 Capital is $60,000. Hence, CAR would turn out to be 8%.

If the capital adequacy requirement set by the regulator is 10%, then the bank is not meeting the requirement at the moment. Suppose the bank can only increase T1 Capital to meet that requirement. In that case, the bank will have to increase T1 Capital by $130,000 to meet the capital adequacy requirement.

9.3 Distinct Features of Risk Management in Islamic Banks

The two most important problems identified from the great financial crisis of 2007–2009 are perverse incentives and de-linking of financial sector growth and activities with the real sector of the economy. Islamic finance principles by basing all financial products with real assets fill the gap and this feature alone is a very important risk management tool inbuilt into the system.

In an article "What Went Wrong", *The Economist* writes:

> *US credit market debt was 168% of GDP in 1981 and over 350% in 2007. Financial assets were less than five times larger than the US GDP in 1980, but over ten times as large in 2007. The notional value of all derivative contracts rose from about three times global GDP in 1999 to over 11 times global GDP in 2007. The notional value of credit default swap derivatives rose from about $6 trillion in December 2004 to $62 trillion three years later. In the US, the share of total corporate profits generated in the financial sector grew from 10% in the early 1980s to 40% in 2006.*[1]

Historically, the rationale for financial intermediation in traditional theory is that they reduce transaction costs and deal effectively with the problems of adverse selection. But, the anomaly is that in practice, the transaction costs have declined, but financial intermediation is still expanding.[2] Islamic financial institutions can reduce high monitoring costs substantially since Islamic modes of financing involve a real transaction. The moral hazard problem arising from the use of funds for purposes other than those intended substantially reduces in Islamic contracts.

On the contrary, from a broad cross section of countries, an illustration of capital to assets ratio against Gini coefficient does reveal that there is an inverse relationship between capital to assets ratio in banks and income inequality as shown in Figure 9.1. The OIC member countries where the banks have higher capital to assets ratios usually have lower inequality of income.

---

[1] *The Economist* (2008). *What Went Wrong.* Print Edition, March 19, 2008.
[2] Allen, F. and Santomero, A. M. (1998). "The Theory of Financial Intermediation", *Journal of Banking & Finance*, 21, 1461–1485.

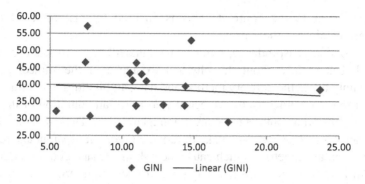

Figure 9.1.   Capital to assets ratio on GINI coefficient.
Source: World Development Indicators 2016.

Thus, in the full-reserve banking system or the system where there is only asset-backed financing or a greater capital buffer, the distribution effects are expected to be more egalitarian. Since remunerative investment accounts in Islamic banking are operated through *Mudarabah*, the capital buffer would be greater in Islamic banking leading to greater solvency and resilience and lesser volatility in net banking spreads due to pass-through of returns in the risk-sharing model.

In Islamic banking, there is inherent risk management technology. Floating rate rentals substitute the use of interest rate swaps. Credit Default Swaps (CDS) are not needed in most cases since almost all financial assets credit creation is backed by real assets and the bank has recourse to them. Delivery-based trade contracts ensure that the transaction is not for speculative purposes only. Price hedging can be ensured through *Salam* and *Murabaha* already which are used for short-term financing. In long-term financing, the rentals are mostly floating.

Islamic banks are not merely interest free. Interest-free nature of Islamic banks is a necessary condition for Islamic banking, but not the sufficient one. Islamic banking transactions need to avoid other elements of fraud, deceit, and uncertainty. Islamic banking transactions are *Gharar*-free transactions. *Gharar* is an element of uncertainty in the contract about the product, price, or other features of the contract. *Gharar*-free transactions ensure mutual benefit by covering and spreading risks of both counterparties to the contract. This is ensured by making each one's obligations clear at the outset.

In Islamic jurisprudence, *Gharar*, i.e. "uncertainty", makes a contract invalid. Uncertainty about the physical existence of the subject matter, uncertainty about the delivery method and date, ambiguities in contract with respect to the contract itself, subject matter, price, and duration of the contract may render a contract to be invalid in Islamic law. Thus, reducing these uncertainties and ambiguities make the contract more transparent and reduce information asymmetries which cause the risk in a financial transaction.

An Islamic bank is normally exposed to certain internal and external risks. External risks are caused by changes in policies and regulations (regulatory risk) or by factors that affect the rates of benchmarks, such as London Interbank Offered Rate (LIBOR). Another risk relates to the fulfilment of obligations by debtors of the Islamic banks (credit risk).

Operational risk arises from activities or processes involving people, infrastructure, and technology. The fiduciary or legal risk might be triggered by non-compliance with the legal rules causing litigation costs and penalties in some cases. *Shari'ah* non-compliance risk is a special type of legal risk that is caused when the Islamic rules governing the financing transactions are not complied with. *Shari'ah* non-compliance may render the contract to be void and the income resulting from the transaction to be considered non-*Halal*.

Finally, market risk is involved in Islamic finance transactions since the Islamic bank needs to buy the asset before it can sell and give it on lease to the client. Hence, an Islamic bank is exposed to the risk related to the subject matter as long as it remains in the ownership of the Islamic bank. In certain cases, the Islamic bank is also exposed to the price risk if there is significant deviation in the market price from the time of purchase of asset to the selling of that asset to the client.

In some respects, Islamic products have different risk characteristics. For instance, *Shari'ah* compliance risk is unique to Islamic banks. The nature of liquidity risk is also different in Islamic banks since the instruments and contracts available for Islamic banks in the money market and treasury operations are different for Islamic banks as compared to conventional banks. Likewise, Islamic banks face greater repercussions if there is a delay in repayment of financial obligations by the clients. Any late payment received in order to maintain financial discipline cannot be taken as income by the Islamic bank. Second, the price of asset in *Murabaha* financing cannot be altered even if the price is not received at maturity.

Finally, new debt cannot be created by rescheduling or rolling over loan as it happens in conventional banking.

Islamic banks also have some unique challenges as compared to conventional banks. They do not have access to the central bank as the lender of last resort in many jurisdictions. Islamic banks also do not invest in Treasury bills in order to meet statutory reserve requirements. In some jurisdictions, they invest in Sovereign *Sukuk* and also face greater cash reserve requirements if there is a lack of Sovereign *Shari'ah*-compliant instruments available. Thus, Islamic banks have to be more watchful and prudent in their financing operations to mitigate liquidity risk.

On the contrary, Islamic banks also have distinct advantages over conventional banks in managing risks. First, all financing provided by Islamic banks is backed by real assets. Thus, Islamic banks do not have uncollateralized loans where there is no underlying real asset. Second, their remunerative deposits are mobilized using essentially an equity-based mode of financing, i.e. *Mudarabah* and *Musharakah*. Thus, if there is a shock on the asset side, it will be widely absorbed in Islamic banking by shareholders of the Islamic banks as well as depositors who have placed their investments in the Profit Sharing Investment Accounts (PSIA).

9.4 Nature of Risks in Islamic Banking

This section identifies the nature of risks encountered in Islamic banking operations, namely credit risk, liquidity risk, market risk, legal risk, exchange rate risk, *Shari'ah* non-compliance risk, equity risk, and commercial non-displacement risk. Figure 9.2 gives a schematic illustration of some of the important risks faced by Islamic banks.

9.4.1 *Credit risk*

Credit risk is generally defined as the potential that the counterparty fails to meet its obligations in accordance with agreed terms. Credit risk also includes the risk arising in the settlement and clearing of transactions.

9.4.2 *Liquidity risk*

Liquidity risk arises when there is a shortage of liquid assets to meet the current liabilities. In the context of banks, especially Islamic banks, it also

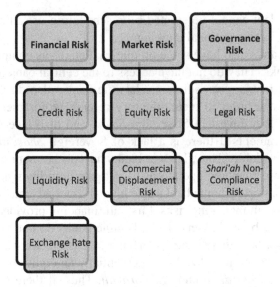

Figure 9.2.   Some important risks in Islamic banking.

arises when there is surplus liquidity which does not generate income for the bank. To manage the liquidity risk, Islamic banks cannot use interest-based money market instruments, such as T-bills, bonds, debentures, commercial papers, and financial derivatives, like forwards, futures, options, and swaps since they violate some of the principles of valid sale in Islamic jurisprudence as discussed in Chapter 7.

9.4.3 *Market risk*

Market risk arises from fluctuations in prices of the subject matter. Commodity risk is also present in *Murabaha*, *Ijarah*, and *Salam*. Islamic banks have to take ownership and possession of the asset before they can sell the asset as in *Murabaha* or give the asset on lease as in *Ijarah*, for instance. Fluctuations in prices from the date of purchase to the date of lease or sale expose the Islamic banks to the price risk.

9.4.4 *Legal risks*

Islamic banks have to comply with prudential regulations issued by the central banks. These guidelines might pertain to *Shari'ah*, but may also involve restrictions or guidelines regarding general operations. For instance, allowable credit limits, mandatory insurance, maintaining capital adequacy, facilitating payments and remittances, and deducting taxes. Legal risks especially arise when there is a conflict between conventional and Islamic laws.

9.4.5 *Exchange rate risk*

Exchange rate risk arises from the exchange rate volatility. This risk often arises in trade finance operations where the price of the asset is often denoted in non-local currency. For instance, an importer in Malaysia wants to import machinery from the USA priced in US dollars through an Islamic bank. If Malaysian Ringgit depreciates in value after the import price is locked, then a greater amount of Malaysian Ringgit will be paid to settle the import price obligation in US dollars. Exchange rate risk becomes further complicated in Islamic banking due to the unavailability of currency options and conventional currency swaps in Islamic banks.

9.4.6 *Shari'ah non-compliance risk*

Shari'ah non-compliance risk arises when banks do not meet all the required stipulations of *Shari'ah* in the execution of contracts. Sometimes, the non-compliance happens due to the negligence at the end of the bank including its staff and sometimes, it is caused due to negligence at the end of the client. For instance, if the client consumes the raw material purchased in *Murabaha* financing before the execution of sale with the bank, then the bank cannot enter into the sale since the raw materials are non-existing after they are used up in the production process.

Thus, it is important that the credit analysts, relationship managers, and field officers are well trained about the nuances and structure of Islamic modes of financing. Field officers need to inspect the goods and ascertain existence and constructive possession and execute the sale after obtaining constructive possession of the asset. Likewise, it is also important that the client is also aware of its role as an agent and buyer. The cooperation by the client in furnishing documents on time and in executing each of the steps as advised will enable the financing transactions to remain compliant with the principles of *Shari'ah*.

9.4.7 *Equity risk*

It refers to adverse changes in market value (and liquidity) of equity held for investment purposes. It covers all equity instruments including *Mudarabah* and *Musharakah*. This risk arises from the uncertainty of investment returns in an equity stake. Not only profit is variable but the value of the investment is also not guaranteed.

9.4.8 *Commercial displacement risk*

This risk arises when the products and services of the bank are not competitive *vis-à-vis* other competitors. If an Islamic bank with the same financial standing as that of a conventional bank pays lesser return on deposits than the conventional bank, then some customers might switch to conventional banks if they are only driven by returns. Similarly, if an Islamic bank offers a house financing product that costs more than a conventional mortgage loan, then some customers driven by cost comparisons alone might switch to the cheaper conventional mortgage loan.

9.5 Tools to Manage Risks in Islamic Product Structures

After discussing the broad risk management framework in Islamic banking, this section discusses the tools which are used in Islamic banks at the operational level to mitigate the various financial risks arising in the financing operations of Islamic banks.

9.5.1 *Tools to manage credit risk*

In Islamic banks, all financing is backed by real assets. This feature itself provides comfort to the banks since in case of default, the subject matter of financing can be liquidated to recover financial obligations. In *Ijarah*, the ownership of the asset remains with the bank during the period of the lease. In Diminishing *Musharakah* as well, Islamic bank retains the ownership of its share in an asset which is let to the client until the client purchases the share in asset of the bank. Thus, in the case of non-fulfilment of payment obligations by the client, the Islamic bank has sufficient recourse to recoup its investment. Apart from reducing risk through these structural differences, the following tools are used to further mitigate the credit risk in Islamic financing contracts.

- **Pledge of assets as collateral:** Any asset owned by the client could be taken as collateral. The client may not be able to sell that asset without the bank's permission. However, the ownership of the asset will remain with the client.
- **Third-party guarantee:** If the client's own guarantee is not completely reliable, then the bank can ask for a third-party guarantee, especially when the client is an associated company or a subsidiary company or when the majority owner is a conglomerate.
- **First and second charge on assets:** The first and second charge rank the order in which the proceeds of the liquidated asset are used to pay off liabilities. If a financier has a secondary charge, then his turn to be paid back from the client's liquidation of the asset will come second or later than the first. All else equal, financiers will prefer to have first charge.
- *Takaful*: *Takaful* can be used to insure a tangible movable or immovable asset. The insurance cost can also be added back to the sale price or rentals.
- **Security deposit (*Hamish Jiddiyah*):** As an alternative to the down payment or security deposit, some advance rental could be taken which may be adjusted. It could also be used as a partial settlement price for the sale of asset. However, any amount received in this case at the beginning of the contract cannot be taken as income for that period.

9.5.2 *Liquidity risk*

Liquidity risk is the potential loss to the Islamic banks arising from their inability to meet their obligations as they fall due without incurring unacceptable costs or losses. In order to manage their liquidity risk, Islamic banks trade in *Sukuk*, equities, and commodities. Sometimes, they also engage in *Mudarabah*- and *Musharakah*-based investments with other banks in the interbank market. The other tools and strategies used to manage liquidity risk are as follows:

- **Diversify sources of funds:** An increase in non-remunerative deposits can reduce the cost of raising funds from the public. Reliance on a few big deposits is risky. It is better to have a widespread deposit base.
- **Reduce the concentration of funding base:** It is better to have an efficient liability mix with adequate availability of short term and long term deposits. Maturity matching on both sides of the balance sheet can solve much of the problem systematically.
- **Rely on marketable assets:** It is better to finance those assets on a priority basis that have a secondary market and that are somewhat standardized and widely used in the real sector of the economy.

9.5.3 *Tools to manage market risk*

It refers to the risk arising from adverse movements in interest rates, commodity prices, and FX rates. Commodity risk is also present in *Murabaha*, *Ijarah*, and *Salam*. The tools used to manage market risks are as follows:

- **Parallel contract (if permissible):** To mitigate the storage risk and avoid inventory cost, the parallel contract can be done for the same date in the case of *Salam*.
- **Binding promise:** A binding promise which is unilateral (one-sided) can be taken to ensure contract enforcement and to guarantee the seriousness of purpose on the client's end before the bank invests depositors' funds to provide financing to the clients. In order to mitigate the risk of fluctuations in price from the date of purchase to the date of lease or sale, the client furnishes a unilateral undertaking to buy the asset subsequent to purchase of the asset by the bank for the client in *Murabaha* or take the asset on rental basis from the bank in *Ijarah*. At this time, the client also agrees to the financial obligations that will emanate from the execution of *Murabaha* and *Ijarah*. Once the Islamic bank obtains this unilateral binding undertaking, it is able to ascertain commitment of the client to purchase the asset on mutually agreed payment terms. Therefore, when the asset is purchased by

Islamic bank and after taking over its ownership and possession, the Islamic bank would sell the asset to the client in *Murabaha* as per the mutually agreed *Murabaha* price or give the asset on lease basis as per the mutually agreed rentals. Thus, any fluctuation in price of the asset subsequent to the purchase of asset by the Islamic bank does not affect the Islamic bank.

- *Takaful* **for asset risk:** *Takaful* can be used to insure a tangible movable or immovable asset. The insurance cost can also be added back to the sale price or rentals.

9.5.4 *Tools to manage legal risks*

The tools used to manage legal risks are as follows:

- **Documenting agreements to make them enforceable:** It is important to have legally enforceable documentation so that all parties to the contract are committed and in case of any dispute or misunderstandings, there is swift resolution possible due to documentation and evidence.
- **Covering contingencies in the design of agreements:** It is important that the roles, rights, and duties of each of counterparties are outlined at the outset in the documentation.
- **Compliance with legal rules of sale and lease:** In some jurisdictions, there might be legal rules governing sale and lease. For instance, if there is Value Added Tax (VAT) on goods, then this should be incorporated in the price. If it is compulsory to have insurance of assets in the lease, then *Takaful* should be taken to comply with the law.
- **Strong internal compliance, due diligence, and audit:** Strong internal compliance is necessary to ensure that external compliance check by regulators does not pose any legal threat. For instance, if the prudential regulations by the regulators limit the debt burden ratio at 33%, then it means that the cumulative financial obligation of the client in financing products should not be more than one-third of his/her net take-home monthly income. Banks can be even more conservative to ensure compliance as well as greater prudence. Likewise, if the central bank requires that the CAR shall be at least 10%, then the Islamic banks need to ensure that they reach this ratio comfortably in order to be more solvent.

9.5.5 *Tools to manage exchange rate risk*

In Islamic banking, exchange rate risk is covered through Forward Rate Cover to fix the cost of the imported goods in local currency in Usance Letter of Credit (LC). The structure based on the concept of *Wa'ad* involves the exchange of currencies at the beginning and promise or undertaking (*Wa'ad*) to carry out another *Bai Sarf* (currency trade) at the future date based on the rate determined today.

9.5.6 *Tools to manage Shari'ah non-compliance risk*

In order to mitigate *Shari'ah* non-compliance risk, the following tools and strategies are employed in practice.

- **Establishing a *Shari'ah* board with resident *Shari'ah* advisor:** It is mandatory to obtain an Islamic banking license for full-fledged Islamic banks and Islamic banking windows to offer Islamic banking products and services. Banks have to establish *Shari'ah* Board with at least one resident *Shari'ah* advisor who looks after the strategic and operational issues requiring *Shari'ah* oversight and approvals.
- **Mandatory *Shari'ah* approval at the transaction level:** It is mandatory in Islamic financial institutions to have every financing transaction approved by the *Shari'ah* advisor from the perspective of *Shari'ah* compliance. This ensures that each financing transaction generating revenues for the bank is *Shari'ah* compliant so that the returns earned by the depositors and shareholders are *Halal*.
- **Periodic *Shari'ah* audit:** In all Islamic banking institutions, it is mandatory to have a periodic *Shari'ah* audit to ascertain that all transactions are executed in full compliance with the principles of *Shari'ah* and the guidelines are approved by the *Shari'ah* advisors. If any discrepancy or non-compliance is found in any financing transaction which makes it void, then the income arising from the transaction is paid to charity. Hence, it is ensured that all the income that is shared with the depositors and shareholders is fully compliant with *Shari'ah* principles.
- **Staff training on Islamic banking products and application:** In order to avoid *Shari'ah* non-compliance due to negligence or lack of awareness and insights about *Shari'ah* rules, regular training

workshops and programs are designed for the staff members of Islamic financial institutions so that they are well versed with the compliance requirements and how to ensure compliance in practice at all times.

9.5.7 *Tools to manage equity risk*

The tools used to manage equity risk are as follows:

- **Seek diversification of capital contribution:** If there is a wider participation of investors in the depositor's pool with different preferences with regards to risk and maturity, then the asset liability management would be adequately handled by the Islamic bank. If only a small number of depositors invest with the Islamic bank with particular risk and maturity preferences, then Islamic banks would be constrained in their financing operations and asset liability management.
- **Using restricted *Mudarabah*:** If Islamic banks engage in *Mudarabah*-based financing with big corporations or financial institutions, one way to limit investment use in particular projects is to use restricted *Mudarabah* rather than unrestricted *Mudarabah*. This can give more control over investment style and direction.

  Islamic banks can also identify particular businesses or engage in transaction-based ventures. This way, Islamic banks would not be exposed to all aspects of business and will not have to share capital expenditure with the client. They can also pre-decide which costs are subject to be deductible in the investment project for the determination of profits and which costs are not supposed to be deducted in the computation of profits in the equity partnership.
- **Using *Musharakah* than *Mudarabah* where possible:** In *Mudarabah*, all capital contribution comes from *Rabb-ul-Maal* (investor) and who is also liable to bear all the financial losses. In financing operations, if Islamic banks provide financing based on *Mudarabah*, then they are exposed to all the financial losses if the loss occurs in *Mudarabah* financed enterprise. Since the client in *Mudarabah* would not have any investment, there is a risk of moral hazard. To mitigate financial risk, Islamic banks can instead use *Musharakah* in which there is capital provided by both parties, and hence, in case of loss, it is shared on the basis of capital contribution ratio. This can check the risk of

moral hazard and ensure greater commitment on the part of the client to avoid financial losses since the client would also have to bear them to the extent of their capital investments.

- **Increased monitoring and control on strategic matters:** If Islamic banks finance small ventures on the basis of equity financing, they can include their stake in the board of directors or management to have influence over strategic decisions. They can also ask for an audit of accounts to ensure the monitoring and verification of accounts. Islamic banks can also limit the period of contract and investment capital. Only if there is sufficiently acceptable performance by the client, there will be renewal of financing and the increase in the limit of financing. This will also encourage the client to avoid cheating in a repetitive contractual relationship.

9.5.8 *Displaced commercial risk*

It refers to the risk that Islamic banks may confront commercial pressure to pay returns that are competitive. Else, if they distribute profits to the investors which yield less return on investment than the competitor banks, then Islamic banks will face commercial displacement risk. The tools used to manage displaced commercial risk are as follows:

- **Using floating rentals in long-term lease:** If Islamic banks provide lease on a long-term basis, there is a greater chance that the benchmark rate would fluctuate during the period of the lease. Using floating rentals would allow the bank to avoid becoming uncompetitive.

- **Using profit equalization reserves and *Hiba*:** In deposit mobilization, Islamic banks cannot guarantee a particular rate of return to the depositors. They can only agree to a pre-agreed profit-sharing ratio and assign weightage to allow greater stake in actual profits to long-term and large investors. In case the profits are less than expected, Islamic banks set up profit equalization reserves to allow smoothing of distribution of profits.

In some cases, Islamic banks unilaterally gift depositors without any stipulation or pre-agreed formula in order to avoid depositors getting less than competitive returns on their investments. However, this cannot be stipulated, and it is also avoided as a norm. In some jurisdictions, where there is less than favourable regulation and attitude towards Islamic banking, these tools can be used in limited and controlled ways to avoid commercial displacement risk.

9.6 Conclusion

This chapter discussed how Islamic banks manage risks. Since Islamic banks have to comply with principles of Islamic finance, they are exposed to greater breadth of risks. However, Islamic banks can mitigate such risks through various ways. In addition to that, Islamic banks are also able to absorb financial shocks due to the risk-sharing model and the fact that they are not obliged to pay stipulated return to depositors. Therefore, Islamic banks have better capacity to mitigate financial risks.

Self-Assessment Quiz

1. In which of the risk management frameworks, is there a greater requirement of capital to RWAs ratio?
   (a) BASEL I
   (b) BASEL II
   (c) BASEL III
   (d) All of the above

2. If Islamic banks pay relatively lesser returns on deposits, it will increase
   (a) Commercial displacement risk
   (b) *Shari'ah* non-compliance risk
   (c) Credit risk
   (d) None of the above

3. Islamic banks by structure have higher solvency since in addition to the equity, their
   (a) Non-return-generating deposits do not require repayment unlike conventional banks
   (b) Non-return-generating deposits do not require any return unlike conventional banks
   (c) Return-generating deposits do not require guaranteed repayment of the original deposit amount unlike conventional banks
   (d) Return-generating deposits do not require stipulated return unlike conventional banks
   (e) Both (c) and (d)

4. In *Ijarah*, if the benchmark rate of return is expected to go down in the future, it is beneficial for the financial institution to use
   (a) Fixed benchmark rate to compute rentals
   (b) Flexible rate to compute rentals
   (c) Both (a) and (b) yield similar results
   (d) None of the above

5. An additional risk faced by Islamic banks in *Murabaha* which cannot be mitigated through even *Takaful* is
   (a) Asset destruction risk
   (b) Asset produces lower profits for the firm that has sought finance to purchase the asset
   (c) No option to reprice asset if payment is delayed and the sale has been executed
   (d) None of the above

Self-Assessment Questions

1. Does undertaking risks related to assets before selling and leasing them mean that that the risk borne cannot be managed or mitigated if it is not altogether avoided?
2. Identify the key features of the BASEL II and BASEL III frameworks.
3. Define mathematically LCR, NSFR, and LR and their required limits in BASEL III framework.
4. List the main components of CET1Capital and AT1 Capital.
5. List the main components of T2 capital.
6. Explain what is CAR and what factors help in increasing this ratio?
7. Though not recognized as pure equity in current regulations, do return-generating investment deposits mobilized through *Mudarabah* with no guarantee of principal and stipulation of returns make the Islamic bank more solvent as compared to conventional banks?
8. Describe the nature of risks in Islamic banks with examples.
9. Discuss how Islamic banks mitigate (i) Credit risk, (ii) Liquidity risk, (iii) Market risk, and (iv) Exchange rate risk.
10. Discuss how Islamic banks mitigate (i) *Shari'ah*-non-compliant risk, (ii) Commercial displacement risk, and (iii) Legal risk.

PART V

Islamic Banking: The Way Forward

Chapter 10

Islamic Social Finance

10.1 Introduction

Due to high levels of poverty and weak governments, most of the Muslim-majority countries are lagging behind in spending on schooling and health services. Hence, the levels of human capital, productivity, and national income remain at lower levels. Muslim-majority countries on average have lower literacy rates and primary school enrolment rates when we compare them with the high-income and middle-income countries as shown in Table 10.1. Similarly, in health infrastructure, life expectancy, and basic facilities like sanitation and water, it is observed that Muslim countries are far behind the high-income and middle-income countries.

Islamic commercial finance products and services primarily cater to the needs of the individuals or institutions which have the capacity of generating enough income to pay the market price of assets financed through Islamic modes of financing. The limited use of equity-based modes of financing in Islamic commercial finance imply that poor individuals with humble and informal business setups by and large remain unserved or underserved. This creates a financing gap where the individuals and small-scale microenterprises remain financially excluded in obtaining financing from the commercial banks.

On the contrary, finance is also required in society for funding public goods. In rich and developed countries, it is possible to mobilize funds from taxes to fund the provision of public goods. But, in a large part of the world, governments have less capacity to fund the provision of public goods and services at a large scale from taxes alone. Due to the weak

175

Table 10.1.   Comparison of socio-economic indicators across country groups.

Indicators/Country Groups	High Income	Middle Income	Muslim
Economic			
GDP per person employed (constant $ PPP, 2011)	76,507	29,631	40,341
Poverty at PPP USD 1.90 a day (% of population)	0.56	5.95	24.58
Gross fixed capital formation (% of GDP)	21.95	24.50	22.87
Education			
Literacy rate (% of adult population)	98.46	93.22	73.46
Net enrolment ratio in primary (%)	96.92	92.34	85.55
Government expenditure on education (% of GDP)	5.19	4.67	3.69
Health			
Health expenditure (% of GDP)	8.75	6.20	5.18
Hospital beds (per 1,000 people)	5.18	3.37	1.98
Improved sanitation facilities (% people)	97.14	81.85	64.53
Improved water source (% people)	99.28	91.89	82.04
Life expectancy (years)	79.06	71.69	66.53

Source: World Development Indicators (2015).

capital markets and less capacity of the government to provide public goods and services on debt-based finance, there is a crucial role for the third-sector institutions to step up in scaling the provision of social safety nets, public goods, and subsidised services in health and education, for instance.

By and large, Muslim countries have lower financial inclusion, especially when it comes to the provision of finance. High levels of poverty, underdeveloped financial markets, and lower tax collection by governments highlight the important role of social finance. Social finance primarily focuses on promoting prosperity and higher living standards of the lower income segments of the society.[1]

In this backdrop, the role of Islamic social finance becomes pivotal. Islamic social finance is a set of market- and non-market-based institutions.

[1] Jones, J. F. (2010). "Social Finance: Commerce and Community in Developing Countries", *International Journal of Social Economics*, *37*(6), 415–428.

Islamic microfinance is a market-based social finance institution that provides financial services including financing for buying income-generating assets. On the contrary, *Zakat* and *Waqf* are social finance institutions that are non-market based. *Zakat* is a compulsory financial obligation to pay a part of wealth and income in identified social causes. In its economic character, *Zakat* is a redistribution tool to redistribute wealth and endowments from the relatively rich to the poor. *Waqf* is an institution that provides an opportunity to extend the benefits of resources widely in present as well as in future periods. It can work as a mechanism for provision of public goods and services in a decentralized way. It also checks confinement of beneficial resources in private ownership. It strengthens social safety nets imbued with the spirit of sharing and social solidarity.

This chapter introduces these Islamic social finance institutions and their depth in terms of current penetration. It also looks at the potential of these institutions and their economic effects.

10.2 Microfinance in OIC Countries

Muslim countries represent a quarter of the global population, but they are generally poorer than non-Muslims as their share in global poverty pool is twice as much as their share in global population.

These poor people need income support as well as finance to ensure that they are able to achieve socio-economic mobility. The reported statistics from financial services providers (FSPs) in Table 10.2 show that microfinance penetration among the Muslim-majority countries is highest in Bangladesh, Pakistan, Indonesia, and Nigeria. These countries are the most populous countries and host a major share of poor people. Nonetheless, the current penetration is minuscule in the face of millions of poor people who reside in the developing world.

By and large, the share of Islamic microfinance in providing micro financial services is not as much as that of conventional microfinance which is interest based. Since a major reason for financial exclusion from financial services among the Muslim population has been the attempt to avoid *Riba*, it is important to enhance the outreach and scale of Islamic microfinance institutions (IMFIs). It will help in boosting the growth of other institutions in Islamic finance ecosystem like Islamic banks and *Takaful* companies. More importantly, it can help in tackling the high level

Table 10.2.   Microfinance outreach statistics.

Country	FSP Count	Active Borrowers	Borrowers Rural	Borrowers Urban	Gross Loans (min $)
Afghanistan	10	152,500	39,800	110,900	141
Azerbaijan	18	208,400	107,800	75,300	911
Bangladesh	29	26,916,400	15,185,000	2,381,300	7,897
Benin	8	620,600	228,200	327,100	207
Bosnia	2	79,400	26,400	53,000	140
Burkina Faso	9	210,200	33,000	46,900	231
Comoros	1	7,700	—	—	17
Coted'Ivoire	4	89,300	300	70,500	306
Egypt	5	911,700	515,500	396,100	136
Guyana	1	3,600	3,200	400	14
Indonesia	5	1,823,800	1,508,600	315,200	236
Iraq	3	63,500	8,600	54,900	108
Jordan	4	246,600	106,300	140,300	150
Kazakhstan	3	246,600	168,400	78,100	280
Kyrgyzstan	12	261,200	182,000	78,500	309
Lebanon	1	72,800	32,000	40,800	72
Mali	5	123,000	90,000	33,000	125
Morocco	5	519,100	227,000	292,100	407
Mozambique	2	7,600	2,500	5,100	1
Niger	10	55,300	22,600	31,500	11
Nigeria	13	1,890,100	668,400	101,700	2,872
Pakistan	33	5,062,200	2,510,100	2,505,200	1,681
Palestine	4	73,300	34,700	34,000	198
Senegal	5	273,200	—	52,400	332
Sierra Leone	1	37,600	29,500	8,100	5
Syria	2	48,600	26,000	22,600	12
Tajikistan	26	314,600	175,900	104,300	349
Togo	4	209,300	71,700	137,600	128
Tunisia	1	329,500	128,000	201,500	196
Uganda	6	296,800	127,600	92,000	510
Uzbekistan	4	39,300	31,000	8,300	1,465
Yemen	3	50,600	12,800	24,700	19

Source: MIX Market.

of poverty through financial development since the governments in poor countries are weak in resource mobilization as well as in governance.

Islamic microfinance is an alternative for people who wish to obtain relief in their income and liquidity constraints to smooth consumption of their own and their family members. Obaidullah explains that there are two broad categories of Islamic microfinance models that are globally used, i.e. charity-based not-for-profit models and market-based commercial models.[2] The former model uses *Qard-e-Hasan*, *Waqf*, and *Zakat* funds for providing non-compensatory loans or non-repayable grants. Market-based commercial models provide micro-credit using *Murabaha* and micro-leasing using *Ijarah*.

The theoretical edge of Islamic microfinance has been studied by several Muslim economists. According to Ahmed, IMFIs appear to have performed better than Grameen Bank.[3] Ahmed expects IMFIs to benefit from the social capital derived from Islamic values and principles. Ahmed reasons that IMFIs can reduce high monitoring costs substantially since Islamic modes of financing involve a real transaction. The moral hazard problem arising from the use of funds for purposes other than those intended substantially reduces in Islamic contracts. Studies find significantly higher compliance rates for the Islamic-compliant contracts (profit-sharing and joint venture) than for the traditional contracts (interest-based)[4]. It is also found in some studies that a low religious orientation corresponds to higher levels of risk and default.[5] Citing another ethical benefit of Islamic microfinance due to its risk-sharing and asset-backed nature, Samad argues that if Islamic microfinance is offered in India, the mass suicides committed especially by the Indian farmers can be contained to a great extent and can be virtually stopped.[6]

---

[2]Obaidullah, M. (2008). *Role of Microfinance in Poverty Alleviation: Lessons from Experiences in Selected IDB Member Countries*. Jeddah: Islamic Research Training Institute.

[3]Ahmed, H. (2002). "Financing Micro Enterprises: An Analytical Study of Islamic Microfinance Institutions", *Islamic Economic Studies*, 9(2), 27–64.

[4]Komi, M. E. and Croson, R. (2013). "Experiments in Islamic Microfinance", *Journal of Economic Behaviour & Organization*, 95, 252–269.

[5]Ashraf, A., Hassan, M. K. *et al.* (2014). "Performance of Microfinance Institutions in Muslim Countries", *Humanomics*, 30(2), 162–182.

[6]Samad, M. A. (2014). "Islamic Microfinance: Tool for Economic Stability & Social Change", *Humanomics*, 30(3), 199–226.

However, in terms of realizing the theoretical and structural potential, we do not find impressive progress. Islamic microfinance is still just 1% of the total global Islamic banking assets. This is despite the impressive growth and stable profits of Islamic commercial banks all over the world. Awareness about Islamic banking is cited as one important hindrance in Islamic banking practice; however, with wide geographical penetration and targeted products for lower segments of the society, the awareness issue can be tackled more directly. It can provide an opportunity for the average Muslims to benefit from Islamic banking and finance on a wide scale.

10.3 *Waqf* as a Non-Market Social Finance Institution

In a largely income-poor Muslim world, there is an enormous need for development spending and infrastructure. However, the size and the scope of the formal-sector financial institutions remain small and concentrated. On the contrary, governments are also weak in terms of effective governance and have limited revenue collection to instigate any meaningful long-term development plans. In this scenario, the role of the third sector becomes highly important. The institution of *Waqf* in the Islamic social finance framework provides a useful vehicle to fill the gap in social intermediation.

Effective social intermediation can enable the surplus households who want to engage in continued philanthropic spending to help resource-deficient households who require income and social assistance. However, financial intermediation in Muslim-majority countries focuses on commercially viable target markets and offers financing products that have income-based lending criteria for eligibility. The majority of income-poor households do not have sufficient or stable sources of income, and they lack asset ownership to qualify as bankable clients.

Could government instead scale up development spending and provide a wide range of welfare services as is the practice in the West? The fact is that welfare states in Europe usually have high tax collection. On the contrary, the governments in Muslim-majority countries have weak tax collection, and the public institutions are generally poorly governed. The World Governance Indicators data reveal that OIC countries have very poor governance performance. None of the OIC countries feature in the top 50 countries with strong governance in 2015 on a composite index which includes voice and accountability, political stability, government effectiveness, regulatory quality, rule of law, and control of corruption.

In such a scenario, third-sector social finance institutions could fill the gap in providing effective social intermediation within the country. In addition to that, across countries, it is widely known that there is a huge disparity in economic conditions between oil-rich and industrializing countries in the Gulf Cooperation Council (GCC) and East Asia, respectively, and the rest of the OIC member countries in Africa and South Asia. With trans-national *Waqf* and country-to-country support programmes among the Muslim-majority countries, *Waqf*-based social intermediation can help to improve the underdevelopment problems of the Muslim *Ummah* (community). *Waqf* is an important institution in the Islamic social framework. It can harness the potential of selfless charitable giving in an effective way for a better economic impact in the targeted social segments of society. Nobel Laureate Angus Deaton shows that in the absence of credit markets for households, they may be able to achieve a high degree of consumption smoothing using buffer stocks.[7] In this regard, *Waqf* provides an opportunity to institutionally share the buffer stock resources in society for both contemporaneous and intertemporal needs.

Under *Waqf*, an owner donates and dedicates an asset (movable or immovable) for the permanent societal benefit. The beneficiaries enjoy its usufruct and/or income perpetually. In the contemporary application of *Waqf*, it can be established by dedicating real estate, furniture, other movable assets, and liquid forms of money and wealth like cash and shares. The Cash *Waqf* is usually formed where the pooled donations are used to build institutions, such as schools, hospitals, and orphanages.[8] It is argued by some writers that Cash *Waqf* can pool more resources and ensure wider participation of individual donors.[9]

One of the important features of *Waqf* is that it provides flexibility in fund utilisation as compared to *Zakat* (almsgiving). *Zakat* funds

---

[7]Deaton, A. (1991). "Saving and Liquidity Constraints", *Econometrica*, *59*(5), 1221–1248.

[8]Sadeq, A. M. (2002). *"Waqf*, Perpetual Charity and Poverty Alleviation", *International Journal of Social Economics*, *29*(1/2), 135–151.

[9]Aziz, M. R. A, Johari, F. *et al.* (2013). *Cash Waqf Models for Financing in Education.* Proceedings of the 5th Islamic Economic System Conference (iECONS2013), Kuala Lumpur, Malaysia.

must be utilised for specific categories of recipients. On the contrary, the institution of *Waqf* can be used to provide a wide range of welfare services to Muslims as well as non-Muslims, and the beneficiaries could also be other living beings. For instance, animal protection programmes and environmental preservation expenditures can be provided more flexibly through *Waqf*. The institution of *Waqf* can transform social capital into social and public infrastructure. It provides a permanent social safety net in the case of perpetual *Waqf* to the beneficiaries.

The institution of *Waqf* complements the institution of *Zakat* since the government cannot take more than a prescribed portion of wealth as *Zakat*. Hence, the private establishment of *Waqf* helps in sharing the burden of the exchequer and also provides a source of contentment for the faithful donor in following the Islamic directives on charitable spending. As compared to individual charity, the institution of *Waqf* is more effective in matching the right targets with objective screening and providing sustainable sources of funds to the beneficiaries. In individual charity, rich people often face difficulty in finding the right targets because their extended families and social circle normally comprise people like themselves.

Besides income support and cash transfers, poor people need training, capacity building, and skills improvement in order to get out of poverty and achieve social mobility. It is often contented that lack of finance and business training requires institutional support to unleash the potentials of micro-entrepreneurs and to establish viable micro-enterprises.[10] Obaidullah explains that growth-oriented micro-finance programmes also need to provide training, insurance, and skills enhancement facilities. In this regard, the institution of *Waqf* can improve the chances of socio-economic mobility by providing a rather permanent, effective, and efficient funding source for the health and education infrastructure. The increased and improved provision of education and health infrastructure funded through *Waqf* can enhance the income-earning potential of beneficiaries.

In Muslim history, *Awqaf* provided public utilities (roads, water, and sewage), educational institutions, and hospitals. Even staunch critics of Islamic economics, such as Timur Kuran concede that the institution of *Waqf* delivered public goods in a decentralized manner in Muslim

---

[10]Haneef, M. A., Muhammad, A. D. *et al.* (2014). "Integrated *Waqf* Based Islamic Microfinance Model (IWIMM) for Poverty Alleviation in OIC Member Countries", *Middle-East Journal of Scientific Research*, *19*(2), 286–298.

economies for a long period of time.[11] Even in contemporary times, *Awqaf* (pl. of *Waqf*) can also directly affect entitlements by providing educational scholarships and health services for the poor. Hence, the institution of *Waqf* can help in capacity building and wealth creation through building human, physical, and financial capital.

The permissibility of making *Waqf* with contemporary forms of wealth like cash and shares increases the flexibility and widens participation. *Waqf* can be used to establish new financial, commercial, and social sector institutions.[12] *Waqf* with large funds can also become a superstructure under which other commercial and welfare institutions can be established. In this regard, Ahmed proposes a *Waqf*-based IMFI.[13] Ahmed suggests that Islamic banks can use income derived from late-payment penalties and other proceeds to establish these institutions. Since commercial banks usually miss the poorer clients, Cash *Waqf*-based Islamic banks can provide more compassionate and egalitarian services. Since the people establishing Cash *Waqf* will not have as much target profit in mind as the investors in commercial banks, the *Waqf* management can use the funds in a more flexible way in financing social needs as well as providing benevolent loans to the ultra-poor. In this regard, the Cash *Waqf* model can be used to provide capital for the *Waqf* bank.

In developing countries, the masses of poor people do not have access to financial services because of either supply-side sluggishness or the unavailability of supporting services. For commercial reasons, microfinance programmes usually miss the ultra-poor and hence commercial microfinance is ineffective in reducing poverty.[14] The evidence from countries with high penetration of microfinance reveals that poverty has not been reduced by much there. The ultra-poor severely lack access to complementary services, which reduces the marginal benefit of access to finance relative to the moderate poor. That is where the institution of

---

[11] Kuran, T. (2001). "The Provision of Public Goods under Islamic Law: Origins, Impact, and Limitations of the *Waqf* System", *Law and Society Review*, 35(4), 841–898.

[12] Mohammad, M. T. S. H. (2011). "Towards an Islamic Social (*Waqf*) Bank", *International Journal of Trade, Economics and Finance*, 2(5), 381–386.

[13] Ahmed, H. (2007). *Waqf-Based Microfinance: Realizing the Social Role of Islamic Finance*. Presented at the International Seminar on Integrating Awqaf in the Islamic Financial Sector, Singapore, 6–7 March.

[14] Saad, N. M. and Anuar, A. (2009). "Cash *Waqf* & Islamic Microfinance: Untapped Economic Opportunities", *Islam and Civilisational Renewal* (*ICR*), 1(2), 337–354.

Waqf could support microfinance beneficiaries in enhancing the non-income aspects of their human capital potential.

It is important to utilise the institutions of *Waqf* and *Zakat* for capacity building of the poor so that they can build skills for income generation and subsequently become marketable clients for microfinance.[15] The *Waqf* model can be used to fund the establishment of training and business support centres. Such non-credit services are essential for enhancing the skills and productivity of workers which can subsequently enhance their chances of gainful employment and achievement of socio-economic mobility.

The institution of *Waqf* implies holding or setting aside certain physical assets by the donor (*Waqif*) and preserving it so that benefits continuously flow to a specified group of beneficiaries or community. A Cash *Waqf* is *the confinement of an amount of money by a founder(s) and the dedication of its usufruct in perpetuity to the welfare of society*. The nature of the expected benefit or purpose of the *Waqf* is clearly stated in the *Waqf* deed or document created for this purpose by the donor (*Waqif*). A traditional example of *Waqf* is that of donating or setting aside a land for construction of a masjid or a school or a hospital. The donor also specifies the trustee-manager(s) who would ensure that the intended benefits materialize and flow to the community. The trustee-manager is described as *mutawalli* or *nazir*.

Historically, in many Muslim societies, *Waqf*-based institutions were the sole providers (with no state intervention) of education, healthcare, water resources, and support for the poor. The list of social services even included the welfare of animals. The institution of *Waqf* by creating community assets has the potential to create robust sustainable institutions that may address educational, healthcare, and other social needs in Muslim societies. Thus, *Waqf* is a viable, sustainable funding option for socially beneficial projects, thereby reducing dependency on public funds.

10.3.1 *Global overview of Awqaf sector*

This section provides a global overview of *Awqaf* sector where the details had been taken from the Islamic Social Finance Report 2014 and 2015

---

[15]Rahim, A. R. A. and Dean, F. (2013). "Challenges and Solutions in Islamic Microfinance", *Humanomics*, *29*(4), 293–306.

published by Islamic Research and Training Institute, Jeddah. In *India*, there are more than 490,000 registered *Awqaf* spread over different states and union territories of India. A large concentration of *Waqf* properties is found in West Bengal (148,200) followed by Uttar Pradesh (122,839). Other states with a sizeable number of *Awqaf* are Kerala, Karnataka, and Andhra Pradesh. The total area under *Waqf* properties all over India is estimated at about 600,000 acres. As the book values of the *Awqaf* properties are about half a century old, the current value can safely be estimated to be several times more and the market value of the *Waqf* properties can be put at INR 1.2 trillion (about US $20 billion). However, the current annual income from these properties is only about INR 1.63 billion, which amounts to a meagre rate of return of 2.7%. Of this amount, the *Waqf* boards are entitled to receive a share at the rate of 7% which is used for the working expenses of the boards. If these properties are put to efficient and marketable use, they can generate at least a minimum return of 10% which is about INR 120 billion (about US $2 billion) per annum. Interestingly, as many as 584 *Waqf* properties have been in unauthorized occupation of the governments and their agencies.

Bangladesh — In Bangladesh, according to a survey conducted by the Bureau of Statistics of the Government of Bangladesh, the total number of *Waqf* properties in the country is 150,593 including 1,400 properties around different "mazars". According to the 1983 Mosque census, out of about 200,000 mosques, 123,006 are *Waqf* properties. It is also claimed that almost one-third of the land of Dhaka city is *Waqf*. Out of 150,593 *Waqf* properties, only 15,300 are registered with the *Waqf* Administration of the Government.

Malaysia — In Malaysia, as at 2012, the *Waqf* portfolio comprises the following: The state of Johor has 1,843 pieces, Perak has 1,749 pieces, Kedah has 1,472 pieces, Melaka has 601 pieces; Selangor has 285 pieces, Terengganu has 236 pieces, Pulau Pinang has 138 pieces, Kelantan has 52 pieces, and the Federal Territory Kuala Lumpur has 30 pieces of properties. Data for *Waqf* buildings indicate that the state of Penang has the highest number of *Waqf* buildings — 160 units — followed by Perak (50 units), Melaka (43 units), Johor (14 units), Federal Territory Kuala Lumpur (4 units), and Kelantan and Terengganu (each with 3 units). Data for *Waqf* by type of properties indicate that out of 6,406 pieces of *Waqf* properties, 1,760 pieces are for Masjids, 900 pieces for Suraus, and

219 pieces for religious schools. A total of 2,446 pieces are for cemeteries, 15 pieces for house dwellings, 125 pieces for buildings, 314 pieces for paddy fields, 46 pieces for coconut planting, 42 pieces for rubber trees, and 8 pieces for gardening. Further, there are 38 pieces of orchards, 87 pieces of village lands, 37 pieces of empty lots, 367 pieces undefined, and 2 pieces of strata title ownership. According to the Department of *Awqaf, Zakat,* and Hajj (JAWHAR) of the government of Malaysia, the 11,091 hectares of land under *Awqaf* are valued at RM 1.2 billion (the US $384 million). Nonetheless, the current statistics indicate that of Malaysia's nearly 13 and a half thousand hectares of *Waqf* land, only two percent of the total area has actually been redeveloped. *Awqaf* hotels are a recent trend in the development of *Waqf* property. Four hotels have been built under the *Waqf* concept in the states of Malacca (Pantai Puteri), Perak (The Regency Seri Warisan), Terengganu (Grand Puteri), and Negeri Sembilan (Klana Beach Resort).

Indonesia — In Indonesia, data obtained from the Ministry of Religious Affairs for the year 2012 indicate that the size of registered land *Waqf* in Indonesia is equal to 1,400 square kilometres and most of them are still idle. The market value of registered land *Waqf* is estimated to be equal to Rp 590 trillion (US $60 billion). Collected Cash *Waqf* by Badan Wakaf is equal to Rp 3.60 billion (US $370,000).

Singapore — In Singapore, as of 2012, the *Waqf* portfolio of MUIS includes 157 properties that comprise 114 shop-houses, 30 residential units, 10 commercial units, two commercial buildings, and one institution. The size of land area under *Waqf* is 406,910 sq. ft. The size of the net area that may be rented out is 447,233 sq. ft. The portfolio is valued at Singaporean $471 million.

Mauritius — The country was among the early states to create a modern and dedicated law of *Waqf,* the *Waqf* Act 1941 under which it set up a Board of *Waqf* Commissioners to protect the community wealth and assets. As of now, there are a total of 377 *Awqaf* comprising 105 family *Awqaf,* 150 religious *Awqaf,* and 122 philanthropic *Awqaf.* The family *Waqf* is classified as the *Waqf-ul aulad.* The first *Waqf* was registered under the *Waqf* Act dated 26th February 1942 and was a family *Waqf* (*Waqf-ul aulad*).

Besides that, many countries have now in place regulations and institutional structures to govern the establishment and operations of *Waqf*. In Indonesia, Badan Wakaf Indonesia is an independent institution established in order to improve and develop the national *Waqf*. Pakistan has independent *Waqf* administrations in each of the four provinces headed by a chief *Waqf* administrator. Similarly, Bangladesh has a similar *Waqf* infrastructure where the *Waqf* Administrator functions as the top authority with an advisory role for *Waqf* committee. Countries in South East Asia, such as Malaysia, Singapore and Brunei Darussalam disallow any significant role for private *Mutawalli* (manager/administrator).

Brunei and Malaysia have their state Islamic religious council(s) or *Majlis* as the exclusive owner and administrator of *Waqf* assets. Thus, it disallows any role of private *Mutawalli* or privately managed *Awqaf*. Nonetheless, Singapore allows private management. Ownership of all *Awqaf* is retained with the state agency, *Majlis Ugama Islam Singapura* (*MUIS*). However, private management is allowed. In non-Muslim majority countries, such as India, Ministry of Minority Affairs looks after the affairs of *Waqf*, but with significant autonomy to *Waqf* boards constituted at the provincial or state levels.

10.4 Overview of *Zakat*

In the Islamic faith, Muslims are obliged to pay *Zakat* on surplus wealth and particular types of production. Furthermore, *Zakat* performs an important function in reducing income poverty. In its fiscal character, *Zakat* levies a charge on surplus wealth and production. The rate of *Zakat* varies by the nature of assets and production process. A 2.5% wealth *Zakat* is levied on all bases of wealth except for the wealth below *Nisab* and the assets in regular personal use like home, personal transport, and furniture.[16] According to the mainstream Islamic jurisprudence, wealth subject to *Zakat* would include the following:

- Gold, silver, and other precious stones and metals held for trade.
- Livestock including goats, cows, camels, and sheep.

---

[16]Mahmud, M. W. and Haneef, S. S. S. (2012). *Issues in Contemporary Zakat: A Juristic Analytical Evaluation*. Kuala Lumpur: IIUM Press.

- Stock-in-trade which is purchased for the purpose of selling.
- Legal currency in the form of notes and coins.
- Financial investments, such as
  - Equity investments.
  - Investment in fixed income securities, such as bonds, debentures, *Sukuk*.
  - Bank investments and money held in bank deposits.
  - Investments in mutual funds.

The ruling for tax on production value is based on the fact that there was a production value tax of 10% (*Ushr*) on the value of production from rain-fed lands. On the contrary, there was a production value tax of 5% on the value of production from irrigated lands. In essence, the irrigated lands had to be provided with the capital in the form of water supply.

According to the World Inequality Database, most of the developed countries have estimated wealth to income ratio ranging from 5 to 6. The Gross World Product is estimated to reach 100 trillion USD by 2020. If the world's average wealth to income ratio is taken as 5, then the estimated global wealth will reach $500 trillion by 2020. It is sufficient to give one dollar a day to 767 million poor people for 1,786 years. Annually, 2.5% *Zakat* on $500 trillion will provide one dollar a day to 767 million poor for 45 years. This redistribution through *Zakat* could assist food-insecure people and contribute towards achieving the second sustainable development goal of zero hunger. Since the amount of potential redistribution is substantially enough, it can help in not only assisting people facing hunger and extreme poverty but also in funding educational and health needs to improve the living conditions and human capital.

Paul Romer, winner of 2018 Nobel Laureate Prize in Economics, worked on the scarcity of ideas with positive externalities. His policy suggestion was that there should be subsidies given and patents approved to engender ideas. But, weakly funded and indebted governments face problems in affording subsidies. Patents might provide incentives to the producers, but at the same time, it has resulted in underprovision and overpricing of life-saving medicines for concentrating large profits of commercial manufacturers. An alternate is to address the ethical concern via culture and values. *Qur'an* says: *Help you one another in good deeds and righteousness, but do not help one another in sin and transgression.*[17] Decentralized provision of public

---

[17]*Al-Qur'an*, Al-Maida: 2.

goods and services through *Zakat* and *Waqf* can enhance the social safety net. Furthermore, investment acceleration can be achieved through institutionalizing *Zakat* which levies a charge on idle wealth. In an economy where there is prohibition of interest, the surplus and idle wealth would accelerate conversion of saving into investment. Thus, it can enhance the scale of decent employment opportunities and contribute to economic growth.

Next, we give a numerical simulation of wealth redistribution under the institution of *Zakat*. Table 10.3 provides the necessary details.

Suppose we have an interest-free economy that comprises 10 rich people each having wealth of $1,010. We also assume that there are 50 poor people each having subsistence level of wealth of $10. Column two shows the aggregate wealth of the rich people. Column three shows the wealth transferred from the rich to the poor each year. Column four shows the aggregate wealth of poor people after wealth transfer. For simplicity, we suppose perfect wealth equality between the people in each of the groups. For the sake of highlighting the effect of wealth redistribution of wealth transfers, we assume that income is generated randomly in this interest-free economy with no interest-based lending allowed. Furthermore, we assume that income earned is consumed in that period to enable us to focus our attention on the wealth redistribution effect of *Zakat* in an interest-free economy. Column five shows the wealth multiple in each year for the two groups. It can be seen that after around 27 years, the wealth multiple will drastically go down from 101 to almost four for the two groups as a whole. Eventually, the wealth recipients will become ineligible for *Zakat* receipts and rather will become part of the *Zakat* payer group.

Table 10.4 presents a similar analysis with the assumption that there is a uniform 5% growth in endowments that rich and poor people experience. It can be seen that this growth does not affect wealth distribution. The redistribution is impactful both without and also with growth. Thus, redistribution is not dependent on the business cycle or growth. Even if growth happens, it is egalitarian in this interest-free economy in the presence of the institution of *Zakat*.

Another interesting aspect is the boost in aggregate demand which is given in the last column of Table 10.4. The marginal increase in surplus wealth would mostly be saved by the rich. Since this wealth is transferred to the poor with little endowments, it is likely to be consumed. Thus, assuming a Marginal Propensity to Consume (MPC) value of 0.9, the last column of Table 10.4 presents the additional increase in aggregate demand

Table 10.3.   Simulation of wealth redistribution under the *Zakat* system.

Year	W_R	Wealth Transfer (R to P)	W_P	W_R to W_P Multiple per Person
0	10,100.00	—	500	101.00
1	9,850.00	250.00	750	65.67
2	9,606.25	243.75	993.75	48.33
3	9,368.59	237.66	1,231.41	38.04
4	9,136.88	231.71	1,463.12	31.22
5	8,910.96	225.92	1,689.04	26.38
6	8,690.68	220.27	1,909.31	22.76
7	8,475.92	214.77	2,124.08	19.95
8	8,266.52	209.40	2,333.48	17.71
9	8,062.36	204.16	2,537.64	15.89
10	7,863.30	199.06	2,736.7	14.37
11	7,669.21	194.08	2,930.78	13.08
12	7,479.98	189.23	3,120.01	11.99
13	7,295.48	184.50	3,304.51	11.04
14	7,115.60	179.89	3,484.4	10.21
15	6,940.21	175.39	3,659.79	9.48
16	6,769.20	171.01	3,830.8	8.84
17	6,602.47	166.73	3,997.53	8.26
18	6,439.91	162.56	4,160.09	7.74
19	6,281.41	158.50	4,318.59	7.27
20	6,126.88	154.54	4,473.13	6.85
21	5,976.20	150.67	4,623.8	6.46
22	5,829.30	146.91	4,770.71	6.11
23	5,686.07	143.23	4,913.94	5.79
24	5,546.42	139.65	5,053.59	5.49
25	5,410.26	136.16	5,189.75	5.21
26	5,277.50	132.76	5,322.51	4.96
27	5,148.06	129.44	5,451.95	4.72

Table 10.4.   Simulation of wealth redistribution under *Zakat* with growth.

Year	W_R	Wealth Transfer (R to P)	W_P	W_R to W_P Multiple	Boost in AD
0	10,100.00	—	500	101	—
1	10,339.88	252.50	752.50	68.70	227.25
2	10,585.45	258.50	1,011.00	52.35	232.65
3	10,836.85	264.64	1,275.63	42.48	238.17
4	11,094.23	270.92	1,546.55	35.87	243.83
5	11,357.71	277.36	1,823.91	31.14	249.62
6	11,627.46	283.94	2,107.85	27.58	255.55
7	11,903.61	290.69	2,398.54	24.81	261.62
8	12,186.32	297.59	2,696.13	22.60	267.83
9	12,475.75	304.66	3,000.79	20.79	274.19
10	12,772.05	311.89	3,312.68	19.28	280.70
11	13,075.38	319.30	3,631.98	18.00	287.37
12	13,385.92	326.88	3,958.87	16.91	294.20
13	13,703.84	334.65	4,293.52	15.96	301.18
14	14,029.31	342.60	4,636.11	15.13	308.34
15	14,362.50	350.73	4,986.84	14.40	315.66
16	14,703.61	359.06	5,345.91	13.75	323.16
17	15,052.82	367.59	5,713.50	13.17	330.83
18	15,410.33	376.32	6,089.82	12.65	338.69
19	15,776.32	385.26	6,475.08	12.18	346.73
20	16,151.01	394.41	6,869.48	11.76	354.97
21	16,534.60	403.78	7,273.26	11.37	363.40
22	16,927.29	413.36	7,686.62	11.01	372.03
23	17,329.32	423.18	8,109.81	10.68	380.86
24	17,740.89	433.23	8,543.04	10.38	389.91
25	18,162.23	443.52	8,986.56	10.11	399.17
26	18,593.59	454.06	9,440.62	9.85	408.65
27	19,035.18	464.84	9,905.46	9.61	418.36

which will happen every year in the interest-free economy with a uniform growth rate of 5% and in the presence of the institution of *Zakat*. This boost in aggregate demand would support the business cycle against economic slumps. Finally, this boost in aggregate demand is not a function of loose monetary or expansionary fiscal policy. Thus, it will not create the problem of inflation or crowding out in the economy.

Therefore, it is clear that taxing wealth can reduce wealth concentration. Islam's worldview with belief in afterlife accountability and the concept of property rights held as trust ensure that the behaviour of economic agents incorporates ethical and equity concerns in their economic choices. By removing extractive institutions like interest on money capital, the income creation process is directly influenced. Then, the income created from the productive enterprise is itself redistributed as flows in the economy by taxing the stock of wealth. Furthermore, the classification of rates on production value tax reveals that there is a lower financial levy on the value of production which intensively uses inputs and greater financial levy when the production comes from the minimal use of inputs.[18]

Ahmad shows in a Keynesian model of the aggregate economy that expenditure multiplier in the presence of *Zakat* and *Infaq* (charity) institutions will be higher than in a capitalist economy.[19] Since *Zakat* redistributes income from rich to the poor with direct incidence, the higher MPC for the poor can also increase aggregate spending. Hence, the redistribution of resources from people with lower MPC to people with higher MPC will boost aggregate spending even with the same level of income as shown before with a simple numerical simulation above.

Lastly, there will be downward pressure on the prices of durable goods with a wealth tax on tradable inventory while allowing an exemption on assets in use. For instance, if the furniture, consumer appliance, or residential facility is unsold at year-end, the seller will have to pay *Zakat* on it. But, if the asset is sold to the buyer before the due date of *Zakat*, then the subsequent owner while using such assets personally will not have to pay *Zakat* on these assets. This will help in checking inflation, clearing markets, and promoting efficient production processes to reduce inventory cost. However, to avoid *Zakat* arbitrage, the government has

---

[18]Siddiqui, S. A. (1982). *Public Finance in Islam*. New Delhi: Adnan Publishers & Distributors.

[19]Ahmad, A. (1987). *Income Determination in an Islamic Economy*. Jeddah: Scientific Publishing Centre, King Abdul Aziz University.

to randomly assign *Zakat* due date for different retailers. It can also enact a policy to levy wealth *Zakat* on tradable inventory as an average of ending and beginning inventory to counter *Zakat* arbitrage.

10.4.1 *Role of Zakat in social finance*

Islamic finance caters to the financial needs of consumers and producers who want to invest and obtain financing in a way so as to avoid interest, speculation, and exploitative exchanges that are impermissible in Islam. While the current coverage in the product mix and outreach is appreciably increasing in Islamic finance, people at the bottom of the pyramid of income distribution find liquidity constraints and remain financially excluded. One way to bridge the gap in commercial finance is to integrate it with social finance institutions. In this regard, *Zakat* can be a useful bridge and catalyst.

In developing an integrated microfinance framework, first, there is a need for differentiating between the different categories of poor people that might be present in any typical developing economy. Let us define two categories of poor people in order to distinguish between moderate poor and ultra-poor. Non-poor people can be with and without investible capital. These four groups require income support, social and public support, and market-based finance. Usually, poor people do not have investible capital. Non-poor people in the proposed integrated financing model are assumed to have an existing income source. To alleviate poverty in a cost-efficient manner on a wide scale, one way is to ensure that the provision of finance is at the enterprise level rather than on individual basis.

In Table 10.5, the numbers in parentheses denote the level of priority. For instance, *Zakat* (1) against ultra-poor implies the highest priority access of *Zakat* funds to this poverty group. *Zakat* (2) against moderate poor implies secondary priority access of *Zakat* funds to this poverty group. In the case of debt-based financing modes like *Murabaha* and *Salam*, *Murabaha* (1) and *Salam* (1) against non-poor people with zero investible capital implies highest priority access of these modes of financing to this group. The priority access may be operationalized either through subsidized mark-up rates or through rationing. The mark-up rates can be used as a way of providing differential priority access. Microenterprise

Table 10.5.   Proposed poverty alleviation framework.

Poverty Groups	Income Support	Social and Public Support	Market-Based Finance
Ultra-poor	*Zakat* (1)	*Bait-ul-Maal* (1) *Waqf*	*Mudarib* in ME, PSR (2)
Moderate poor	*Zakat* (2) *Qard-e-Hasan* (1)	*Bait-ul-Maal* (2) *Waqf*	*Mudarib* in ME, PSR (3)
Non-poor with zero investible capital	*Qard-e-Hasan* (2)	*Bait-ul-Maal* (3) *Waqf*	*Murabaha* (1) *Salam* (1)
Non-poor with investible capital	Not applicable	Not applicable	*Murabaha* (2) *Salam* (2) *Musharakah* *Rabb-ul-Maal* in ME, PSR (1)

is abbreviated as "ME" and Profit-Sharing Ratio is abbreviated as "PSR" in Table 10.5.

Carefully designed household income and expenditure surveys can be used to identify ultra-poor. These people will be escalated to the moderate-poor category after a certain period. During the period in which they are treated as ultra-poor, they will enjoy higher PSR than moderate-poor people in microenterprise *Mudarabah* as *Mudarib*. They will not be provided with any debt with or without mark-up to avoid indebtedness before they reach a sustainable income and asset base to increase chances of poverty exit. Hence, they will have zero indebtedness, but no source of finance unless they get share from profits of microenterprise. Hence, they will have no incentive to underperform, shirk, or free-ride. Their consumption needs can be fulfilled through *Zakat* and *Bait-ul-Maal*. Their educational and health needs can be met through especially designed *Waqf*-based educational and health centres. These support services are as much important as the actual finance. Provision of education and training, better coordination and networking, and technical assistance through *Waqf* and *Zakat* funds are necessary for the effectiveness and sustainability of Islamic Microfinance. Hence, creating synergies between micro equity finance and skills enhancement facilities and programmes will help in lifting the people out of poverty with not only increased income opportunities but also enhanced skills.

Moderate-poor people who are relatively better off will be provided with *Qard-e-Hasan*, but they will have lesser PSR as compared to ultra-poor in microenterprise *Mudarabah*. They will not be able to access debt-based modes of finance and will have lower priority in *Zakat* distribution and support from *Bait-ul-Maal*. They would want to show themselves as ultra-poor, but then they will not have the availability of *Qard-e-Hasan*. If they want to access subsidized debt-based modes of finance like *Murabaha* and *Salam*, they will have to show themselves as non-poor with zero investible capital. But, in that case, they cannot remain *Mudarib* in micro-enterprise. Also, they will have to make frequent rental or instalment price payments on the financing facility they avail. They will also enjoy least priority in access to *Zakat* funds and support from *Bait-ul-Maal*. Hence, the moderate-poor people will have no clear incentive without any trade-offs to show themselves in any lower or higher poverty group.

Non-poor people without investible capital would have some source of income which enables them to avoid poverty. The presence of an already existing source of income would qualify them to obtain debt-based finance using *Murabaha* and *Salam* at a subsidized mark-up. They will not be able to invest in microenterprise *Mudarabah* with the highest PSR unless they show themselves as non-poor with investible capital. In that case, they will not qualify for *Qard-e-Hasan* or any income support from *Zakat* or *Bait-ul-Maal*. They will also be disqualified from debt-based microfinance at the subsidized mark-up. If they show themselves as poor, then they will not be able to obtain debt-based finance at subsidized mark-up. They will also not be able to keep their existing income-earning occupation intact if they enter *Mudarabah* as *Mudarib*. Hence, these people also will not have any incentive to show in a higher or lower poverty group. The presence of multiple *Mudarib* in *Mudarabah* enterprise will provide the delegated monitoring offered by group lending mechanism in conventional microfinance. Hence, the monitoring will be ensured at the horizontal level of the organization rather than having a single distant monitor at the vertical level that has all the stakes at risk as a financier (*Rabb-ul-Maal*).

Finally, the non-poor people with investible capital will qualify for debt-based finance at market benchmark-linked rates. It will encourage them to use equity-based finance using the mode of *Musharakah*. They could also use their investible capital to enter in microenterprise *Mudarabah* as *Rabb-ul-Maal*. They will enjoy the highest PSR in order to incentivize their participation for creating a sustainable loop of funding for the microenterprises. But, these people would have an incentive to show themselves as non-poor with no investible capital so as to avail subsidized mark-up financing. That is where the credit assessment is an important activity. Banks as delegated monitors can do the credit assessment more efficiently. Tax incentives can be provided to the investment made and profits earned from microenterprise *Mudarabah* so as to incentivize investment participation. Here again, the non-poor people will not be able to hide their investible capital since the presence of multiple *Mudarib* in *Mudarabah* enterprise will provide the delegated monitoring in the micro-equity financing.

10.5 Conclusion

Islamic commercial banks cannot cater to every individual person, enterprise, and institution requiring finance. Islamic banks are one of the pillars in Islamic finance architecture, but there is more to offer by other institutions. Islamic social finance fills the gap by providing income support as well as microfinance where Islamic commercial banks do not operate due to scale diseconomies and risk aversion. There are ample set of institutions for helping ultra-poor and extreme poor to fulfil their deficit in endowments in order to ensure basic consumption expenditure on necessities. These include *Zakat*, *Waqf*, and *Sadaqah*. For people who are poor or vulnerable to become poor, but have skills and capacity to engage in micro-entrepreneurship, Islamic microfinance comes to the picture by providing a set of short- and long-term debt-based and equity-based modes of financing. These market- and non-market- based institutions together contribute to enable socio-economic mobility for people to come out of poverty. Hence, Islamic social finance institutions are an important part of Islamic finance architecture to enable inclusion of everyone in Islamic finance.

Self-Assessment Quiz

1. If a poor person is suffering food insecurity and requires support for basic consumption, which Islamic instrument is the most appropriate
   (a) *Murabaha*
   (b) *Qard*

(c) *Zakat*

(d) None of the above

2. If a poor person needs to buy an income-generating asset and wants to pay the cost of the asset in instalments over a long period of time covering the useful life of the asset, which Islamic mode of financing is most suitable to be used by Islamic microfinance?

(a) *Murabaha*

(b) *Ijarah*

(c) *Salam*

(d) *Istisna*

3. Using Cash *Waqf*, which of the following public projects can be funded?

(a) School

(b) Hospital

(c) Water filter plant

(d) All of the above

4. What is the potential impact of *Zakat* on macroeconomic outcomes?

(a) Increase in aggregate demand and redistribute resources from the rich to the poor

(b) Increase in aggregate demand and no redistribution impact

(c) No impact on aggregate demand and redistribute resources from the rich to the poor

(d) Decrease in aggregate demand and redistribute resources from the rich to the poor

5. In the integrated Islamic social finance model, socio-economic mobility is enhanced through graduated support and financing to extreme poor in which sequence

(a) *Qard, Zakat, Mudarabah, Musharakah,* and Islamic debt-based modes of finance

(b) *Zakat, Mudarabah, Musharakah, Qard,* and Islamic debt-based modes of finance

(c) *Zakat, Qard, Mudarabah, Musharakah,* and Islamic debt-based modes of finance

(d) None of the above

Self-Assessment Questions

1. List the reasons why commercial banks are averse to finance ultra-poor and extreme poor.
2. Why financial inclusion is less in financing-side products as compared to deposit-side products?
3. Explain how the institution of *Zakat* can help the poor in income support and income redistribution?
4. Explain the potential of *Waqf* in the provision of public goods and services?
5. Why are the mark-up rates in microfinance higher as compared to commercial banking?
6. Explain the difference between *Zakat* and *Waqf*.
7. If there is a need for a water filter plant that requires land and machinery, which Islamic social finance institution can be used and why?
8. If a poor person has a need for long-term fixed asset for generating income through self-employment, which Islamic mode of financing can be used by IMFI and why?
9. If a poor person has a short-term need for purchasing inventory for cash sale in a small retail business, which Islamic mode of financing can be used by IMFI and why?
10. Explain the graduated finance approach using social finance to enable socio-economic mobility.

Chapter 11

Islamic Banking in the Digital Era

11.1 Introduction

The fusion of finance with technology termed as "Fintech" in popular discourse is promising to enable financial inclusion more rapidly than banks which have a scarce presentation in rural areas and which still by and large rely on a brick and mortar model for expediting financial inclusion. This presents an opportunity for Islamic banks to compete afresh with new ground rules in digital space where they and conventional banks are equally new and inexperienced.

Given the rapid rise of payment facilitation through non-banking apps, banks are going to face increased commercial displacement risk and disruption to their payment facilitation function. It is interesting to see how and when they join the Fintech revolution by enabling online banking and mobile banking and offering spending incentives to retain customers on their payment gateways.

This chapter explains the fundamental changes in the way of banking in foreseeable future. It also highlights the important challenges that these changes will pose to Islamic banks in particular. Furthermore, disruptive technologies will present opportunities in digital space that were not there before. Finally, the chapter discusses how to cope up with disruption and sail through the era of disruption to enter a new era of construction with new and exciting possibilities.

11.2 The Risk of Security in Digital Space

Accenture and the Ponemon Institute in a report, "Cost of Cyber Crime Study", look closely at the costs that financial services companies suffer when responding to cybercrime incidents. The study applies a costing methodology that allows year-over-year comparisons. It is found that

> *The average cost of cybercrime for financial services companies globally has increased by more than 40 percent over the past three years, from $12.97 million USD per firm in 2014 to $18.28 million USD in 2017 — significantly higher than the average cost of $11.7 million USD per firm across all industries included in the study. The analysis focuses on the direct costs of the incidents and does not include the longer-term costs of remediation.*

A *Forbes* report highlights several statistics regarding banks and cybercrime. Cybercrime costs banks more to recover from than businesses in any other industry. The rate of breaches in the financial sector has increased by 300% over the past five years. Banks are breached by hackers 300 times more frequently than firms in other industries. Strikingly, cybercrimes cost banks over $1 trillion each year.

While the typical bank's network perimeter is strictly guarded, these findings show that in 100% of cases examined by Positive Technologies, the penetration testers were able to gain full control over a bank's network infrastructure. In more than half of the tested banks (58%), attackers got in via unauthorized access to financial applications. Moreover, in 25% of the banks, penetration testers were able to compromise the workstations used for ATM management.

Thus, cyberattacks pose almost an existential threat to banks if the privacy and confidentiality are breached. If private details like debit card number, personal identification number (PIN), and personal information are leaked, then it enhances the risk of unauthorized access to accounts and fund transfers.

11.3 *Shari'ah* Non-Compliance Risk in Digital Space

While the technology, security, and financial risks might be common between Islamic and commercial banks, Islamic banks face an important type of risk, i.e. *Shari'ah* non-compliance risk. It is highly important that Islamic transactions abide by the principles of *Shari'ah*. If the bank card of an Islamic bank is used in payments for non-compliant goods and services, then it will be considered breach of the rules of *Shari'ah* compliance.

In financing transactions, if the customer is charged rents in Islamic lease contracts before the delivery of *Ijarah* asset in usable condition, then such a charge cannot be taken or recorded as income. Likewise, if an asset is already consumed and used up in the production process before the Islamic bank could sell it to the client in *Murabaha* contracts, then it is no longer possible for an Islamic bank to earn any income from such transactions. Thus, timing of the steps is important in Islamic transactions. In order to ensure this, the algorithm in an Islamic smart contract should comply with the principles of Islamic finance. However, technology will not reduce the significance of *Shari'ah* compliance. Rather, it will allow *Shari'ah* compliance to be more robust and less costly.

11.4 Commercial Risk via Disruptive Technologies

Disruptive technologies will change the cost structure and hence pricing. This will lead to increased commercial displacement risk. When the price is the same, the competition shifts to other attributes. But, if, on the grounds of cost, banks become more costly, there will be less loyalty and switching costs for the consumers.

Alternate payment networks including e-wallets, digital currencies, and platforms like PayPal, Paytm, and Payoneer are already displacing banks from the remittance and payment function.

In the case of financing operations too, peer-to-peer (P2P) lending enabled by smart contracts can displace commercial banks. Non-banking financial intermediation through crowdfunding and P2P lending creates new possibilities to avoid intermediation costs. In order to survive, banks have no choice than to embed digitization in their financial services.

11.5 Coping with Technology Risk in Digital Space

In the digital fund transfers, convenience is important, but transparency and legal compliance are even more important. It is important to detect and control money laundering to offshore regions. It is vital to ensure that funds transferred for criminal intent, such as terrorism financing, are detected and chased to the source in order to avoid the misuse of endless possibilities offered by the digitization of financial transactions.

Use of digitization in financial services is necessary, but it needs to guard against operational security risks posed in the cyberspace. There is need for increased vigilance and monitoring by updating Standard Operating Procedures (SOPs) for monitoring. For instance, it is important to provide digital access only through biometric verification using thumb or face recognition. Including requirement of PIN to access digital services and to authorize every transaction through one-time passwords (OTP) can also limit unauthorized access.

Convenience and efficiency matters, but it should not compromise security and safety. The employees of the bank need to be trained as to what they can and cannot ask along with the knowledge of what they should ask to ascertain proper identification in phone banking.

In the Islamic product structures, the cash flows might be similar, but they occur in a sequence which is important to be followed linearly. Hence, there is a need for customized upgradation to incorporate the principles and protocols of Islamic product structures in digital smart contracts.

The interface and communication in mobile apps need to have customized nomenclature. The words "loan", "interest rate", and "principal" are not the correct words to be used in Islamic product structures. It is because Islamic banks do not loan out money, and hence, they do not charge interest on money loans. Since they provide asset-backed finance, the term "principal" which is used in a loan contract is also not appropriate. Likewise, if Islamic banks distribute periodic profits to the depositors, it is not akin to interest. Hence, the term "interest" needs to be avoided and replaced with an appropriate term that signifies the true nature and essence of the transaction. Likewise, any communication and promotion needs to avoid such words too. For instance, an Islamic mortgage calculator using the mode of Diminishing *Musharakah* shall represent the instalment breakup in purchase amount of units and rental amount rather than showing interest payment and principal repayment.

Financial accounting and financial reporting also need to appropriately record transactions. For instance, payment received on late payment cannot be taken in income account. Payments received as advance rentals cannot be treated as income right away. An asset purchased by an Islamic bank from a vendor cannot be simultaneously sold without recording its ownership and possession in the balance sheet of the Islamic bank. Thus, such distinctive features in Islamic finance need to be incorporated in financial accounting and reporting.

Lastly, there is a need for ensuring platform security including website for online banking and mobile applications for mobile banking. Thus, the platforms must be guarded against viruses, malwares, and trojans. Customers also need to be repeatedly informed to avoid sharing personal information on any platform or with anyone in order to avoid unauthorized access.

For ensuring maximum security and performance, a sandbox is an isolated testing environment that enables users to run programs or execute files without affecting the application, system or platform on which they run. Software developers use sandboxes to test new programming code. Cybersecurity professionals use sandboxes to test potentially malicious software. Fintech Techpreneurs use sandboxes to bring innovation and robustness to their products. Thus, sandboxes can be used to improve the products and services in digital space.

11.6 Coping Up with Commercial Risks in Digital Space

It is important to invest more in technological infrastructure than physical infrastructure. As payment facilitation function faces stiff competition from mobile wallet accounts, it will be important to invest in technology infrastructure. In today's world, logging into a mobile app is just like entering a physical branch. In fact, it is more efficient as it reduces the shoe leather cost related to branch visit and it enables the customer to avoid rush and inflexible timings. A mobile app of a bank is a gateway to do banking 24 hours a day and 7 days a week. What might still be tempting customers to not increase their use of mobile and online banking is the apprehension about security, privacy, and confidentiality. In some cases, it might also have to do with the user-unfriendly nature of the interface and procedures. Thus, investing in providing a secure, convenient, efficient, interactive, and enriched service through mobile and online banking is as important as investment in physical infrastructure of a bank.

In order to ensure user friendliness, multiple input methods, multiple languages, and customization of user interface are some of the aspects which can give customer control over the way he or she would like to operate. However, efficiency need not result in compromise on security. There is a need for multi-layered security protocols to avoid breach of privacy, confidentiality, and unauthorized access. Since such problems often reoccur, strong vigilance and update are necessary to avoid any mishap and irreversible distrust. Most people might remain unaware of the financial soundness of a bank. However, they engage in the mobile and online banking personally. Hence, any cyberattack which results in a loss of private confidential data is going to create distrust, and this would have a more widespread effect through the spread of negative word of mouth.

Data are valuable in providing tailor-made solutions and suggestions. Much of the credit analysis can be done through the use of the details of transactions and activities in the account. These data can be used for suggesting other products like insurance, mutual fund investments, and personal finance.

As the penetration of mobile and online banking grows, there will be a need to leverage physical infrastructure by offering one-window operations to facilitate payments and investments and avail other financial services like credit and insurance in digital space. Cheques are already being replaced by online fund transfers. Thus, the transactions that required repeated visits to the bank for remittance, deposit, and payments will now be increasingly done in digital space on smartphones.

Digital-savvy customers are likely to stick with those banks which offer extensive network externalities. If doing banking with a particular bank enables app-based payments for food, utilities, travel, education, health, telecom, Internet, e-commerce, groceries, and donation, then a customer is likely to stick with that bank than another bank which does not offer an extensive list of possibilities when it comes to payments facilitation.

Likewise, if a particular bank has no or slab-based processing charges for interbank transfer, then it is likely to attract and retain most customers to use its platform for small and large payments as compared to a bank which has flat and inflexible processing fee for interbank transfers. The days when banks used to compete on characteristics like being open on Saturdays or having late operating hours are gone. Now, the competition will move towards the digital space where convenience, efficiency, flexibility, security, and overall service experience matter more than the physical attributes of a branch.

As barriers to entry like minimum balance requirement are removed, opening a bank account would be easier. However, to generate more activity and avoid open but dormant accounts, there is a need for an active bank–vendor relationship to offer exclusive discounts to retain customers. As the competition grows, it will not be enough that a particular bank card can be used at a point of sale terminal. More often than not, the customer would use among different bank cards the one which offers discounts. Since the discount schemes change frequently, there is a need for an engaging and customized communication with the customers. Mailing a print copy of a list of hundreds of outlets where the bank card has a discount incentive is costly as well as less engaging. Most consumers do not bother to open such mails after sometime if they have to sift through pages of promotional material. Interactive searches and in-app messages are more engaging and less costly.

On the lending side too, P2P lending has a lot of potential if the trust is built through effective documentation and monitoring which ensures transparency. Blockchain provides new possibilities in recording and monitoring thereby limiting the need for third-party verification. Blockchain technology offers access to all stakeholders in a transaction to track and monitor information without the need of verification by a third party.

Smart contracts using Blockchain technology bring automation in the contractual relationship between two parties including the enforcement of terms and conditions of the contract. The self-executing programmes or algorithms electronically store the terms of the contract and execute when the stipulated conditions are met. This presents an exciting opportunity for Islamic banks to minimize the role and engagement of costly labour hours in monitoring the mundane details of the contractual process. This can allow Islamic banks to reduce redundancies, bottlenecks, and administrative lags. As a result, the cost can be reduced and this will allow Islamic commercial banks to remain competitive and avoid commercial displacement risk in dual banking systems.

Thus, Islamic commercial banks have to embed Blockchain in their monitoring function in order to avoid disruption in their intermediary function. Smart Blockchain Islamic *Sukuk* have been launched in the recent past. Such issuances will compel the investment banks to adapt to the new frontiers in Fintech in order to avoid being driven out of the value chain in capital market transactions.

11.7 The Budding Industry of Islamic Fintech

Earlier, we had looked at the challenges and risks that emanate from technology. However, technology also provides solutions for reaching new markets, customer base, and opportunity to cross-sell as well as economize outreach and delivery of the financial services.

Now, there are companies that specialize in doing the Shari'ah compliance check and provide Shari'ah advisory services digitally. Wahed Invest is an America-based, Halal-focused investment firm. It is the first robo-advisor firm aimed towards Muslim investors with a Shari'ah-compliant platform. Algebra by Farringdon Group also offers Shari'ah-compliant robo-advisory investment services. In addition to that, Blossom Finance provides impact investment platform.

There are platforms that are aiming to take up the financial intermediation function through P2P lending. Based in Dubai, Beehive is the first P2P lending platform in MENA. Using innovative technology, it directly connects businesses seeking fast and affordable finance with investors who can help fund their growth. Beehive is certified as a Shari'ah-compliant P2P finance platform by the Shari'ah Review Bureau (SRB). Beehive has worked with prominent Islamic legal advisors and Islamic finance industry experts to develop a structure that allows them to process investments in a Shari'ah-compliant way. There are other players like Maliyya that provide global Shari'ah-compliant P2P financing platform as well.

Even for consumers, InsureTech companies provide insurance services. StrideUp is another Islamic Fintech app that helps consumers to buy property in a Shari'ah-compliant way.

In social financial intermediation, there are Islamic Fintech companies providing crowdfunding platform and the opportunity to make impact investments. Ethis Crowd platform features high-impact investments in property projects to build affordable houses supported by local government programmes. On the contrary, Kapital Boost is a Singapore-based crowdfunding platform that matches SMEs in need of financing with global investors looking for attractive investment opportunities which support community growth. The use of Islamic financing structures for asset purchase financing and invoice financing ensures that the products and operations are ethical and transparent and cater to the needs of Muslims worldwide.

Islamic Fintech players also assist in achieving the best use of big data and artificial intelligence. MyFinB is a Big Data and Analytics company that helps banks and consultants evaluate a high volume of financial data and turn them into strategic insights using artificial intelligence. MyFinB's latest innovation includes incorporating Shari'ah modules onto its engine to evaluate listed and unlisted companies for compliance and quality assurance. Using a RoboBanker, they make bankers' jobs easier by generating good leads, shortening processing time to evaluate credit risks, monitoring their exposure effortlessly and, detecting red flags. With MyFinB, banks are able to manage their risk-weighted assets better. They are able to reduce NPLs and operating costs substantially and to improve their loan margins.

Traditional Islamic financial institutions are adopting the Fintech solutions. Kuwait Finance House, Dubai Islamic Bank, and Bank Syariah Mandiri are some of the Islamic banks that have adopted Chatbot solution. Al-Rajhi Bank and Kuwait Finance House have adopted Robotic Process Automation (RPA) to automate the workflow system for retail financing and to conduct customer due diligence.

These are some of the many examples of Islamic Fintech companies starting to play an active role in facilitating the use of financial services by embedding technology to provide convenience to both the consumers as well as financial service providers. Apparently, Fintech may seem to challenge traditional financial service providers. However, if the traditional financial service providers join the Fintech wave, then they can benefit from technology and achieve bigger gains with a large existing customer base, greater outreach, infrastructure, investment, and economies of scale. On the contrary, Islamic Fintech companies can provide innovation, cost efficiency, and the opportunity to leverage technology in reaching the digital-savvy customers.

11.8 Conclusion: Way Forward

There are challenges with opportunities with digitization in financial landscape. One of the important challenges is in the domain of security and monitoring in allowing payment facilitation through mobile wallet accounts and how to still ensure know your customer (KYC) and anti-money laundering protocols in compliance.

Coming to Islamic microfinance, it appears that on the supply and institutional side, the major hurdles in penetration of Islamic microfinance include scale inefficiency, high outreach costs, and lower impact. Since the size of financing provided to the clients in microfinance is smaller, the high fixed costs of credit analysis, documentation, monitoring, and *Shari'ah* compliance are hard to cover from the competitive markup rates in the market, especially through a brick and mortar model. Thus, Islamic microfinance assets contribute approximately 1% in total Islamic finance assets. There is a need to bring inclusivity in the Islamic finance ecosystem given the high levels of poverty in the Muslim world generally. Fintech provides an opportunity to cut costs, widen outreach, and help to scale the operations.

Fintech provides an opportunity to improve efficiency through digitization of processes and operations, thereby enabling the provision of finance to small-scale microenterprises. Microfinance outreach is still below the requirement and potential target market in a lot of Muslim majority countries. Millions of people in Pakistan, Nigeria, Indonesia, and Bangladesh are poor and are financially excluded from accessing formal financial services. It is interesting to see how Fintech can help in increasing outreach, reducing the cost of administration, and monitoring the financing side clients. Artificial intelligence can be used in client screening and suggesting the appropriate terms of financing to ensure financial stability and socio-economic mobility.

An important challenge going forward is geographical diversity in outreach. Given the high demand for microcredit in rural areas, it is interesting to see how the services and infrastructure of banks and telecommunication companies can be leveraged in increasing the scale and outreach of microfinance in rural areas.

An important enabler in financial inclusion is financial literacy. It is highly important that mobile and online platforms should be user-friendly, multi-lingual, and foolproof against security breaches. For Islamic banks, the challenge is dual. People have a hard time understanding financial terms, let alone Islamic terms which are readily used in Islamic financial products and services. Hence, there is a need for increased care and effort in popularizing Islamic finance and making it mainstream by reaching to the common people in ways convenient and comfortable to them.

Thus, it is hoped that Islamic banks with surplus liquidity will think of embedding technology in their products and services so that they are able to compete on cost with the large conventional banks that have economies of scale. Technology has provided an opportunity for smaller Islamic banks to change the path of their cost curves by achieving efficient delivery and operations and excelling in service quality. With growth in assets and capital, it is also expected and hoped that in future, Islamic banking services would also cater to the bottom of the pyramid population to actualize the vision of Islamic banking to be the banking of the first choice for everyone, including Muslims and non-Muslims and including all segments of population, regardless of their socio-economic status.

Self-Assessment Quiz

1. Which of the following function or revenue source of banks is facing the most risk due to Fintech?
   (a) Payments
   (b) Long-term corporate financing
   (c) Short-term corporate financing
   (d) All of the above

2. Mobile wallet accounts can be used to
   (a) Pay utility bills
   (b) Funds transfer
   (c) Make donations
   (d) All of the above

3. Unauthorized access to accounts can result in
   (a) Loss of private information including transaction history
   (b) Unauthorized debits
   (c) Unauthorized fund transfers
   (d) All of the above

4. What are the security checks applied in banks in digital banking to reduce the risk of unauthorized access
   (a) Passwords and PIN
   (b) Transaction-specific OTP
   (c) Do not allow fund transfer altogether and only allow balance check and making requests for chequebook and bank statement
   (d) Only (a) and (b)

5. How can technology aid in banking in different ways for the financial institution
   (a) Cross-selling based on digital transactions history
   (b) Customized promotions and marketing
   (c) Reduce cost of outreach
   (d) All of the above

Self-Assessment Questions

1. Explain how innovation in technology can create disruption for traditional ways of banking in different functionalities.
2. Open the mobile app of a bank with which you have an account. List the various transactions and things that you can do using the mobile app.
3. What is cybersecurity? Describe with example why banks need to be vigilant about security threats.
4. List and describe the security checks used in mobile banking and online banking to reduce the risk of unauthorized access.
5. Discuss how Fintech can help in improving efficiency and scaling up operations.
6. Discuss how Blockchain provides an opportunity for Islamic banks to reduce the administrative cost and lags in executing Islamic finance transactions.
7. Can P2P lending reduce the need for intermediary? Discuss why there may still be a need of intermediary.
8. Compare the characteristics of a mobile wallet account and a bank account.
9. Discuss the potential of customized marketing to the clients using digital data.
10. Discuss how developments in technology bring opportunity to ensure effective and efficient *Shari'ah* compliance.

Chapter 12

Mainstreaming Islamic Finance: The Way Forward

12.1 Introduction

Islamic finance has now penetrated in many countries in different continents including regions where the Muslim population is in majority as well as regions where it is not the case. The governments of Western Europe as well as those in East Asia have issued Islamic securities to finance their needs using Islamic asset-backed financing modes and instruments. Now, the challenge that Islamic banks face is how to ensure mainstreaming of Islamic banking. Despite the presence in many countries, Islamic banking is still not the dominant or even significant portion of overall banking in Muslim-majority regions like Indonesia, Pakistan, and Bangladesh, for instance. Increase in penetration is needed to achieve scale economies, efficiency, and room for more innovating product design and pricing for a distinctive economic impact. This chapter discusses the major challenges and opportunities that Islamic banks face in expansion and outreach. The challenges relate to taxation, liquidity management, and product design. However, there are opportunities to contribute to financial inclusion, development finance, public finance, and bringing inclusivity in the system by way of microfinance. The next two sections in this chapter elaborate more on these issues.

12.2   Challenges in Making Islamic Finance Mainstream

12.2.1 *Lack of support for tax neutrality*

Tax neutrality in the context of tax regulations on financial products refers to providing the same treatment to products where the economic substance, effects, and implications are the same. Horizontal equity principle demands that individuals and businesses with similar income characteristics and business processes must be treated equally.

Islamic banks have to undertake unique risks and get involved in financial transactions in order to ensure *Shari'ah*-compliant income from financial intermediation services. They cannot merely lend money to earn compound interest. They provide asset-backed financing for which they have to take ownership of real assets. Only after obtaining ownership and physical or constructive possession of these real assets, they can sell these assets at a profit or provide usufruct of the asset to earn rental income. Thus, this unique form of participatory intermediation involves asset ownership and multiple asset transfers.

This could create several tax issues, such as duplication of duties in assets transfer, registration, and multiple sales for indirect taxes and in the tax treatment of income for direct tax purposes. Islamic banks or their customers have to pay double duties since at least two sale contracts are usually involved in Islamic banking products, i.e. one between the bank and the vendor and subsequently, a sale transaction between the bank and the client. Double taxation in the form of Goods and Services Tax (GST), Value-Added Tax (VAT), registration duties, or stamp duties could create an extra transaction cost in the Islamic banking products. As a result, these products may become unattractive and uncompetitive either from the point of view of the client or from the point of view of the Islamic financial intermediary. The burden of effects depends on demand and supply elasticities. If the demand is more inelastic than supply, then greater incidence of the additional indirect tax burden falls on the consumer. On the contrary, if the supply is more inelastic than demand, the greater incidence of the additional indirect tax burden falls on the financial institution.

The additional levies could render Islamic banking products uncompetitive, and hence, their growth and penetration, especially in Muslim societies, could be hindered where financial inclusion is already at a dismal level. Muslim-majority countries are predominantly developing countries at early stages of economic development and have weak institutional settings. Thus, they rely mostly on the bank-based financial system than on market-based system.

If tax distortions result in additional tax impact on Islamic banking products, then it will result in failure to utilize the potential household savings that do not reach financial markets and institutions due to uncompetitiveness arising from distortionary tax treatment. Tax distortions may influence the portfolio choice of banks and compel them to take undue risks, which could ultimately increase systemic risks.

Debt bias induces excess leverage due to the interest tax shield available on debt finance as compared to equity finance. If the interest tax shield is not available for Islamic banks that do not exactly create money-based debt claims, then they will be at a disadvantage. Conventional tax systems recognize the tax deductibility of interest payments, but not dividend payments. The interest tax shield reduces the weighted average cost of capital for firms. If such tax shield is not available in Islamic banking products due to the returns not arising purely from a debt claim, then using Islamic products could appear to be more costly after tax adjustments. Furthermore, differences in the treatment of Islamic and conventional finance can create international tax arbitrage opportunities if left unchecked.

Finally, the disposal of assets may be subject to capital gains tax in some jurisdictions. In *Tawarruq*, the client obtains liquidity by purchasing a commodity for a higher deferred price and selling it at a lower spot price. If the difference in price is not treated as the cost of finance, then the client will not be able to deduct the cost for income tax purposes.

Following are the key steps in the taxation framework governing Islamic banking products which can allow a level playing field for Islamic banking:

- Tax systems should base treatment on economic substance and move away from distortionary transaction taxes. It is vital to treat the economic substance of Islamic instruments similar to conventional instruments for levelling the playing field.
- Tax neutrality to *Sukuk* issuance shall apply to both listed as well as non-listed *Sukuk*.
- Rather than enacting new regulatory regime, the current regulatory impediments may be overcome through changes to existing laws to ensure equal treatment between the Islamic financial products and their conventional counterparts.

- The economic substance in generic and mainstream Islamic banking transactions is similar to their substitutes in conventional banking. However, in some cases, the results could differ. For instance, the economic benefits arising from the real assets in the form of rent in Islamic lease stop in the event of asset destruction or its non-usability. Thus, the laws should accommodate compliance to *Shari'ah* principles in such circumstances. Else, if *Shari'ah* compliance is ignored, it can create commercial displacement risk from a predominantly faith-conscious client base.

12.2.2 *Constrained liquidity management*

In Islamic banking, deposit mobilization has much less contractual frictions than creating a *Shari'ah*-compliant financing asset. In providing finance, it is important that finance is provided for the genuine purchase of an asset whose ownership, possession, and risk has to be borne by the bank so as to be able to earn any profit or rents on the sale and use of asset.

Investment with other banks on short-term basis is also not easy for Islamic banks. The use of money market instruments like repo, reverse repo, T-bills, and financial derivatives like forward, futures, options, forward rate agreements, and swaps is not permissible for Islamic banks since these instruments involve *Riba*, *Maysir*, or *Gharar*. Thus, when Islamic banks have surplus liquidity, they face a constrained set of short-term liquid investments due to the small number of *Sukuk* in the markets.

Furthermore, Islamic banks also have no facility of lender of the last resort from the central bank. Since the central bank provides this facility to the conventional banks on the basis of interest-based lending, Islamic banks are unable to use this facility. To manage surplus liquidity, it is important to have greater breadth of exchange-traded liquid *Sukuk* for different maturities so that Islamic banks can productively use surplus liquidity in a diverse set of investment options.

12.2.3 *Constraints in product design, pricing, and efficiency*

Islamic banks do not have complete product alternatives for all kinds of conventional finance solutions. According to the World Islamic Banking Competitiveness Report, there are 38 million customers globally with Islamic banks with average product holding of 2.1 which is significantly lower than class leading average of 4.9. This represents untapped cross selling potential in Islamic banking with an existing and growing customer base.

While it is indeed appreciable that not all conventional practices are replicated as is by Islamic banks, but such lacking in solutions and alternatives cannot completely be attributed to this factor alone. Distress financing, educational financing, health financing, and microfinance are areas where if Islamic product alternatives can be developed and adequately marketed, it will increase the size and scope of Islamic banking. Furthermore, it will validate the position of Islamic banks as having solutions for all classes and stratum in the economy and not just for the big corporations looking to expand with new assets acquisition.

It is easier for a customer to switch from a conventional banking deposit to an Islamic banking deposit than to convert a conventional debt-based liability to an Islamic financing product. Hence, the full product range will enable Islamic banks to better use their growing deposits and increase the market share expeditiously. From the commercial point of view, this is an essential requirement for the Islamic banks to improve their advance to deposit ratio and reduce spreads.

On the contrary, the financing operations that are overly dependent on asset–backed debt-based modes of financing create several issues.

First, in times of recession, Islamic banks have limited product range for firms that require finance in already ongoing projects in which large investments had been made to setup business, but financing is required to meet rising variables costs of energy and utility prices.

Second, in a recession, purchasing new assets for expansion is not the first thing most firms would do or can afford to do. Hence, if Islamic banks remain stuck in debt-based modes of financing, they will have to start offering buyback or sale and leaseback type of products, which are not preferable or ideal from the *Maqasid-e-Shari'ah* perspective.

Islamic banking products may generate higher transaction costs than conventional finance, especially due to the necessity in some cases to set up additional intermediaries between suppliers and demanders of funds. For instance, in *Tawarruq* used in treasury operations, agency fees are paid to the transacting intermediaries. In situations where use is made of Islamic banking products which are outside of the prescribed and recognized list of contracts, then additional legal fees paid to prove the economic substance for approval may involve additional costs as well as time delays.

In Islamic banking, financing is mostly provided for the purchase of an asset whose ownership belongs to the bank before second leg sale is executed. Once the client and the bank agree to the contract's financials, i.e. sale price, it cannot be changed. In this case, the problems of moral hazard and adverse selection become even more significant. If there is increased use of flexible financing options where payoffs to the bank are not fixed to the historical prices of assets, it will be more equitable to both the bank's shareholders and depositors.

Generally, in Islamic banking, each financing contract requires thorough documentation and ascertainment of genuine purchase of an asset. However, if the Islamic banks can identify stable growth companies with widely used tangible products for consumers and industries, then they can provide equity financing facility which is more inclusive, egalitarian, and flexible in the allocation of funds.

12.3 Future Opportunities for Growth

12.3.1 *Financial inclusion of faith-conscious target segment*

There are a lot of Muslim-majority countries where domestic credit to GDP ratio is very low. Table 12.1 provides statistics on domestic credit provided by financial sector and by banks in particular in selected OIC member countries. It is revealed that in 34 out of 54 countries, domestic credit by finance sector as a percent of GDP is lower than 50%. Moreover, it is further discovered that in 17 out of 54 countries, domestic credit by finance sector as a percent of GDP is even lower than 30%. Other than Lebanon, none of the OIC member countries has even as much value of this ratio as the average for the middle-income countries.

On the contrary, for middle- and high-income countries, this ratio stands at 188% and 149%, respectively. On the contrary, in 41 out of 54 countries, domestic credit by banks as a percent of GDP is lower than 50%. Moreover, it is further discovered that in 33 out of 54 countries, domestic credit by banks as a percent of GDP is even lower than 30%. On the contrary, for middle- and high-income countries, this ratio stands at 101% and 80%, respectively. None of the OIC member countries has even as much value of this ratio as the average for middle-income countries.

Thus, there is a huge portion of non-banking population that will be new to both conventional and Islamic banking. Another striking feature in

Table 12.1. Credit services by financial sector and banks in OIC.

Country	Domestic Credit by Finance Sector (% GDP)	Domestic Credit by Banks (% GDP)	Country	Domestic Credit by Finance Sector (% GDP)	Domestic Credit by Banks (% GDP)
Albania	58.82	30.74	Libya	43.39	17.62
Algeria	72.74	24.16	Malaysia	143.12	119.33
Azerbaijan	13.18	19.99	Maldives	64.94	28.29
Bahrain	90.89	73.72	Mali	32.30	25.34
Bangladesh	64.06	46.77	Mauritania	42.86	28.56
Benin	26.96	23.85	Morocco	110.22	62.08
Bosnia	62.01	54.79	Mozambique	32.89	22.67
Brunei	28.37	34.40	Niger	21.98	14.08
Burkina Faso	34.03	29.81	Nigeria	21.20	10.91
Cameroon	19.27	15.20	Oman	66.81	70.43
Chad	22.48	9.62	Pakistan	58.28	18.89
Comoros	17.89	15.40	Qatar	132.80	76.66
Cote d'Ivoire	39.07	26.18	Saudi Arabia	38.78	53.97
Djibouti	37.24	32.06	Senegal	35.39	28.26
Egypt	91.81	25.55	Sierra Leone	23.20	5.71
Gabon	23.13	12.93	Sudan	31.11	12.37
Gambia, The	37.57	6.63	Suriname	45.23	28.25
Guinea	23.11	9.56	Tajikistan	15.63	11.41
Guinea-Bissau	21.36	11.91	Togo	48.76	36.79
Guyana	68.94	37.33	Tunisia	93.34	67.46
Indonesia	47.24	32.74	Turkey	83.28	64.16
Iran	77.65	66.06	Uganda	25.54	14.85
Iraq	6.97	8.64	UAE	91.28	75.72
Jordan	109.18	78.32	West Bank	56.61	49.90
Kazakhstan	38.23	23.77	Yemen	30.12	5.64
Kosovo	45.16	41.00	Low income	25.91	20.40
Kuwait	79.90	88.68	Middle income	148.80	101.60
Kyrgyzstan	22.35	23.76	High income	188.44	79.20

Muslim-majority countries is the lower savings ratio and, consequently, a higher savings-investment gap. This creates a hurdle in fostering capital formation and economic growth. It also creates external sector imbalances due to the large current account deficit.

Table 12.2 shows the savings–investment gap in some OIC countries.

In only 17 out of 51 OIC countries, the savings–investment gap is positive. Two-thirds of the countries in the sample have a negative

Table 12.2.   Savings–investment gap in selected OIC countries.

Country	Savings (% GDP)	GFCF (% GDP)	Gap	Country	Savings (% GDP)	GFCF (% GDP)	Gap
Afghanistan	20.79	19.17	1.62	Kuwait	35.29	17.98	17.31
Albania	16.28	24.17	−7.90	Kyrgyz Republic	26.68	31.16	−4.48
Algeria	37.83	41.36	−3.53	Lebanon	−2.77	17.16	−19.93
Azerbaijan	32.97	20.63	12.33	Malaysia	28.53	24.40	4.13
Bahrain	28.80	28.66	0.15	Mali	13.99	19.96	−5.96
Bangladesh	35.24	31.23	4.00	Mauritania	19.38	57.39	−38.01
Benin	12.33	25.77	−13.45	Morocco	27.68	29.07	−1.39
Bosnia	13.86	18.59	−4.73	Mozambique	9.20	25.68	−16.47
Brunei	55.64	40.89	14.75	Niger	20.23	33.66	−13.43
Burkina Faso	17.19	22.81	−5.63	Nigeria	18.26	14.72	3.54
Cameroon	18.23	22.40	−4.17	Oman	19.43	25.09	−5.66
Comoros	12.03	17.52	−5.49	Pakistan	18.50	14.82	3.68
Cote d'Ivoire	14.57	20.79	−6.22	Saudi Arabia	34.91	21.39	13.51
Djibouti	23.65	24.20	−0.55	Senegal	20.42	24.95	−4.54
Egypt	10.37	16.25	−5.88	Sierra Leone	3.36	17.98	−14.62
Gabon	38.38	21.41	16.97	Sudan	15.09	18.67	−3.59
Gambia	12.04	17.01	−4.96	Suriname	50.34	37.54	12.80
Guinea	8.58	19.47	−10.89	Tajikistan	23.09	26.63	−3.53
Guinea-Bissau	8.42	10.82	−2.40	Togo	21.73	25.27	−3.55
Guyana	30.19	31.09	−0.90	Tunisia	8.87	18.69	−9.82
Indonesia	31.63	32.29	−0.66	Turkey	26.60	29.67	−3.07
Iraq	19.59	14.40	5.19	Uganda	18.35	24.14	−5.80
Jordan	9.35	16.67	−7.31	Uzbekistan	41.90	29.76	12.14
Kazakhstan	26.03	21.89	4.14	West Bank	12.63	23.20	−10.57
Kosovo	23.60	28.73	−5.13	Middle income	30.76	28.69	2.07
				High income	23.07	21.33	1.74

savings–investment gap. In almost half of the countries in the sample, the gross savings to GDP ratio is lower than 20%, whereas the average gross savings to GDP ratio in middle-income countries is 30.8%. If we delve in to gross domestic savings to GDP ratio, it stands at below 20% in 32 out of 56 countries in the sample where the data are available on this indicator. Besides poverty and lower per capita incomes, one of the other significant reasons why savings ratio is lower in Muslim countries is that faith-conscious individuals tend to avoid interest-based banking and savings instruments. Even besides the religious and ethical appeal of interest-free banking, effective marketing can enable Islamic banks to penetrate and increase their presence and size in Muslim-majority countries.

According to the FINDEX database of the World Bank, the proportion of adult population holding bank accounts in 25 out of 48 OIC countries surveyed by World Bank in 2011 stood below 20%. In 2014, 17 out of 45 countries surveyed by World Bank had less than 20% of the adult population holding a bank account. Appreciably, in 2017, only 3 out of 46 countries had less than 20% of the population holding bank accounts. Nonetheless, still 32 out of 46 countries have less than half of the population holding bank accounts in OIC member countries. On the contrary, the average for middle-income and high-income countries on this indicator is 65% and 94%, respectively. This highlights the need for interest-free banking in these Muslim-majority regions. Due to the prohibition of interest, Muslims, in particular, need financial solutions which are *Shari'ah* compliant. Table 12.3 gives statistics on account penetration in selected OIC countries.

Apart from the Muslim-majority regions, there is substantial potential for further penetration of Islamic banking in other regions. Due to the growing interest in interest-free banking in many regions including Western Europe, East Asia, and Central Asia where there is significant Muslim population, the governments in non-Muslim-majority countries have also embarked on providing a level playing field to Islamic banking. These countries aim to achieve inclusivity in their financial system which will also allow these countries to boost savings, investments, spending, and economic growth while also allowing their faith-conscious citizens to achieve consumption smoothing and asset acquisition through a form of banking which achieves these aims in a faith-compliant manner. Tax neutrality exists in developed markets of Europe and emerging markets of Southeast Asia which allows an opportunity for Islamic banks to penetrate in these markets.

Table 12.3.   Account penetration in selected OIC countries.

Country	2011	2014	2017	Country	2011	2014	2017
Afghanistan	9.01	9.96	14.89	Mali	8.21	20.08	35.42
Albania	28.27	37.99	40.02	Mauritania	17.46	22.87	20.87
Algeria	33.29	50.48	42.78	Morocco	—	—	28.64
Azerbaijan	14.90	29.15	28.57	Mozambique	—	—	41.67
Bahrain	64.51	81.94	82.61	Niger	1.52	6.71	15.52
Bangladesh	31.74	30.99	50.05	Nigeria	29.67	44.44	39.67
Benin	10.46	16.62	38.49	Oman	73.60	—	—
Bosnia	56.21	52.69	58.84	Pakistan	10.31	13.04	21.29
Burkina Faso	13.35	14.36	43.16	Qatar	65.88	—	—
Cameroon	14.81	12.18	34.59	Saudi Arabia	46.42	69.41	71.70
Chad	8.96	12.43	21.76	Senegal	5.82	15.42	42.34
Comoros	21.69	—	—	Sierra Leone	15.34	15.58	19.81
Cote d'Ivoire	—	34.32	41.33	Somalia	—	38.66	—
Djibouti	12.27	—	—.	Sudan	6.90	15.27	—
Egypt	9.72	14.13	32.78	Syria	23.25	—	—
Gabon	18.95	33.01	58.60	Tajikistan	2.53	11.46	47.02
Guinea	3.69	6.96	23.49	Togo	10.19	18.25	45.29
Indonesia	19.58	36.06	48.86	Tunisia	—	27.43	36.91
Iran	73.68	92.28	93.98	Turkey	57.60	56.68	68.59
Iraq	10.55	10.97	22.67	Turkmenistan	0.40	—	40.58
Jordan	25.47	24.62	42.49	Uganda	20.46	44.45	59.20
Kazakhstan	42.11	53.91	58.70	UAE	59.73	83.74	88.21
Kosovo	44.31	47.80	52.27	Uzbekistan	22.50	40.71	37.09
Kuwait	86.77	72.91	79.84	West Bank	19.43	24.24	25.02
Kyrgyzstan	3.76	18.47	39.94	Yemen	3.66	6.45	—
Lebanon	37.03	46.93	44.75	Low income	13.36	22.88	34.85
Libya	—	—	65.67	Middle income	43.44	57.54	65.31
Malaysia	66.17	80.67	85.34	High income	88.26	92.83	93.71

The UK traditionally has looked more at the legal form of transactions than their economic substance. Thus, the need for specific legislation for Islamic finance was needed to remove tax distortions. In 2003, double charge to Stamp Duty Land Tax (SDLT) was removed which benefitted

Islamic finance.[1] SDLT provisions were extended to equity-sharing arrangements in 2005 and to companies in 2006.

The UK tax rules are designed to ensure that the direct tax treatment of *Murabaha* is equivalent to paying or receiving interest on a loan, but these rules only apply if the difference between the purchase price and the resale price equates, in substance, to the return on an investment of money at interest. In the UK, the holders of *Sukuk* are treated as a Western bond-holder, provided that (i) the returns are similar, (ii) *Sukuk* is listed on exchange, and (iii) the issuer accounts for the *Sukuk* as a financial liability under International Accounting Standards (IAS). If all of these three conditions are met, then *Sukuk* will be re-characterized as a security of the issuer in the same way as a conventional bond. Returns paid out on the *Sukuk* will be treated as interest paid by the issuer to the *Sukuk* holders and will be deductible or taxable accordingly.

In 2010, Luxembourg tax administration issued a guideline on the treatment of *Murabaha* profit. According to the guideline, the *Murabaha* profit shall be taxed on a linear basis over the period of the transaction, regardless of the actual payment dates of the *Murabaha* profit. It is a significant relief because otherwise the tax will have been applied right at the time of sale straight away. To avail this facilitation, the financial institution shall clearly state the objective of reselling the commodity to the buyer within a period of six months from the date of purchase at an agreed price which includes a markup. The remuneration to the financial institution must be spread over the period of deferment for accounting and tax purposes based on a straight line method.

In France, compensation paid by *Sukuk* issuers is, for tax purposes, treated just like the interest on a traditional bond offering and is deductible from taxable income.[2] In addition, the compensation paid to non-resident *Sukuk* investors is exempt from withholding tax in France, regardless of whether an offering is governed by French law or the laws of another country. In July 2010, the French government made certain amendments to its laws in order to facilitate *Sukuk* issuances. The amendments removed double stamp duty and the payment of a capital gains tax on property.

---

[1] Mashayekhi, A., Hicks, R. *et al.* (2007). *Islamic Finance in the UK: Regulation and Challenges*, Vol. 9. London: Financial Services Authority.

[2] Di Mauro, F., Caristi, P. *et al.* (2013). *Islamic Finance in Europe*. European Central Bank, Occasional Paper No. 146.

The Republic of Ireland in its Finance Act 2010 introduced a new provision providing VAT exemption for certain Islamic financial products that are comparable to non-Islamic financial products that qualify for an exemption from VAT. The amendments were aimed at giving the same tax treatment to Islamic finance transactions as their conventional equivalents if the economic substance is similar. Nevertheless, duplication of the stamp duty in Islamic mortgage is an issue which needs to be addressed.

Next, we take a brief look at the tax neutrality accorded to Islamic finance in the two most important emerging markets of South East Asia, i.e. Malaysia and Singapore.

Malaysian income tax legislation treats "profits" to be similar to interest making the taxability or deductibility of "profits" similar to the treatment of interest in a conventional financing agreement as per Income Tax Act Section 2(7). All of the other requirements of Malaysian tax law governing when interest is taxable or deductible are then applicable. Malaysian tax law accords tax neutrality to Islamic finance. As a result, there is no additional capital gains tax to be paid on disposal of the asset and no duplication of stamp duties on the transfer of assets in order to comply with *Shari'ah*. Some of the tax incentives for Islamic finance in Malaysia include the following:

- 100% stamp duty exemption on foreign currency instruments executed by Islamic financial institutions.
- Stamp duty exemption on instruments executed pertaining to Islamic banking and *Takaful* activities in foreign currencies until December 31, 2016.
- Stamp duty exemption on instruments executed pertaining to Islamic securities issued in all types of currencies as approved by the Securities Commission (SC) until December 31, 2016.
- *Shari'ah*-compliant loan instruments are given a 20% stamp duty exemption when they are used to finance the purchase of homes.
- Exemption of Real Property Gains Tax (RPGT).
- Tax exemption to interest income received by non-residents from Islamic financial institutions.
- Tax exemption for Islamic banking and *Takaful* companies on income derived from Islamic banking businesses conducted in international currencies, including transactions with Malaysian residents.

Malaysia has put in place a process for advance determination of whether a transaction does or does not constitute Islamic finance. For those transactions which are certified as being Islamic finance transactions, the tax laws can be modified relatively easily to give Islamic finance transactions a tax-neutral treatment. When intermediate transactions are necessary to bring about the Islamic finance structure, the intermediate transactions can be disregarded for tax purposes as per Section 2(8) of the Income Tax Act. Thus, Malaysia has undertaken important steps to provide Islamic finance with appropriate banking and tax regulations.[3]

In Singapore, the first tax incentives came in 2005 from the Minister of Finance. Under Section 43Q of the Income Tax Act, a concessionary tax rate of 5% is accorded to income derived by a company from the prescribed *Shari'ah*-compliant activities, i.e. lending, fund management, and investment advisory services. The aim has been to reduce tax inefficiencies and asymmetries for providing a level playing field to Islamic finance. If effective return/markup derived by the financial institution from the prescribed Islamic financing activity is economically similar to interest in conventional financing, such return or markup will be regarded as interest for Singapore income tax purposes. In addition to that, banks would be able to recover GST paid on the purchase of an asset under a prescribed Islamic finance arrangement in full. Finally, under section 74 of the Stamp Duties Act, the amount of stamp duties to be remitted would depend on the type of prescribed Islamic financing arrangement. Either, the full amount or amount in excess of $500 would be remitted.

Thus, we see that especially after the financial crisis of 2007–2009, developed markets had opened doors for Islamic finance by introducing favourable tax regulations. Federal Government of Australia in the Budget 2016 announcement has pledged to enhance access to asset-backed financing by removing key barriers to the use of asset-backed financing arrangements imposed by Australia's current tax laws. Part of the reason for tax-friendly policies is to do with the fact that Islamic banking is

---

[3] Hegazy, W. (1999). *Islamic Finance in Malaysia: A Tax Perspective*. Proceedings of the Second Harvard University Forum on Islamic Finance: Islamic Finance into the 21st Century, Cambridge, Massachusetts: Center for Middle Eastern Studies, Harvard University, pp. 215–224.

potentially less prone to systemic risks by using real underlying assets, risk sharing, and prohibiting the sale of debt.[4]

12.3.2 *Public infrastructure financing*

Providing tax neutrality to Islamic banking products can help in utilizing household savings in obtaining funds for both commercial and development finance projects. Finance of public infrastructure requires huge capital expenditures that are funded through the issuance of long-term bonds. *Sukuk*, as an alternative investment vehicle in Islamic finance, can be utilized to obtain finance from a wide array of investors.

In an empirical study of 119 non-OECD countries using panel data, it is revealed that lack of financing is one of the major obstacles for minimal use of renewable energy in developing countries.[5] Financial sectors of these countries are often underdeveloped and are unable to efficiently channel loans to produce renewable energy.

Islamic banks have grown faster than conventional banks in their financing operations, except in financing to the government.

Part of the reason is that Islamic banks cannot provide finance for debt swap, debt repayment, and deficit finance where no asset is involved. However, in most developing countries, the governments pay more than 50% of their tax revenues in servicing debt and spend very little in development. Often, these governments trim development spending to cover other non-discretionary current expenditures. Islamic banks can finance the government for the purchase of infrastructure that can be used in development projects.

Through the issuance of more *Sukuk*, the ambit of investment class assets will expand, and it will enable the Islamic-conscious individual and institutional investors to effectively diversify their portfolios. It will increase liquidity of these *Sukuk* and generate wider interest among all investors in the economy to consider investing in these investment vehicles.

---

[4]Ahmed, A. (2010). "Global Financial Crisis: An Islamic Finance Perspective", *International Journal of Islamic and Middle Eastern Finance and Management*, 3(4), 306–320.

[5]Brunnschweiler, C. N. (2009). *Finance for Renewable Energy: An Empirical Analysis of Developing and Transition Economies*. Center of Economic Research at ETH Zurich, Working Paper 09/117.

This will dampen the liquidity risks for Islamic banks and allow them to narrow their spreads and improve their advance to deposit ratios.

12.3.3 *Investments in Islamic microfinance*

Islamic microfinance refers to a set of financial products and services that are compliant with the principles of Islamic finance and are offered to the people who are otherwise not able to access banking services given their lower incomes, endowments, and asset ownership. *Shari'ah* compliance is the most significant value proposition for Islamic finance. For Muslims who want to comply with Islamic injunctions, conventional banking and microfinance are not usable options.

Half of the global poverty resides in Muslim world while the Muslim population is quarter of the total global population. Currently, less than 1% of Islamic financing assets are involved in micro financing. Many potential clients in densely populated Muslim-majority countries like Bangladesh remain financially excluded since they do not want to borrow on interest and the scale of Islamic microfinance is inadequate.[6] Islamic microfinance institutions have limited outreach as compared to their conventional counterparts.[7] The scale of Islamic microfinance still remains minuscule and there is a need for scaling up operations, increasing efficiency, and enhancing product range along with non-financial and technical support in business management and skills upgradation. Scaling up operations should not be a problem when it comes to the required amount of funds since Islamic institutions have ample liquidity at their disposal.[8]

There is need to bring inclusivity in the Islamic finance ecosystem given the high levels of poverty in the Muslim world generally. Hence, there is a need to devise an institutional structure to achieve scale, efficiency, and impact. The use of Fintech in functional operations of Islamic microfinance can help in achieving efficiency. The use of Fintech can ensure transparency, effective monitoring, and reducing transaction costs.

---

[6]Mamun, A., Uddin, M. R. *et al.* (2017). *An Integrated Approach to Islamic Microfinance for Poverty Alleviation in Bangladesh*. Üniversitepark Bülten|Universitepark Bulletin.

[7]Ahmed, H. (2002). "Financing Microenterprises: An Analytical Study of Islamic Microfinance Institutions", *Islamic Economic Studies*, 9(2), 27–64.

[8]Dusuki, A. W. (2008). "Banking for the Poor: The Role of Islamic Banking in Microfinance Initiatives", *Humanomics*, 24(1), 49–66.

Islamic finance is rich in its product offerings. *Qard-e-Hasan, Murabaha,* and *Ijarah* cater to the liquidity and working capital needs as well as leasing of fixed assets. On the contrary, equity-based modes of financing, such as *Mudarabah* and *Musharakah*, can satisfy the mutual risk-absorbing and -sharing needs of the micro-entrepreneurs.[9] In order for Islamic microfinance to achieve comprehensive appeal and accessibility, there is a need for multiple approaches, whereby the destitute, disabled, and unbankable clients are served with charity programmes and relatively better-off clients are served with microfinance programme for wealth creation.[10]

Even with a small outreach, Islamic microfinance has created a significant impact in allowing people to supplement their purchasing power with microfinance. Users of Islamic microfinance credit services in Pakistan experienced an increase in liquidity and profits. They experienced a rise in income and spending on non-durable and durable consumption.[11] In another impact evaluation study, it was found that the gross revenues, net profits, consumption, employment, and expenditure on business investment increased significantly upon receiving the loans.[12] For sustainable and substantial impact, provision of capacity-building support and effective service delivery through better coordination, networking, and technical assistance through *Awqaf* and *Zakat* funds is also necessary.

Problems facing conventional Microfinance Institutions (MFIs) include non-exit from the trap of poverty and indebtedness, high rates of dropout, moral hazard, and economic sustainability of the programmes. Islamic microfinance not only can promote financial inclusion but can also allay concerns of mission drift. Islamic microfinance with its exclusive range of equity financing products and *Qard-e-Hasan* offers a more humane and flexible way of financing to the poor clients.

---

[9]Rahman, A. R. A. (2010). "Islamic Microfinance: An Ethical Alternative to Poverty Alleviation", *Humanomics*, 26(4), 284–295.

[10]Obaidullah, M. and Khan, T. (2008). *Islamic Microfinance Development: Challenges and Initiatives.* Islamic Research & Training Institute. Policy Dialogue Paper No. 2.

[11]Mahmood, H. Z., Abbas, K. *et al.* (2017). "Islamic Microfinance and Household Welfare Nexus: Empirical Investigation from Pakistan", *Journal of Global Entrepreneurship Research*, 7(1), 18.

[12]Riwajanti, N. I. and Asutay, M. (2015). The role of Islamic micro-finance institutions in economic development in Indonesia: A comparative analytical empirical study on pre and post-financing states. In H. A. El-Karanshawy *et al.* (Eds.), *Access to finance and human development — Essays on zakah, awqaf and microfinance.* Doha, Qatar: Bloomsbury Qatar Foundation.

Integrating Islamic microfinance with operational third-sector welfare institutions and programmes and with Islamic social and redistributive institutions, such as *Zakat, Awqaf,* and *Takaful* will enhance the financial stability of Islamic microfinance institutions.[13] Islamic institutions like *Sadaqah, Waqf,* and *Zakat* can provide direct support to the poorest of the poor clients either in cash or in kind to satisfy their essential survival needs before engaging them in microcredit services.[14]

Thus, it is pertinent to use these institutions and product structures in a comprehensive package ensuring integration, scale, sustainability, outreach, and efficiency by effectively embedding technology in operations. If Islamic banks enter into microfinancing, they can benefit from high recovery rates and spreads in this sector.

12.3.4 *Use of Fintech in Islamic banking*

In Islamic finance contracts, use of technology can help in completing different steps involved in a typical Islamic finance transaction more quickly and efficiently. It will also ensure efficient monitoring and fulfilling documentary requirements. To capitalize on the advantages of Fintech, standardization in *Shari'ah* rules is vital. Standardized standard operating procedures can enhance the scope of automation for incorporating Fintech in the contract mechanics and execution.

Islamic banks face the challenge of efficiency given that they need to participate more intensely in the Islamic finance contracts. If the additional procedures and documentation for ensuring *Shari'ah* compliance can be done more efficiently with Fintech, then it will bring efficiency in Islamic banking products and operations.

Furthermore, Fintech can help in effective marketing and cross-selling of financial products in Islamic banking by providing interactive exchange of information and communication with the customers. Furthermore, Fintech would make the financial markets more competitive by reducing information asymmetries and enabling comparison of product features across financial institutions.

---

[13] Akhter, W., Akhtar, N. *et al.* (2009). *Islamic Micro-Finance and Poverty Alleviation: A Case of Pakistan.* Proceeding of the 2nd CBRC, Lahore.

[14] Ali, A. E. E. S. (2015). "Islamic Microfinance: Moving Beyond Financial Inclusion", *European Scientific Journal, 11*(10), 297–310.

The average score on mobile phone penetration in Muslim-majority countries is similar to the average for middle-income countries, i.e. 103 out of 1,000 people, according to the data for 2018 provided by FINDEX database of World Bank. However, it is not the case with the number of ATMs and branches per 1,000 people in Muslim-majority countries. The average number of branches in Muslim-majority countries is around 10 per 100,000 people as against 12 and 20 in middle-income and high-income countries, respectively, according to the World Bank data for 2018. Likewise, the average number of ATMs in Muslim-majority countries is around 25 per 100,000 people as against 36 and 66 in middle-income and high-income countries, respectively, according to the World Bank data for 2018.

These empirical data highlight an opportunity for Islamic banks. They might be having a disadvantage when it comes to the physical infrastructure. However, Fintech opens an all new opportunity to reach the customers more efficiently and engage with them in a more interactive way.

12.4 Conclusion

The discussion in the chapter identified potential future challenges which include the lack of a level playing field in regulatory frameworks and constraints in liquidity management. The chapter also highlighted growth opportunities by noting that Islamic banks have the potential to contribute to financial inclusion and development finance. This chapter also discussed the issue of tax neutrality for Islamic banking products. We discussed the tax issues that arise in Islamic banking products in direct and indirect taxes in asset ownership, multiple transfers, and treatment of income and disposal of assets. We also looked at the prevailing tax framework for Islamic finance in diverse geographic regions including the developed markets of Europe and emerging markets of South East Asia.

Self-Assessment Quiz

1. Tax neutrality implies that
   (a) There are no taxes on banking transactions
   (b) There is tax preference or relaxation granted in comparison to other similar institutions

(c) There is similar tax treatment for transactions having similar economic substance

(d) None of the above

2. Which of the following is the likely impact of Fintech for the future of banking?
   (a) Marginal role of banks in financing and payments facilitation both in branch and online banking
   (b) Increased use of online and mobile banking over branch banking
   (c) Cost of transactions to go up
   (d) None of the above

3. Few of the reasons why Islamic microfinance constitutes a small part of Islamic finance assets include
   (a) High costs of outreach, documentation, and monitoring
   (b) Lack of demand for Islamic microfinance
   (c) Lower profit margins on financing products
   (d) Higher rates of default

4. In liquidity management, which of the following are challenges for Islamic banks?
   (a) Islamic banks do not have lender of last resort facility
   (b) Islamic banks cannot invest in treasury bills and such money market instruments which are based on interest
   (c) Islamic banks have lack of *Shari'ah*-compliant, short-term marketable investment options
   (d) All of the above

5. In development finance, Islamic commercial banks can contribute in the following ways:
   (a) Providing new debts for repaying older debts
   (b) Provide interest-free loans to developing countries
   (c) Provide finance for purchase of fixed assets infrastructure
   (d) None of the above

Self-Assessment Questions

1. Explain the concept of tax neutrality. Do Islamic banks deserve to have tax neutrality?
2. If tax neutrality is not provided to Islamic banks, how do they suffer and face greater commercial displacement risk?

3. What are the additional constraints that Islamic banks face in managing liquidity in terms of choice of liquidity instruments?

4. What are the additional constraints that Islamic banks face in market risk due to non-flexibility in repricing if the terms of contract relating to payments are not met by the financing client? Give an example to illustrate the point.

5. What are the constraints that Islamic banks face in product design, especially in offering short-term working capital financing products?

6. Describe through statistics the potential ground for Islamic banks to contribute in financial inclusion both in terms of market gap as well as the willingness to use Islamic banks among general public.

7. Explain how Islamic banks can reduce the savings–investment gap in Muslim-majority countries. What effect will it have on the macro-economy of Muslim-majority countries if the savings and investment rates increase?

8. Briefly describe the developments in offering tax neutrality to Islamic banks in the selected countries of (i) Europe and (ii) East Asia.

9. Discuss how to scale-up Islamic microfinance through the use of Fintech to reduce outreach, monitoring, and documentation costs.

10. Discuss how Islamic finance can be used to mobilize deposits for impact investments and development finance through *Sukuk*.

Answers to Self-Assessment
End of Chapter Quizzes

Chapter 1
1. a
2. a
3. a
4. c
5. c

Chapter 2
1. b
2. e
3. b
4. d
5. d

Chapter 3
1. c
2. d
3. a
4. a
5. a
6. d
7. a

8. d
9. a
10. a

Chapter 4
1. c
2. d
3. e
4. c
5. d

Chapter 5
1. c
2. a
3. a
4. a
5. a

Chapter 6
1. c
2. c
3. b
4. b
5. a

Chapter 7
1. a
2. c
3. d
4. a
5. a

Chapter 8
1. d
2. d
3. b
4. b
5. c

Chapter 9
1. c
2. a
3. e
4. a
5. c

Chapter 10
1. c
2. b
3. d
4. a
5. c

Chapter 11
1. a
2. d
3. d
4. d
5. d

Chapter 12
1. c
2. b
3. a
4. d
5. c

Index

Printed in the United States
By Bookmasters